Using ORACLE to Build Decision Support Systems

Using ORACLE to Build Decision Support Systems

W. H. Inmon

QED Information Sciences, Inc.
Wellesley, Massachusetts

P.O. Box 82-181
Wellesley, MA 02181

Library of Congress Catalog Number: 90-43675
International Standard Book Number: 0-89435-356-X

Printed in the United States of America
90 91 92 10 9 8 7 6 5 4 3 2 1

Library of Congress Cataloging-in-Publication Data

Inmon, William H.
Using ORACLE to build decision support systems / W. H. Inmon.
p. cm.
Includes index.
ISBN 0-89435-356-X
1. ORACLE (Computer system) 2. System design.
3. Decision support systems. I. Title.
QA76.9.D3I545 1990
005.75'65—dc20

90-43675
CIP

To Mike Loper and Dave Dodge—
two people who believe in the
importance of building bridges

Table of Contents

Preface

ORACLE—ORACLE Corporation's database manager—is a powerful piece of software that has many capabilities. ORACLE can be used in the production environment and in the DSS environment. A previous work—*ORACLE: BUILDING HIGH PERFORMANCE ONLINE SYSTEMS*, QED, 1989—explored ORACLE and high-performance, high-availability systems. This book explores ORACLE in the end-user, DSS environment.

As in the case of using ORACLE to build production systems, building DSS systems begins with understanding and establishing the DSS environment. Simply taking the technology of ORACLE and building DSS systems without understanding the larger issues of the DSS environment is a prescription for disaster.

The DSS environment is typified by free-form access and usage of data, high flexibility of data structures, the ability to construct systems quickly, and so forth. In short, the DSS environment supports heuristic, nonrepetitive processing on which decisions about the management of the company are made. But unlocking the promise of the DSS/ORACLE environment requires a thorough grounding in the issues of the DSS environment.

The issues of the DSS environment include:

- the credibility of data;
- the accessibility of data;

- the ability to create views of data spontaneously;
- the ability to efficiently manage large amounts of data; and
- the ability to manage data efficiently in a read-only mode.

The effective DSS/ORACLE environment addresses these issues. There is a definite pattern that shops fall into as they build the effective DSS/ ORACLE environment. That pattern—called a *paradigm* in some circles—is described fully in the book *DATA ARCHITECTURE—THE INFORMATION PARADIGM*, QED, 1989. This book addresses how the paradigm can be applied in a ORACLE environment. Refer to this book for a very detailed explanation of the paradigm.

The world of DSS processing is, for many organizations, an unexplored world. In the 1970s and the 1980s, many shops built operational systems which gathered much data in one form or the other. Much more can be done with that data than just support operational systems for which its data was originally collected. Opening up the possibilities for using the data that has been accumulated is the role and challenge of DSS and ORACLE.

At first glance, merely pulling data into ORACLE from the operational base seems to be enough to start building DSS systems. But after enough people pull DSS data from operational systems in a more or less random pattern, a really confusing, disorganized ORACLE environment is created. At this point, the worth of DSS processing comes into question.

The DSS manager must look at the long-term consequences of building DSS systems across the organization and resist the temptation to haphazardly build DSS systems quickly. This book describes the longer term vision of what the ideal DSS environment in ORACLE should look like.

This book is for managers, developers, database administrators, data administrators, information center professionals, endusers, and students of computer science. In short, practically anyone interested in the progression of information technology and the usage of information technology beyond the building of operational systems will find this book useful.

The author wishes to acknowledge the assistance, guidance and thoughts of, and conversations with the following people:

John Zachman, IBM
Jeff Caplan, AMS
Mike Loper, AMS

Dave Dodge, AMS
Alan Pitt, AMS
Steve Barnes, AMS
Terry Murphy, AMS

In addition, many thanks to Shirley Mahorney for help in manuscript preparation and to Dan Chaffin for graphics support.

WHI

CHAPTER 1

The Effective DSS/ ORACLE Environment

For years the world has known how to build operational systems. High performance, transaction processing, and management of large databases are well-documented in theory and in practice. Using the data that has been gathered by the operational system is another matter. Merely collecting and organizing data for operational purposes is not enough. Taking operational data and merely shoving it at the end-user is not enough either.

With ORACLE the opportunities for effective DSS processing are enabled by the ability to dynamically link data and the ability to access data in a heuristic manner. As a tool, ORACLE is quite useful for providing a foundation for DSS processing. Historically, ORACLE has appeared just as operational systems have matured and have provided a basis for the data on which DSS processing can be done. But merely bringing in ORACLE and pulling data from operational systems *does not provide a foundation for effective DSS processing.*

To build the effective DSS environment requires that the issues of timeliness, believability, efficiency of processing, and technology be addressed. As shall be seen in this book, the issues of effective DSS processing are every bit as complex as the issues of operational processing. And (interestingly!) the issues and techniques of DSS processing are very different from the issues and techniques of operational processing. ORACLE, in its versatility, provides a technical foundation for both operational and DSS processing.

THE DIFFERENT ENVIRONMENTS

Knowing how to effectively build and use the DSS environment starts with an understanding of how the DSS environment is different from the operational environment. The DSS/ORACLE environment and the operational environment both run on computers, access data that is stored magnetically, run under ORACLE, and are controlled by programs. And there the similarities between the DSS/ORACLE and the operational/ORACLE environments end. In practically every other way the two environments are very different, even diametrically the opposite of each other in many cases.

Some of the major differences between the DSS and the operational environment include:

- the development life cycle;
- the way requirements are gathered and used;
- the way DSS and operational systems are used;
- the redundancy of data;
- the way hardware is used;
- the type of data that flows through the environments;
- who is building and using the environments;
- the orientation of data and processing—is it centralized or decentralized;
- whether data or processing shares the spotlight.

Each of these differences between the DSS/ORACLE and operational/ORACLE environments will be discussed.

The System Development Life Cycle (SDLC)

The notion exists that *all* systems have a common SDLC, which looks typically like that shown in Figure 1.1.

Figure 1.1 shows the classical system development life cycle. The classical phases are feasibility, analysis, design, programming, testing, system test, and, finally, implementation. When the first SDLC was drawn up (and formed the heart of most methodologies), it was assumed that *all* systems would be developed under the life cycle. Had the assumption been that all *operational* systems would be developed under the SDLC, the underlying methodologies might not have fallen into the poor reputation that they have earned. Instead, for the most

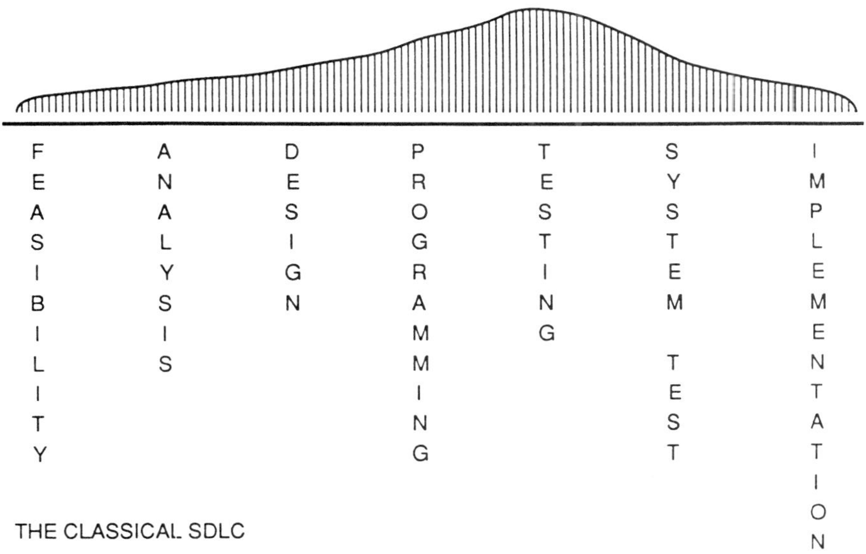

FIGURE 1.1 Manpower utilization over the classical system development life cycle.

part, the SDLC was touted as the *general* approach to developing systems applying to both operational *and* DSS systems.

Unfortunately DSS systems usually are not built using the SDLC. Often another, very different development life cycle applies to DSS processing, as shown by Figure 1.2.

The development life cycle shown in Figure 1.2 in many ways is the reverse of the classical SDLC. Figure 1.2 shows that DSS development often begins with programming, then progresses to design, analysis, and, finally, feasibility. At the end of the process an *answer* is achieved.

The essence of DSS processing is an iterative, heuristic approach. For example, the DSS analyst first decides to find out how many accounts have made orders over $250,000. In the next iteration, the analyst determines how many orders over $250,000 have been made in the last six months. Next, the analyst determines how many orders over $250,000 have been made in the past six months where more than 10% of the goods have been returned. Finally, the analyst finds out who has made orders over the past six months of over $250,000 in which where there have been 10% or more returns. At each step in

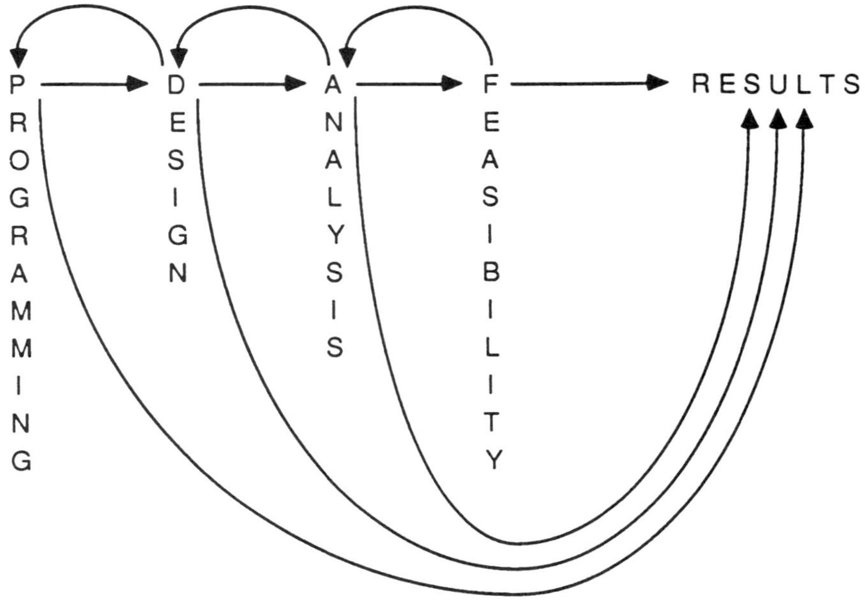

FIGURE 1.2 The heuristic system development life cycle for DSS processing.

this heuristic analysis, the analyst must complete the analysis before deciding what the next step is.

To explain this *backward* looking DSS life cycle, begin with the programming phase. The programming tools used in DSS analysis are designed for very quick development and quick change. Furthermore, the type of work done in DSS processing can often be accomplished by programs that can be run very quickly. Thus, it is usually the best ploy to simply write a DSS program and see what happens in the DSS environment.

If the desired result is achieved from the DSS program that was run, fine. But oftentimes there are reasons why the desired result is not achieved. In some cases there is too much data to be quickly manipulated by ORACLE. More likely there is a need to access other data than that originally envisioned and specified in the DSS program. At this point, some *design* and reanalysis takes place in order to accomplish the objective.

After the design occurs and the DSS program is rerun, another result is obtained. In some cases obtaining this result is enough. But often the result that has been calculated is analyzed and it is decided that a different, or a more refined result is needed. After this analysis, another iteration of design and programming is required, followed by another execution of a program.

At some point during this heuristic process the final, desired result is obtained. But not always. After all the heuristic processing that has occurred, it sometimes becomes questionable whether it is feasible to continue DSS processing. In other cases it is feasible to achieve the desired result, but the analysis, design, and programming cycle must be repeated so often that DSS processing is discontinued. It is no wonder then that unsatisfying results are achieved when the classical SDLC is applied to DSS processing. The classical SDLC simply was not made for DSS processing. But the classical SDLC is not the only gross misfit in the DSS/ORACLE environment.

Requirements Are Created by Starting with the Output

In the classical operational environment the system requirements are gathered beginning with the output. Typically reports, screens, and other system output are gathered. Once gathered, the system designer assimilates and organizes the output. Typically the data from the output is collected and is *normalized*. Once organized, the designer determines what input is available, then goes about the task of figuring out how to transform the input into the desired output.

This time-honored approach works fine for operational data and processing because operational data and processing are essentially stable and are based on the fundamental day-to-day operations of the enterprise. But DSS data and processing are not based so much on the day-to-day operations of the enterprise, as on the *perception* of the day-to-day operations of the enterprise. In other words, the DSS world changes every time a manager or analyst changes his or her mind about how the day-to-day world of the enterprise should be measured.

For example, the marketing manager decides to calculate all quarterly sales. The first iteration of the report shows all sales that the sales force has closed. This is an interesting number, but the accountant views the report and has a different version of quarterly sales. The second iteration of the report is one that calculates all payments received for sales, which is quite different than sales that have been booked. And the production control manager requests a third iteration of quarterly sales—all sales orders fulfilled. In short, the DSS analyst continues to change the report based on who is looking at data and what their interpretation of the data is.

The result is that the *outputs* of the DSS world constantly change. It is never stable. Any design that begins with the output—the reports, screen, other forms of output—for DSS processing is doomed because DSS processing is inherently stable.

Figure 1.3 depicts this fundamental difference between operational and DSS processing.

Figure 1.3 shows that operational processing is an interactive player at the detailed, up-to-the-second level with the enterprise. The operational world has a profound effect on the enterprise. The DSS world on the other hand merely measures or views different perspectives of the enterprise. It is these perspectives that are constantly changing.

So there is no point in trying to use *output* to design a DSS system. The DSS system will change faster and more often than it can be *fixed* or maintained.

The flexibility of ORACLE greatly enhances the ability of the analyst to *roll with the punches*, as the changes in perception are made. But if the data does not exist in the first place on which ORACLE can operate, then all the flexibility in the world will do no good. That is why it is said that the effective DSS/ORACLE environment first depends on the building and understanding of the environment and, second, on the technology underlying ORACLE.

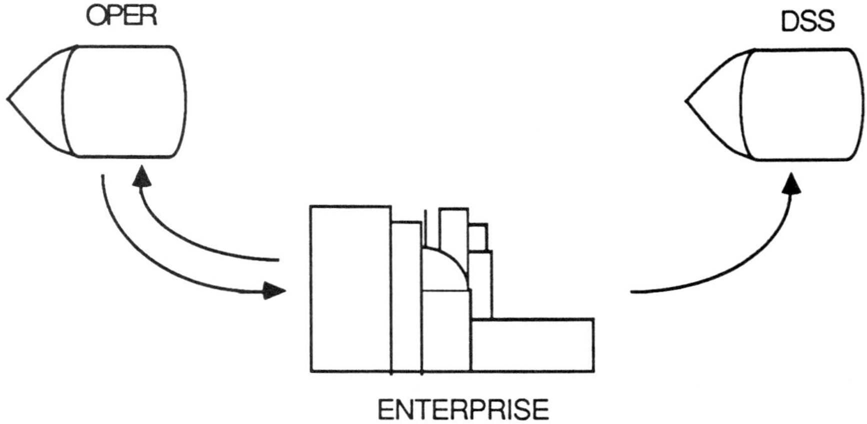

FIGURE 1.3 The fundamental difference between operational and DSS processing.

The Way DSS and Operational Systems Are Used

Operational systems are vehicles—a means to an end. Consider some classical operational systems:

- bank teller systems—a vehicle to achieve accurate and timely information to assist tellers in making detailed decisions;
- airline reservations systems—a vehicle to keep track of what flights are available, who is sitting where on a flight, what seats are available, and so forth;
- manufacturing control—a vehicle to organize and manage large amounts of complex parts and assembly information with very complex interrelationships;
- insurance policy management—a vehicle to manage large amounts of complex policy, claims, and expense information with periodic processing requirements.

In case after case, operational systems provide a vehicle by which business intercourse is achieved efficiently and accurately. ORACLE, as a technology, is regularly used to achieve operational aspects of the environment.

But DSS systems, as a class of systems, are normally not used as a vehicle. DSS systems are used to produce an analytical result. They are an end—not a means to an end—for the most part.

Consider some typical DSS systems:

- trend analysis—how have most recent revenues and costs varied in comparison to previous revenues and costs;
- actuarial—how many blue Thunderbirds in Mississippi had accidents in 1965;
- demographic analysis—of our existing customer base, how many customers are females who live in zip codes where the average income is greater than $30,000 per family per annum;
- ad hoc reporting—how effective was the ad showing the little girl with a flower being blasted by a nuclear bomb.

The essential difference in how operational systems are used and how DSS systems are used is shown by Figure 1.4.

Figure 1.4 shows that operational processing is a day-to-day functional component of the business and directly affects how one part of

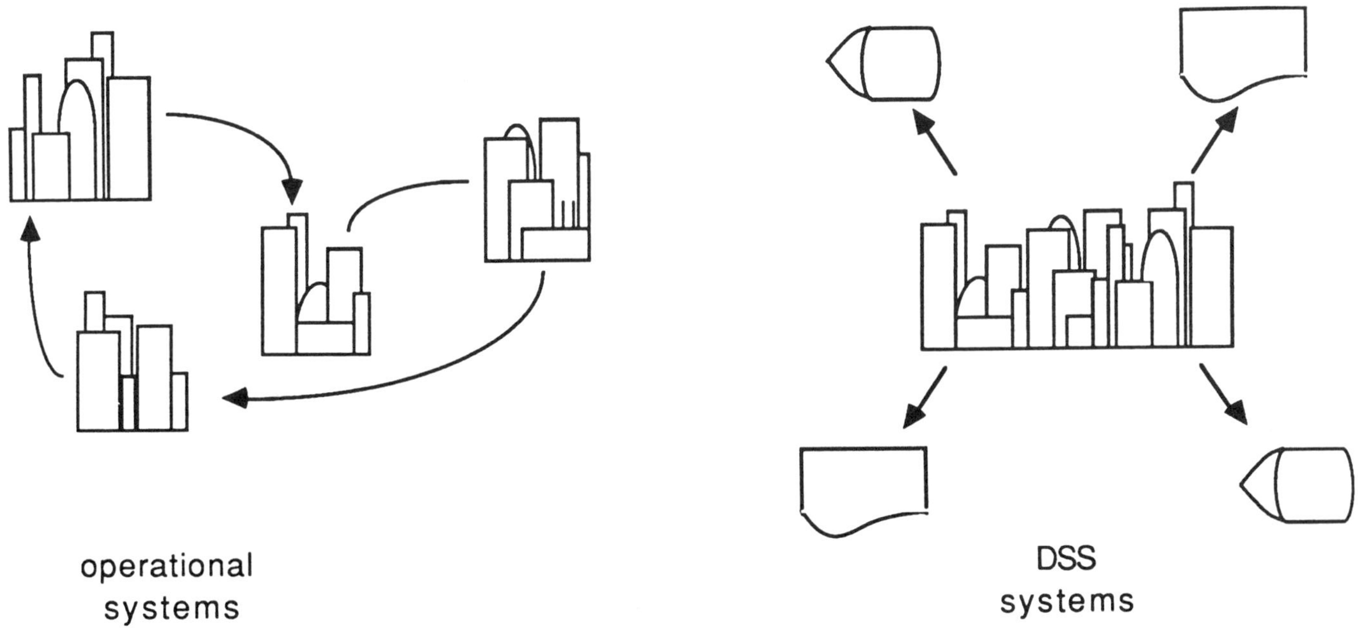

FIGURE 1.4 Operational systems interact with and are an integral part of the business environment; DSS systems measure the business and indirectly influence the business, but do not interact with the detailed day-to-day aspect of the enterprise.

the business interacts with another part of the business. But DSS processing rarely if ever has a direct, immediate effect on the business of the enterprise. Instead, DSS processing measures some aspect of the business of the enterprise that is then used to make decisions as to the direction of the enterprise. There is an indirect effect that DSS processing has on the business, and that effect is shown by Figure 1.5.

Figure 1.5 shows that DSS processing measures or captures one or more aspects of the business of the enterprise. Then the results of the DSS processing are fed to decision makers, and, with the input from other sources, decisions are made as to how the business is run. Those decisions in turn influence the enterprise.

For example, suppose a bank uses DSS processing to determine that many of its customers are from upscale zip code areas but do not have access to top-of-the-line banking services. The business decision is made to start to offer new upscale banking services and to use the upscale zip codes as a starting point for advertising and promotion. In such a manner, DSS processing has an indirect effect on the business.

ORACLE supports this nonoperational usage of data through the ability of the user to access ORACLE data retroactively and to easily and quickly change the way DSS processing is done. If in DSS, ORACLE had to go through traditional technologies such as COBOL, the speed of development and change that could be achieved would be such that DSS processing could not be supported.

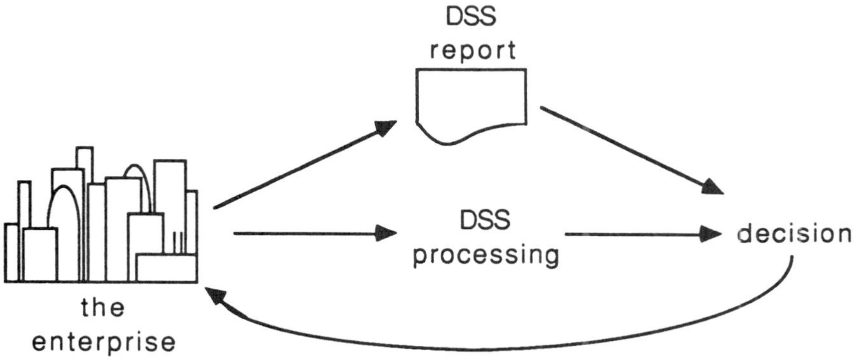

FIGURE 1.5 How DSS processing indirectly influences the business of the enterprise.

Redundancy of Data

When an operational environment contains much redundant data, it is in trouble. The problems of redundant data in the operational environment are legendary and are well-documented. Only a single aspect of redundant operational data will be explored here, but the reader is alerted that there are *many* other problems with redundancy of data in the operational environment.

One of the problems with redundancy of data in the operational environment is that of the integrity and believability of the data. Suppose there are three account files for the same customer; i.e., there is a file for account 1234 for customer = Columbia Electronics for receivables, another file for account 1234 for customer = Columbia Electronics for open orders, and yet another account file for account 1234 for customer = Columbia Electronics for past order activity. The same data credit rating is redundantly stored in all three places, as shown in Figure 1.6.

For reasons known only to the clerks and managers of receivables, open orders, and past order activity, Columbia Electronics has a different credit rating in each place. Depending upon where a clerk looks, trying to respond to an interaction with Columbia Electronics very likely will produce inconsistent results.

If Columbia Electronics credit rating is G for GOOD and it is stored in only one place, then Columbia Electronics will be treated consistently well from every part of the business that must deal with Columbia's credit rating.

Of course, where there is a single nonredundant occurrence of data, there can be no mistaking the credit rating. The redundancy of data opens the door for inconsistency of data in operational processing.

But redundancy of data in the DSS environment is another matter

FIGURE 1.6 One problem with redundancy-believeability of data. What is the credit rating for ACCT 1234?

entirely. It is both useful and mandatory. Redundancy of data in the DSS environment is simply a fact of life. For example, imagine a personal computer environment being fed by ORACLE where there are 450 personal computers and only a single floppy disk. Such a scenario is, of course, absurd. To give users the freedom they need to make use of the technology that enables DSS processing such as personal computer redundancy, is simply a reality that must be dealt with.

Instead of fighting redundancy, ignoring it, or trying to minimize it in the DSS environment, the proper stance is to try to control it. Some of the techniques that typically are used to control DSS redundancy in the ORACLE environment are:

- identifying *official* foundation DSS/ORACLE data;
- using time stamping throughout the foundation;
- limiting the number of iterations of refinement there is for DSS data;
- ensuring that there is a short and unambiguous path back to the foundation data from redundant DSS data at all times.

ORACLE provides a sound foundation for the handling of large amounts of data and the control of the extract process that is required for the management of DSS redundancy.

Hardware Usage

One of the most obvious, most marked, and most profound differences between the operational and the DSS environment is that of the pattern of hardware utilization. The pattern of hardware utilization is independent of whether ORACLE is running on a single machine or multiple machines. Operational processing uses hardware in a static fashion, while DSS processing uses hardware in a binary fashion, either heavily using hardware or hardly using hardware at all.

For example, in an on-line, operational environment where production operational processing is being done, the processor is used sometimes at 80% and sometimes at 100%. But at the end of the day the arithmetic means around 90% is a proper statement of how the online, operational processor is being used.

Contrast that static pattern of utilization with that of a departmental DSS computer. During the end of the month, when reports are being run, the departmental processor is used at 100% nearly all the time. But during the first and middle of the month the departmental processor is hardly used at all, at around 5%. While the arithmetic mean usage for the departmental processor can be calculated, it is a fairly meaningless number because the pattern of utilization is binary. Either the departmental processor is being used heavily or it is hardly being used at all.

The difference in the pattern of hardware utilization is illustrated by Figure 1.7.

Another way the difference in hardware utilization can be shown is by the difference in processing at the DASD level. In general, operational processing tends to access and operate on small units of data on DASD in a more or less random order. For example, a manufacturing control system will need to access data as products and subassemblies are completed and as raw goods and components are needed in the production process. At any moment in time the processing done by the manufacturing control system is accessing and operating on many small units of data which are not related to any great extent.

Contrast this pattern of DASD utilization in which small units of data are accessed in a random pattern with that of DSS processing. As an example of access and control of data during DSS processing, there is a desire to analyze which customers are the most likely prospects to sign up for new telephone services. To do this analysis first requires accessing a large, homogenous block of data (all the customers), then carefully analyzing the data based on its characteristics. Much data

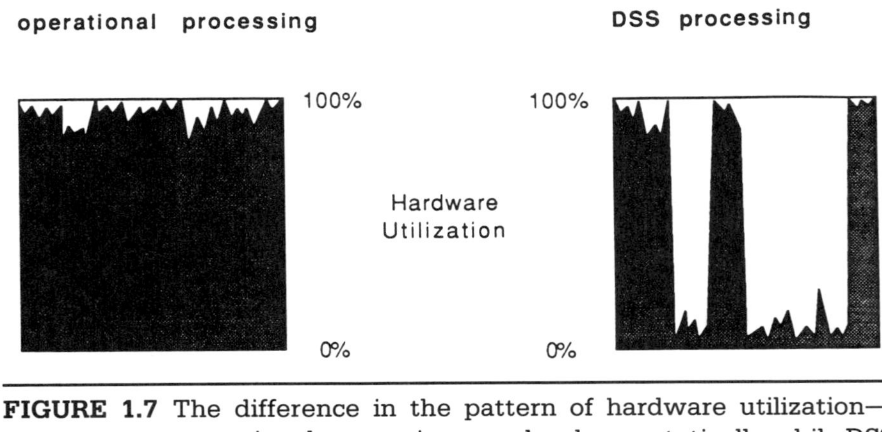

FIGURE 1.7 The difference in the pattern of hardware utilization—operational processing uses hardware statically while DSS processing uses hardware in a binary fashion.

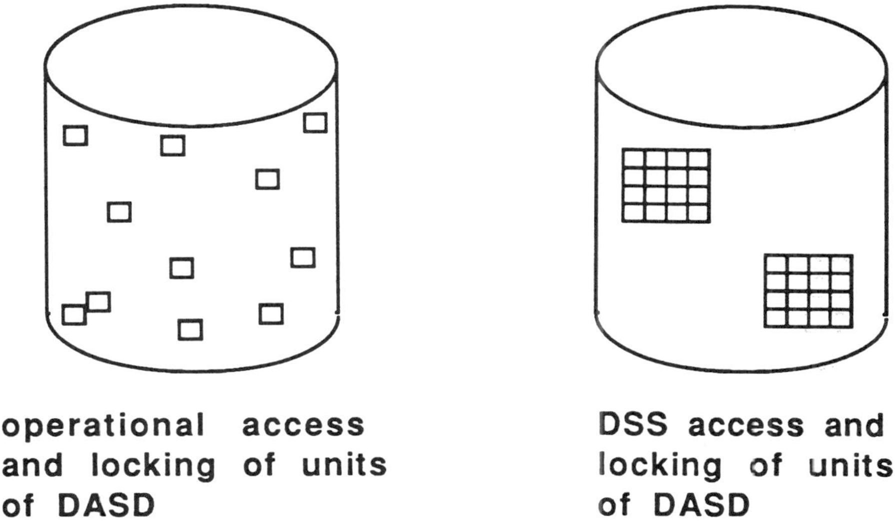

FIGURE 1.8 Access and locking of DASD units.

that is closely related is accessed all at once in a sweep of a database based on the need to access all prospects.

The difference in the pattern of access of data is shown by Figure 1.8.

The indexed organization of data in ORACLE and the ability to access data a set at a time facilitates the DSS access and manipulation of data.

The Type of Data that is Used in Each Environment

There is a very fundamental difference between the operational and the DSS environments in the type of data that flows through and is used in each environment. Primitive data is the type of data that is primarily found in the operational environment, and derived data is the type of data that is primarily found in the DSS environment. (For an in-depth discussion of the differences between primitive and derived data, refer to *DATA ARCHITECTURE: THE INFORMATION PARADIGM*, QED Information Sciences, Inc., Wellesley, Mass.)

Primitive data is detailed data, accurate up to the second. Derived data is usually data that is calculated and reflects the status of data as of some moment in time.

As an example of primitive data in an operational environment, consider the information processing that occurs in the insurance environment. At any moment an insurance agent may access the policy system and find detailed information about a policy which is accurate and current—what car does a customer have insured, what types of coverage are included, when was the policy in force, until when does the policy stay in force, which dependents are also covered, and so forth. Each of the pieces of data about a policy that are available to the agent are detailed and accurate and are examples of primitive data.

As an example of derived data in a DSS environment, consider the work done by an actuary. In studying how to set rates, the actuary looks at accident information across the industry. Some summary data is done showing the accident rate of all females versus all males. Other accident information is the summary of all accidents by age; i.e., how does the driving of all 25 year olds compare to 26 year olds to 27 year olds, and so forth.

Another analysis done by the actuary is on the effect of seat belts. In 1987 Colorado passed a law mandating seat belts. How does the severity of accidents prior to 1987 compare to the severity of accidents after 1987 in Colorado.

All of the data developed by the actuary then is derived data. Of course, the derived data, at some point is calculated from primitive data.

The differences between primitive and derived data are many. Some of the major differences are listed in the table below.

ORACLE is equipped to handle both operational and DSS processing. ORACLE has the infrastructure required to manage data and transaction integrity. At the same time, through set-at-a-time pro-

Table I-1 Differences Between Primitive and Derived Data.

	primitive	*derived*
level of detail	detailed	summarized
audience	clerical	managerial
response time	stringent–3-5 seconds	relaxed–1 min-24 hours
processing nature	repetitive	ad hoc, nonrepetitive
structure	static	constantly changing
updating	individual units are updated	sets of data are calculated

cessing and the ability to scan large amounts of data, ORACLE can do the processing required for DSS processing.

COUNT vs SELECT Processing

One of the interesting issues of DSS/ORACLE processing is exactly what type of processing is occurring. It is a temptation to say that DSS analysts simply specify search criteria and then get all data that applies. For example, a DSS analyst submits a query to the effect:

"GIVE ME INFORMATION ABOUT ALL CUSTOMERS WHO HAVE ORDERS BACKLOGGED AND WHO ARE FROM COLORADO"

The ORACLE request that might be generated would be:

```
SELECT *
FROM CUSTFILE
WHERE STATE = 'COLO' and ORDERDATE < CURRENTDATE
```

The output from the computer looks like:

1—AHERN CHEMICAL, 5935 SANTA FE, DENVER, 500 CASES, DUE SEPT 15
2—WAXMAN CAMERA, 6910 LARIMER, DENVER, 15 CARTONS, DUE SEPT 17
3—HUGH M WOODS, 8915 KIPLING, LAKEWOOD 175 CRATES, DUE SEPT 19

The analyst is either lucky or experienced in that the computer has returned an amount of information that is digestible. If the analyst makes this type of request on a regular basis, the analyst may know what to expect. But what if another analyst had entered the request:

"GIVE ME INFORMATION ABOUT CUSTOMERS WHO HAVE ORDERS BACKLOGGED"

The SQL request might look like:

```
SELECT *
FROM CUSTFILE
WHERE ORDERDATE < CURRENTDATE
```

This request is very similar to the previous one, except that all customers, not just Colorado customers, are being queried. The computer returns:

```
1 - AJAX COMPANY, 140 MEDWOOD, FT DAVIS, TX
    25 CASES, DUE SEPT 19

2 - AHERN CHEMICAL, 5935 SANTA FE, DENVER, CO,
    500 CASES, DUE SEPT 15

3 - ALLIED VAN, 1950 TINCUP, SAN ANTONIO, TX,
    50 CARTONS, DUE SEPT 15

4 - AMDAHL CORP, 9810 FREMONT, NEWARK, CA,
    150 CASES, DUE SEPT 17
        .        .        .
        .        .        .
        .        .        .
        .        .        .
        .        .        .
```

In all, the computer returns 950 companies. The amount of data simply is too much to be useful in a single sitting. Whatever the analyst was looking for is probably lost in the morass of data that was returned.

What the analyst must do is refine the request so that only a reasonable amount of data is returned. Based on what the analyst needs, the analyst may ask for all companies backordered from New Jersey, may ask for all backorders made before September 17, may ask for all backorders more than 50 cases, and so forth.

One way to determine how much data will be returned as a result of a request is to first count how many occurrences of data qualify under a criteria, rather than actually ask for the data itself. Finally, when there is a reasonable amount of qualified data, the analyst actually accesses the data. As an example of the heuristic approach, an analyst inquires how many customers there are with backorders—the reply is that there are 950 companies. The next query asks how many companies there are with backorders where the backorder is more than 50 cases of goods. The reply is 432 companies qualify. Next the analyst asks how many companies have backorders for more than 50 cases where the order was made before September 17. The reply is that 194 companies fit that description. Then the analyst asks how many companies there are where there are backorders of more than 50 cases made before September 17, where the company is in California, Oregon, or Washington. The reply is that there are 14 companies that fit that description. Now the analyst seeks the actual qualified information. The net result of the heuristic search is that most processing is of the COUNT variety, not the retrieve data variety.

SQL uses the COUNT(*) facility for this heuristic type of processing.

Depending on the index structure, it may be *much* more efficient to count occurrences of data than it is to actually retrieve the raw data. Where is COUNT more popular than RETRIEVE? COUNT is more popular where there is:

- heuristic, ad hoc, nonrepetitive analysis going on;
- an experienced analyst manipulating the process.

RETRIEVE is more popular where:

- repetitive analysis is occurring where only small amounts of data satisfy the query;
- analysis is being done by inexperienced analysts and the request has been *prepackaged.*

Why is the COUNT versus RETRIEVE form of analysis an issue? It is an issue because where COUNT processing is regularly done, COUNT processing can be *very* efficient. On the other hand, for whatever reason, if *only* RETRIEVE processing is done, it is very difficult to organize RETRIEVE data so that it can be randomly retrieved efficiently in bulk.

The DSS/ORACLE analyst/designer then is alerted that a little prescience as to the kind of processing that DSS data will be used for can lead to very significant gains in performance when there is even the faintest pattern of DSS processing.

The Operational/DSS Communities

Very different communities are served by the operational and the DSS processing. In general, operational processing serves the needs of the clerical organization, where the customer meets the organization and where the day-to-day commerce is carried on. DSS processing serves the needs of middle and upper management communities who are charged with directing the mid-term and long-term objectives of the enterprise.

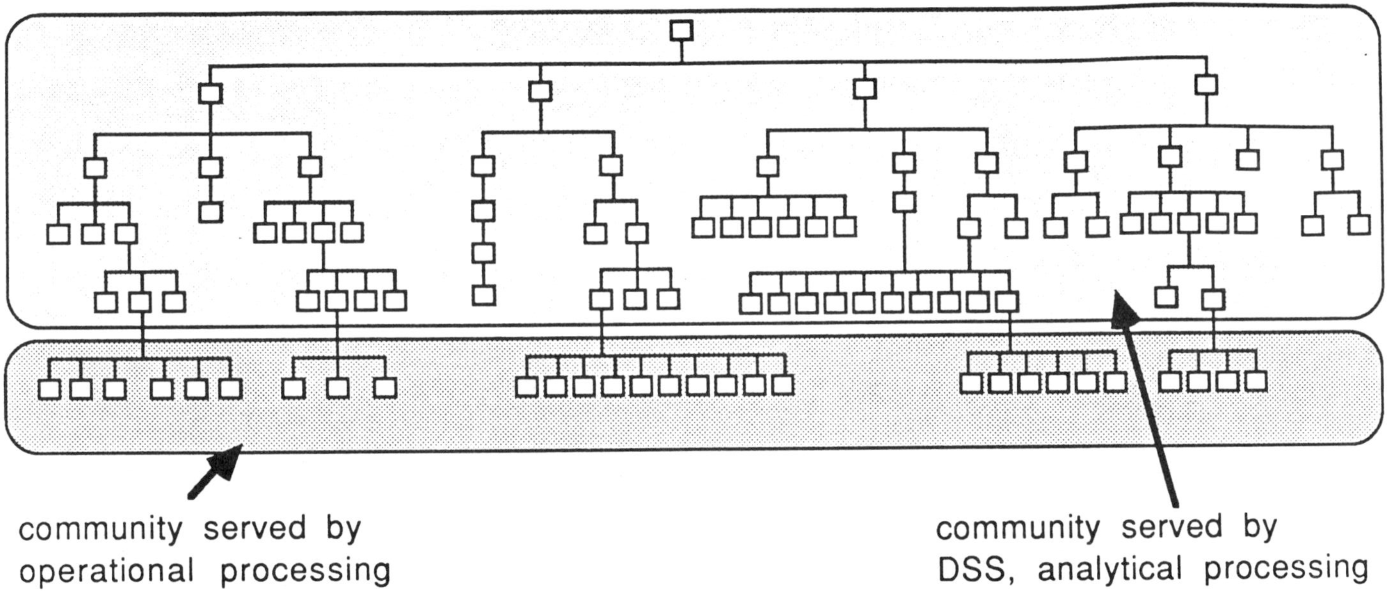

FIGURE 1.9 The communities served by operational and DSS processing are very different.

For example, consider a bank teller system. A bank teller system most decidedly is operational in nature. The community served is the teller and the ATM community at the lower rungs of the organization chart. Contrast the bank teller system with that of an Army DSS organization that looks at strength of military manpower and material around the world. The Army DSS organization looks at different threats, then, based on the threat, determines the Army's readiness posture. The information gleaned in this type of DSS processing is for upper and middle management and has little immediate applicability to the soldier in the field. Figure 1.9 shows how different communities are served by different types of systems.

The Orientation of Data and Processing— Centralized/Decentralized

Most (but not all!) operational data and processing is centralized, and most (but not all!) DSS processing is decentralized. The standard configuration for operational processing is shown in Figure 1.10.

In Figure 1.10, a centralized processor controls data, communications, and the processor. Such a configuration is typical for a bank, an insurance company, a government agency, a retailer, and so forth.

But not all operational processing is done in a centralized fashion. Decentralized flavors of operational processing are depicted as well by Figure 1.11.

In Figure 1.11, there are several, small, remote processors that occasionally exchange data with a larger processor. The smaller processors are autonomous in that when not exchanging information with the central processor they can be used for practically any purpose. At the central processor information is gathered and assimilated. Collectively, the remote processor is organized and assimilated by the central processor. This type of processing configuration is typically found in insurance, manufacturing, some types of banking, and so forth.

Whereas, in one form or the other, operational processing is oriented toward centralized processing, DSS processing is oriented towards decentralized processing, as depicted by Figure 1.12.

Figure 1.12 shows that each unit of DSS processing has its own input of data. Once the data is captured, it "belongs" to the DSS unit. There is very little, if any, coordination of processing among the different DSS processing units.

ORACLE serves the DSS centralized processing needs very nicely in its capacity as a *hub*. In this manner, ORACLE can collect data from a wide variety of sources, either centralized or decentralized.

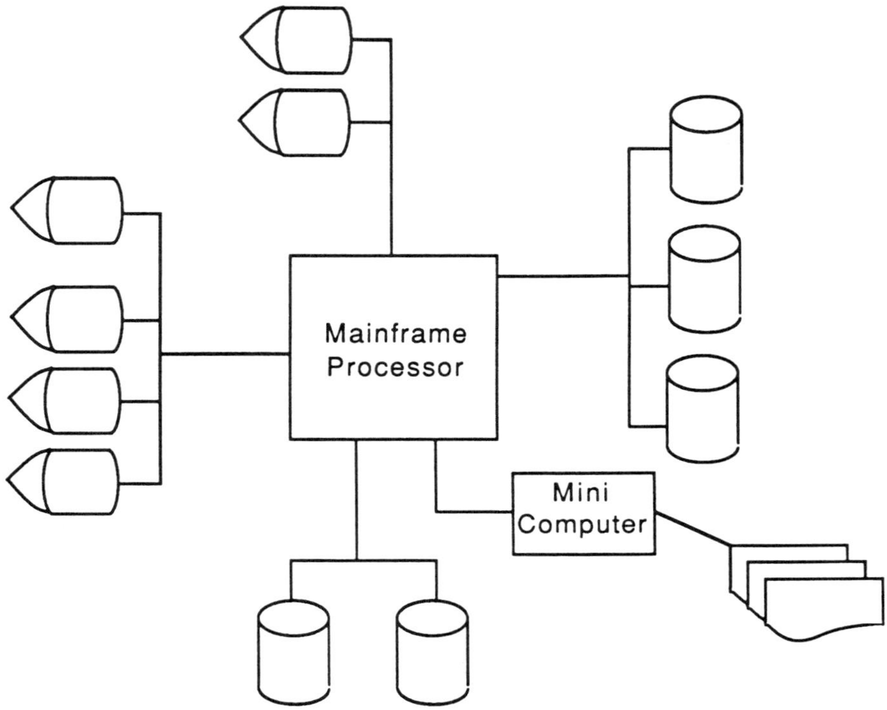

FIGURE 1.10 A typical operational environment, where data/processing are centralized.

Once collected in ORACLE, the DSS processing can be done centrally, or ORACLE can be used to selectively pass the data to other smaller processors, such as mini computers or personal computers.

The Focus on Data or Processing

In operational systems, it is imperative that the designer focus on processing. The *business rules* are of the utmost importance in the design and construction of operational systems, and the business rules shape how processes are to be built. Without a proper gathering and organization of the business rules, the operational system will not execute properly. Some examples of a business rule in a manufacturing environment are:

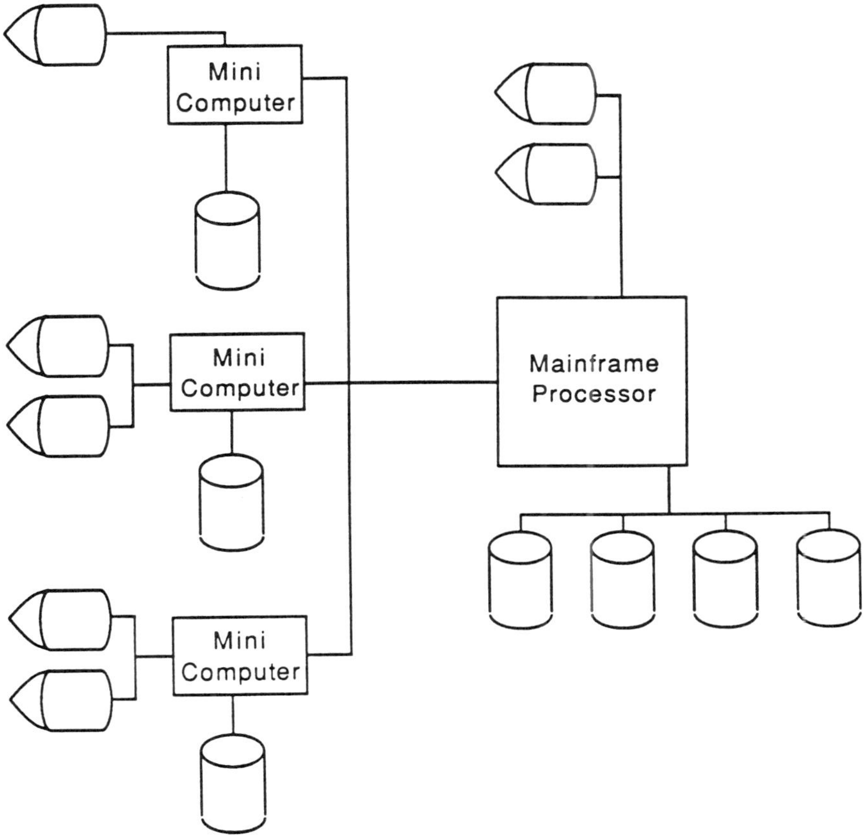

FIGURE 1.11 A distributed operational environment where some processing is done centrally and some is done remotely.

- when quantity is lower than 10% capacity for units measured in bins, set restock to yes;
- when unit cost is more than .50/unit, order approval must be at foreman or higher level;
- when lead time is less than five days, the quantity on hand may go to zero without setting restock to yes;
- when part is a raw good, production control belongs to external expediters, and so forth.

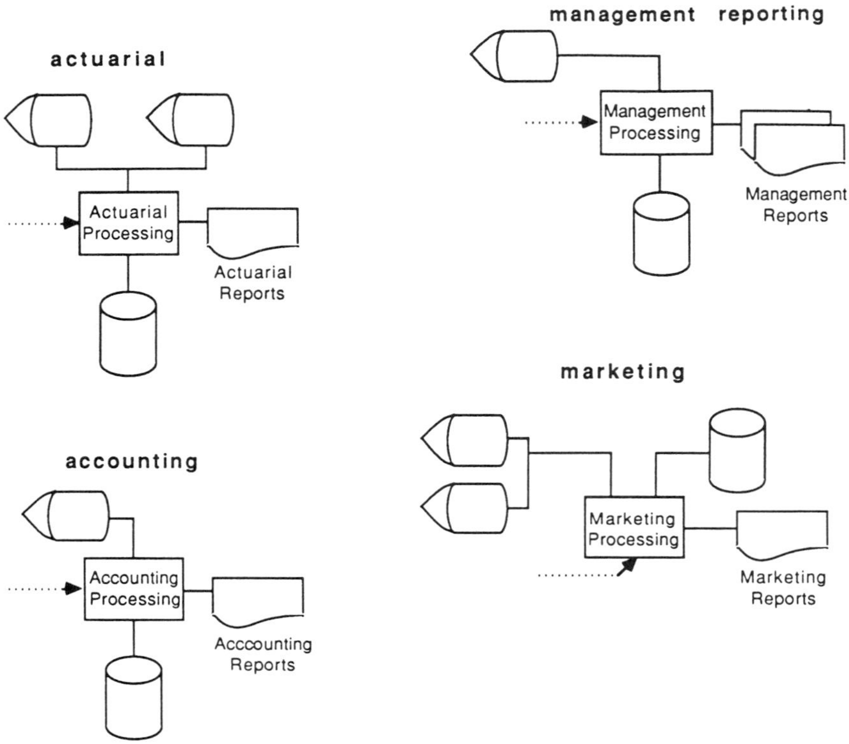

FIGURE 1.12 A DSS environment with its autonomous reporting.

The rules of processing then are essential to the world of operational systems. Data, too, is important to operational systems. In terms of priorities, if the processing is not done properly in operational systems, then the data does not matter.

But the reverse emphasis is true for DSS processing. Data is much more the focus of DSS processing. In a sense, data is the detritus of operational processing. The path of where we have gone and what we have done is left in terms of data. And in that sense, the DSS analyst is more interested in measuring what has happened than in the rules that caused things to happen. The result is that the data becomes the focus of the DSS analyst, not the business rules that caused the data to occur in the first place.

THE EFFECTIVE DSS ENVIRONMENT— IN SUMMARY

The very first step in establishing the effective DSS/ORACLE environment is to understand what the DSS/ORACLE environment is and to understand that the DSS/ORACLE environment is very different from the operational environment.

The canons and practices of design that apply to the operational environment do not apply to the DSS/ORACLE environment in many cases. For instance in the DSS environment:

- redundancy of data is necessary and is absolutely acceptable practice;
- decentralized processing is the norm;
- autonomy of processing is the norm;
- repetitive processing is not the norm;
- achieving ends—producing calculated results—is the norm, not achieving means to an end
- serving upper/middle management is the norm;
- operating on archival detailed data or summarized data is the norm;
- using hardware in a binary fashion—either heavily or lightly—is the norm, and so forth.

QUESTIONS: CHAPTER 1

1. Transaction processing is typically found in ______________ systems.
2. Some of the major differences between the DSS and the operational environment include (list 5).
3. Does the standard SDLC apply to DSS systems? Y/N
4. A word to describe DSS processing in general is ______________.
5. The technology found in the DSS typically IS/IS NOT highly flexible.
6. Name some typical DSS processes.
7. Normally, operational systems strive for as little redundancy of data as possible. T/F
8. Redundancy IS/IS NOT a fact of life in DSS processing.
9. The pattern of hardware usage in operational processing is STABLE/UNSTABLE.

10. The pattern of hardware usage in DSS processing is STABLE/ UNSTABLE.
11. The manner in which ORACLE accesses data is ______________ .
12. Data is organized by means of a randomizer in ORACLE. T/F
13. Data whose existence depends on a single occurrence of an entity of the corporation is ______________.
14. Data whose existence depends on multiple occurrences of an entity of the corporation is ______________.
15. All derived data is calculated. ALL/SOME calculated data is derived.
16. Operational data serves the ______________ community.
17. DSS data serves the ______________ community.
18. Operational processing CAN/CANNOT be centralized or decentralized.
19. In operational processing, requirements analysis is a __________.

CHAPTER 2

Effective DSS/ORACLE Systems—The Issues

The first blush of DSS processing came with 4GL technology and the personal computer. In the early days of DSS processing the notion was born that success in DSS processing was achieved by placing data, hardware, and software in the hands of the end user or DSS analyst. Given the state of technology prior to 4GLs and personal computers, it is true that easy-to-use, easy-to-change technology was on the critical path to success in DSS processing. But time has proven that merely placing the right technology and data in the hands of the end user is not enough. The *right* data must be given to the user at the *right* time in order for DSS processing to be successful. There is a big difference between just data and the *right* data and giving users data and giving users data at the *right* time.

With ORACLE, pulling data from various mainframes became a possibility. But merely pulling data from one environment to the next is an insufficient foundation on which to base DSS processing. Certainly there is a need to address the technical issues of DSS processing. But solving the technical problems of DSS/ORACLE processing is not enough to solve the larger DSS/ORACLE problems.

The difference between the DSS/ORACLE environment and the *effective* DSS/ORACLE environment is highlighted by the following three criteria:

- accuracy and credibility of data;
- timeliness of data; and
- cost of providing and using data.

Once the DSS/ORACLE environment is established where data is provided that satisfies these criteria, the environment can be called an *effective* DSS/ORACLE environment.

DSS—What's in a Name?

DSS stands for *d*ecision *s*upport *s*ystems. In its most proper sense, DSS is a noun. It is proper to say:

- the DSS environment is used for management support.

But the term—DSS—has become so commonly used that the expression *DSS systems* is also widely used. *DSS systems* is an anomaly—a redundancy of terms. "DSS systems" really says: Decision Support Systems systems, which of course does not make sense.

However, since there is an understanding of what DSS is, why it is so important, and what the issues are; and as long as the terminology does not get in the way of communication, DSS systems is quite acceptable.

ACCURACY AND CREDIBILITY OF DATA

The issue of credibility arises innocently enough, but is perhaps the largest, most insidious issue facing the builders of DSS/ORACLE systems. The issue of credibility arises when two (or more!) users or DSS analysts arrive at very different conclusions based on the DSS processing they have done, when in fact the conclusions ought to be at least consistent, if not identical.

As an example, suppose top management of an insurance company wishes to determine some simple information. The management asks the marketing department and the accounting department for this month's new revenues. Management expects to have some differences of opinion because the accountant's perspective of data is not the same perspective as the marketeer's perspective. But management does at least expect the answers to be compatible.

In a few days a meeting is held and marketing announces that monthly revenues are $2,750,000, and accounting announces that revenues are $1,350,000. Management is shocked. The two figures are significantly different. If management were to base serious decisions on each set of data, the decisions would be very different. A decision based on marketing's perspective of the world would be very bullish and aggressive while a decision based on accounting's view of the world would be very bearish and defensive. Yet it is still the same company that marketing and accounting are talking about, so who is correct and why are there such deep differences. Who is to be believed, and who is not to be believed.

Upon investigation, it turns out that marketing is looking at all premium payments made for the month. This includes payments made for policies that are not yet in force and for reinsurance payments. (A payment for a policy not in force occurs when a policy is applied for but the risk is not yet accepted.) In addition, it turns out that marketing is looking at payments made up to the last calendar day of the month.

Accounting, on the other hand, has a somewhat more restricted view of the world. Accounting does not count premiums for policies not in force (because the insurance company may reject the risk) and does not count reinsurance policies. In addition, accounting has used information accurate up to the 25th of the month.

When these differences are accounted for, the large difference of opinion between accounting and marketing is very understandable.

But what if management had never forced the issue and caused such a reconciliation to be done? What if marketing and accounting had continued to do DSS processing independently, as is the case with most DSS processing? What kinds of decisions would the marketeer and the accountant be making based on their best understanding of the data? The two organizations very likely would be working autonomously and inconsistently. Given enough DSS processing and enough differences of opinion, the corporation would have been pulling in many different directions, all at once.

At some point, management would ask the questions: If we are doing all this DSS processing and we can't believe the results and/or we can't work in a consistent fashion, then why are we doing DSS processing at all?

In other words, what is the worth of DSS processing in the face of major inconsistencies and major gaps of credibility?

The road to lack of credibility of DSS processing begins innocently enough. The very desire for autonomy by the end-user is the original springboard of lack of credibility of DSS processing. Consider the very simple scenario, as shown in Figure 2.1.

In Figure 2.1 there is a base of operational data. Five separate

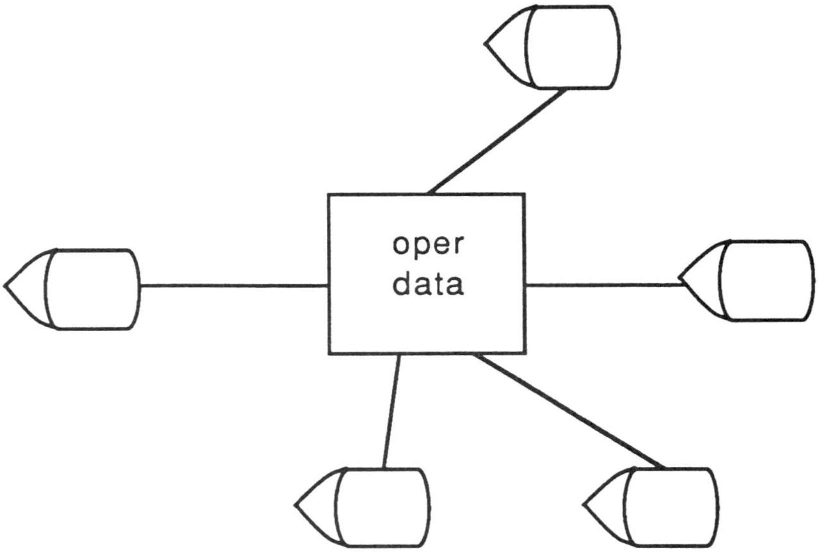

FIGURE 2.1 A simple perspective of DSS processing.

users are accessing the data. If there is a difference of opinion among the five users, it is easy enough to decide whose data and processing is correct and whose data and processing is incorrect. But the configuration shown in Figure 2.1 is not very realistic. It applies only to a very small organization or to organizations who have just embarked on doing DSS processing. A much more likely scenario is shown in Figure 2.2.

Figure 2.2 shows that there are *many* more DSS analysts than shown in Figure 2.1 and that some of the analysts are very near to the operational data and some are not. With the much more realistic scenario in Figure 2.2, it is obvious that is it not possible to reconcile the differences of opinion that will arise. There simply are too many analysts, too little time, and too much complexity.

Furthermore, the number of DSS analysts shown in Figure 2.2 is only 50 or so. Many organizations have *many* more DSS analysts than that shown in Figure 2.2. The large numbers of analysts—each doing his own thing—exaggerates the problems of credibility of DSS processing. Why is the lack of credibility of DSS processing so predictable? Why is it so pervasive?

In the face of much DSS processing and many analysts, the crisis

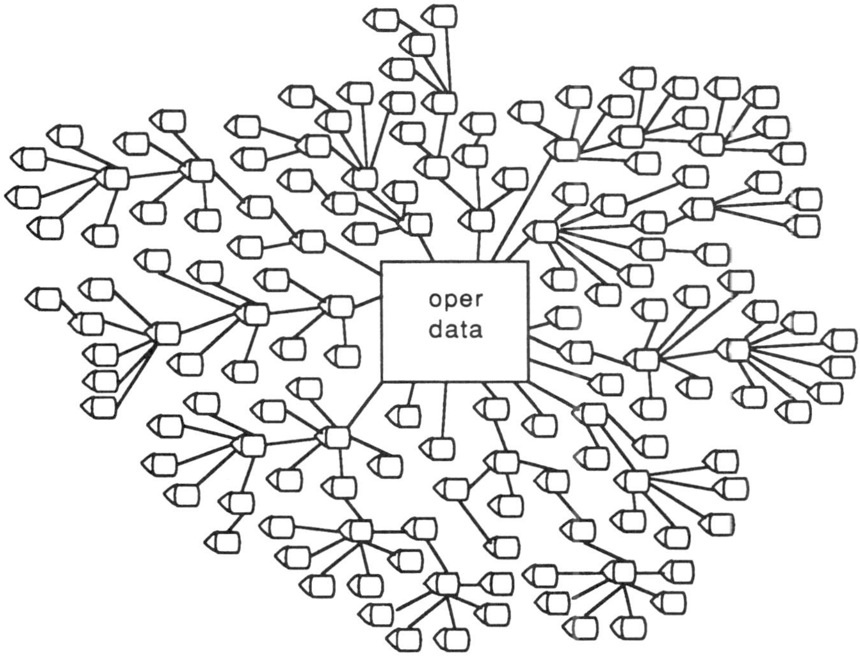

FIGURE 2.2 A more realistic perspective of DSS processing.

of credibility of DSS processing is predictable because of one or all of five factors:

- the lack of consistency in the timing of the extract of data;
- the lack of consistency in the algorithms used to extract data;
- the indeterminate levels of extraction that occur;
- the introduction of external data into the stream of analysis; and
- the lack of consistency in original sources of data to begin with.

Each of these reasons for the lack of credibility will be explored.

Inconsistency of Timing

Marketing reports monthly sales of $500,000. Accounting reports monthly sales of $750,000. But marketing is using data as of the 25th of the month and accounting is using data as of the 31st of the month. Is there any reason to believe the data would be the same? Of course not. The operational data changes from one moment to the next. The only real surprise would be if the data *had* been the same! When data does not have the same time basis, reconciliation is practically impossible.

Figure 2.3 depicts the problem of trying to compare data that has been extracted at different moments in time (data with different time bases).

Inconsistency of Algorithmic Selection Criteria

Engineering reports weekly production of 23,000 units of product. Production control reports weekly production of 17,000 units of product. Who is right? Upon closer inspection, it is found that engineering has chosen to count *all* production for the week. Production control, on the other hand, has opted to count all production minus rejected goods minus parts put in production but not completed in previous weeks. Both engineering and production control have their own perspective of what makes up production. And both have a very different perspective. Figure 2.4 shows how the difference of opinion is propagated to the DSS processing that is done through different algorithmic selection criteria.

When subset A of data is compared to subset B of data and when the populations are very different, there should be no surprise that the conclusion drawn from analysis are very different.

Indeterminate Levels of Extracts

A close examination of Figure 2.2 shows that *most* end-users/DSS analysts do not get the data upon which they make decisions from the operational environment. Instead they get their data indirectly from some other DSS analyst or source of data. It is common in a large

FIGURE 2.3 The timing of extracts is one reason why inconsistent DSS figures may be created.

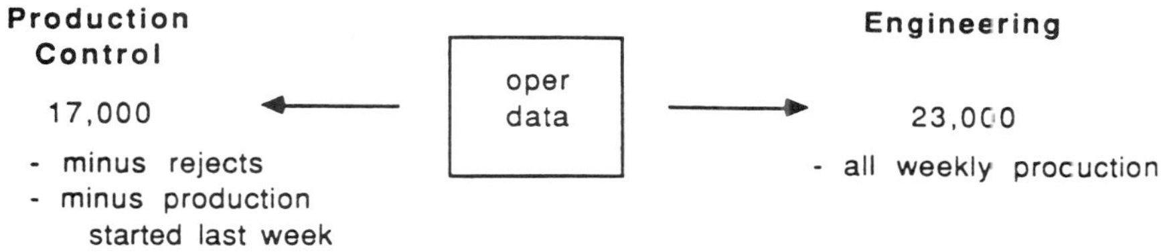

FIGURE 2.4 The algorithmic selection criteria is another reason why inconsistent DSS figures may be created.

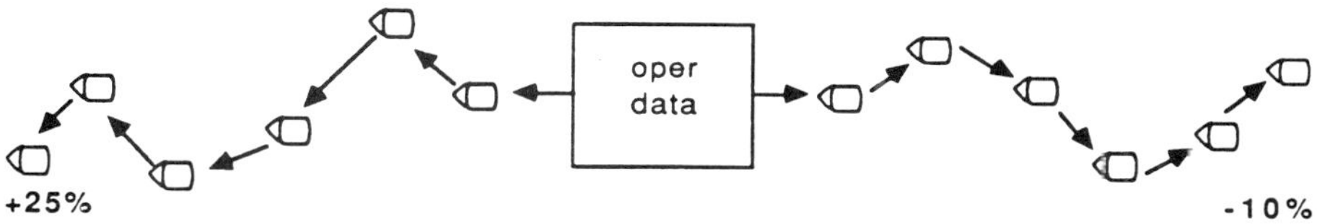

FIGURE 2.5 The circuitous route of extracts that occurs when there are an indeterminate number of extracts.

organization to have less than 5% of the data used in DSS processing come directly from the operational environment, especially where the personal computer is the medium of choice for DSS processing (or at least much of DSS processing) and where floppy disks are freely passed from one end user to the next. Figure 2.5 shows a typically circuitous flow of extracts, away from the source.

One analyst says +25%. Another analyst says −10%. Trying to reconcile who is right and who is wrong, or even why there are such differences of opinion is a tortuous exercise, especially where the passing of floppy disks is involved. And the diagram shown in Figure 2.5 *only* shows six levels of extraction. In reality, six levels of extraction is fairly tame. It is not uncommon to find ten to twelve levels of extraction in a large corporation. Each level of extraction introduces its own complexities and allows the other reasons for lack of credibility to be exaggerated or magnified.

Introduction of Extraneous Data into the Stream of Analysis

As bad (and as realistic!) as the stream of extracts are as shown in Figure 2.5, there is at least a common source of data. It is unfortunately very

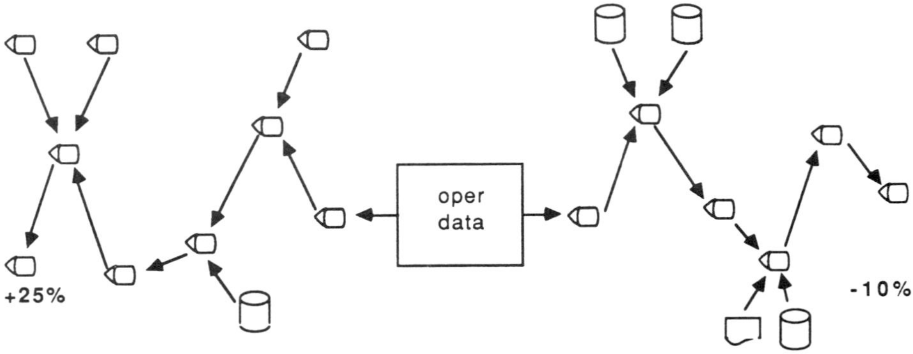

FIGURE 2.6 The introduction of extraneous sources of data into the stream of analysis makes reconciliation of inconsistent DSS processing very, very difficult.

common to have other, extraneous data, whose origin is unknown, interjected into the stream of analysis. The phenomenon of introducing data with unknown sources is especially rampant where the personal computer is widely used. Figure 2.6 shows such a typical jobstream.

The data may come from manual entry (using Lotus 1-2-3, for example), from borrowed disks, and so forth. Once entered into the stream of analysis, there is very little anyone can do about reconciliation of data, and the lack of credibility of DSS data grows.

Inconsistent Sources of Data

A final factor leading to the lack of credibility of DSS data is the lack of a consistent source of data to begin with. The marketing department personnel do their analysis of results from a file created by the field agents, who directly report their activities. And accounting personnel do their analysis based on billables. There may or may not *ever* be any coordination or reconciliation of the field agents' information with that of the accounts billable information. And, if the field agents and the accounting department personnel are never in synch to begin with, it is no surprise that the DSS analyses based on the different sources are not in synch.

Each of the factors that contribute to the lack of credibility of DSS processing are exaggerated by the number of users doing DSS processing. With only a few DSS analysts, the factors that lead to lack of credibility can be overcome with time, patience, and a desire to do credible DSS processing. But in a short amount of time, the number of people doing DSS processing (coupled with the attitude of end-user autonomy that comes with DSS processing) creates complexities that cannot be overcome reasonably with time and patience. It simply is not reasonable to expect a large, complex organization to become imbued with a motivation for credibility.

The scenario described here is typical of most modern data processing/end user organizations. The problems of credibility of DSS processing described here are the very antithesis of the environment needed to create and maintain the effective DSS organization.

Data Definitions—Breaking the Tie

One of the essential activities of satisfying the DSS needs of an organization is to arrive at a common definition of data. Once having determined a common definition, the designer can achieve some degree of reconciliation. For example, marketing support calls a customer someone who uses or might use the services of the enterprise. But accounting calls a customer a person or an organization who has established an account.

While these definitions sound very similar, and, in fact, for many customers are equivalent, they are not the same. For example, does marketing allow an organization to be a customer? It does not according to marketing's definition. And does accounting allow a prospect who has not established an account to be a customer? It does not according to accounting's definition of a customer.

To achieve reconciliation, a broader definition of a customer that meets both marketing's and accounting's needs can be built:

- Customer—a person or an organization that holds or might have an interest in holding an account for the purposes of using the service of the organization.

The best resolution of conflicting definitions is to broaden the definition.

Broadening the definition does not always work well—for a wide variety of reasons. In this case, the data designer of DSS systems can *break the tie*, or satisfy a whole host of reasons why organizations cannot agree on a common definition. The designer can add the qualifiers to data so that, upon examining the data, each organization can determine whether the data meets its own definition.

For example, if marketing and accounting cannot agree on a common definition of customer, the DSS analyst can create a data element—customer (whatever that is!) and attach several attributes to it. For example:

```
CUSTOMER
    @ACCOUNT ESTABLISHED? (Y/N)
    @DATE ACCOUNT ESTABLISHED
    @INDIVIDUAL/ORGANIZATION
    @SERVICES USED
```

With the above data, accounting can weed through *customers* that do or do not have accounts; marketing can weed through individuals or organizations. If the differences of opinion cannot be solved at the definition level, they can be resolved at the data element level by carrying *all* the data used for data qualification.

Of course, when accounting tallies the number of customers to be 4,000 and marketing tallies the customers to be 10,000, there is still a debate as to who is correct. But, building *all* definition criteria into the system at the outset provides a firm foundation for sorting out differences of opinion and for making adjustments as the definitions change.

TIMELINESS, EASE OF ACCESS OF DATA

Credibility of data is hardly the only issue facing the organization that is motivated to create the effective DSS organization. An equally powerful motivation (and a much more obvious motivation) is that of being able to get to data in a timely, easy-to-access manner.

There are two aspects to the issue of timeliness and ease of access of data:

- What time and what effort are required to get at data already in place; and
- What time and what effort are required to position data properly to be used for DSS processing.

Both aspects of timeliness and ease-of-access of data must be satisfied in order for DSS processing to be effective. Both aspects will be illustrated in examples.

Getting to Data that is Already There

One day, the manager of a large insurance company called the data administrator in and asked for a simple report to find out, for all policies in force, how long had the policies been in force and if the policies were to elapse, when would they elapse.

The manager reminded the data administrator the information about policies was already to be found in systems that were up and running. Indeed, the policy systems—of which there were literally hundreds—are depicted by Figure 2.7.

The data administrator set out to determine what would be required to produce a report that carried common data across all the policies of the company. The data administrator decided that three activities needed to be done:

1. Locate the basic policy data needed;
2. Extract the basic policy data, and place it in a common location (in an ORACLE table) with other basic policy data; and
3. Make available the programmer and analysis resources needed to accomplish 1. and 2.

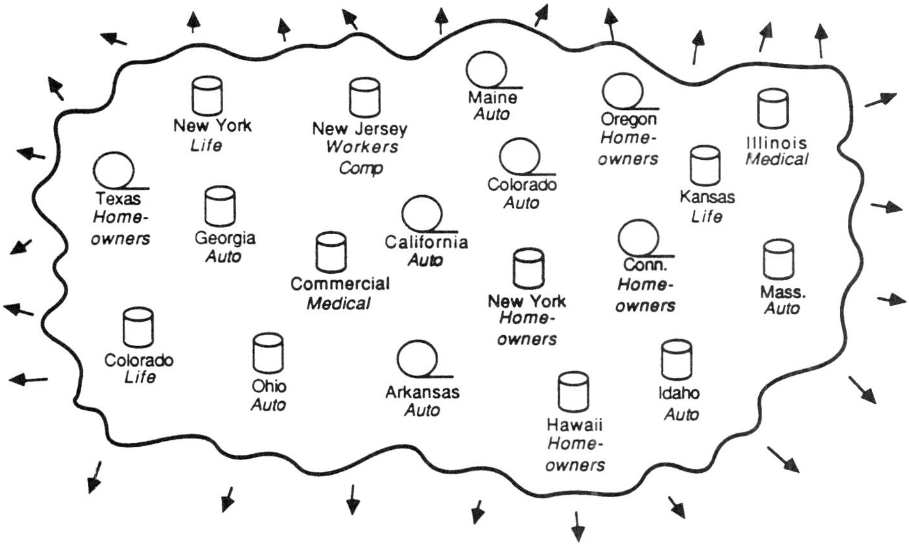

FIGURE 2.7 The existing policy systems—a sample.

The data administrator attempted to estimate how long it would take to produce the desired report. Figure 2.8 shows that the data administrator had to look at literally hundreds of master files and databases on which basic policy data might be found.

The next step in producing the simple policy report required that the basic policy information, once found, be collected in a common place (i.e., in an ORACLE table). To do this a program had to be written wherever basic policy information existed, and basic policy information existed in hundred of places, as shown by Figure 2.9. In addition, the extract program had to be written in the *native* language and environment, such as VSAM, IMS, IDMS, FOCUS, etc.

Figure 2.9 shows that *many* programs had to be written. The extract programs were simple enough, but there were a lot of them, and the interface to each of the individual systems was inconsistent—in terms of format, technology, and so forth.

The third step in producing the desired policy report is a function of the first two steps. The more programmer analyst resources were required, the more of an obstacle this step became.

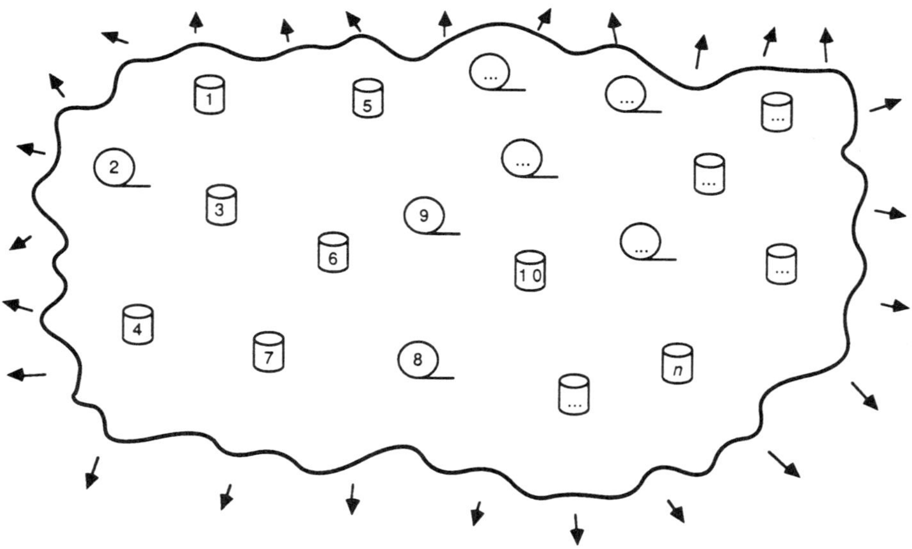

FIGURE 2.8 The number of databases/files that must be examined to determine where and if basic policy information exists.

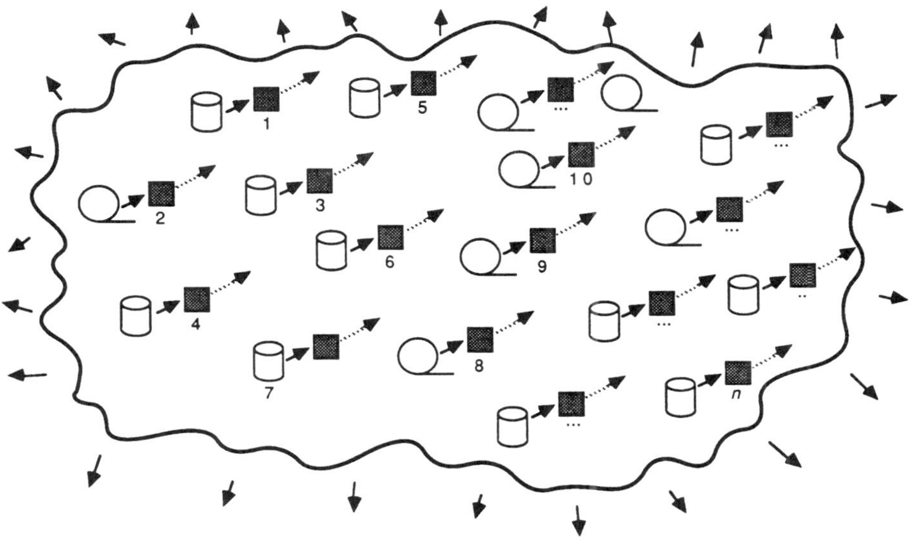

FIGURE 2.9 The number of extract and collection programs that have to be written to collect the basic policy information.

The data administrator made the following estimate:

1. locate policy data—6 months;
2. build collection programs—6–12 months;
3. wait for programmer/analyst resources—3–12 months; and
4. produce report—15–30 months.

The data administrator reported that, given top priority, the new report would take 15 months to produce. Without top priority even more time would be required.

The manager requesting the report was perplexed. His stance was that the data already existed in house, so why would it take so long to get to the data? And why were so many programming resources required?

This (true!) story illustrates the futility of DSS processing if the results cannot be delivered in a timely manner. It is a sure bet that if the basic policy report is produced one to three years after requested, that the manager requesting the report:

- will be gone;
- will have forgotten why the report was needed in the first place;
- will have changed his or her mind as to what was needed;
- or, *all* of the above!

The usefulness of the information requested will be lost before the information can be gathered!

The second issue of timeliness of information is related to the speed of the flow of information. An interesting exercise is to measure how long the news of an event takes to flow through the systems of an organization. The flow can be called the *information cycle*.

For example, an insurance agent sells a policy on a Friday afternoon. On Monday, the agent electronically records the sale of the policy. The information cycle begins on Monday, when the news of the policy becomes electronically known. The question now is, how long is the information cycle? When will the sale of the new policy show up in the company's policies in force count? When will the sale of the new policy show up in the actuary's risk portfolio? When will the sale of the new policy show up in the account premium's receivable portfolio?

In some companies there is a very short information cycle. In other companies, the information cycle is long. And, in other companies, the information cycle is complete for some types of information and incomplete for other kinds of information. For example, in some companies, the sale of a policy might not *ever* show up in the actuary's risk portfolio.

Unless the information cycle can be shortened and made consistent, the DSS information that flows through different levels of extracts can never be consistent or timely.

COST OF PROCESSING

After the major issues of DSS processing are recognized—credibility and timeliness—there remains the issue of cost of DSS processing. The ultimate in futility of DSS processing is expressed in the following statement by a manager of an oil company:

"We have over 6,000 people doing DSS processing and have had them doing 'their thing' for over nine years now. We are running under four mainframes and countless personal computers. If we pulled the plug on the whole complex, the oil business would go right on operating without blinking an eye. The effect of all this DSS processing on the running of the company is nil."

Regardless of the reasons for the opinions of this manager, the fact is that many resources have been dedicated to DSS processing and there has been *very little* discernible payback.

There are some guidelines that relate to resource utilization in the DSS environment. They are:

- The end user, *at all times*, should pay for resources consumed for DSS processing. The best of all worlds is one in which the end user actually owns the hardware, software, and operations of the computer used to do DSS processing. It is patently a mistake to treat DSS costs like operational costs, and to try to *allocate* resource costs based on percentage of usage, as is typical of operational processing.
- Only the minimum amount of data should be stored for DSS processing. It is a temptation to store huge amounts of data as a contingency for unknown DSS processing. The cost of storing huge amounts of data for unknown purposes can be horrendous.

As an example of the last cost-related issue, a drug company was planning a DSS system. The foundation of the system was to be the moving of stock on their shelves for the past ten years' time. There were:

1. lots of drugstores;
2. lots of shelves;
3. lots of items on each shelf; and
4. lots of activity for each item.

The drugstore, as a basis for their DSS processing, desired to keep the following data:

number of stores × number of shelves × number of items × activity × 10 years

The result was a staggering amount of data. The cost of storing (not to mention manipulating the data) was horrendous. (In fact, the cost was so high that the company immediately rejected the attempt to do DSS processing that way.)

The intent was to put the massive amount of data into ORACLE. From the standpoint of ORACLE handling the amount of data, there was no problem. But the amount of processing required huge amounts of daily detailed processing. At this point ORACLE became a problem. (Indeed, any DBMS would have been a problem in terms of the volume of data to be processed.)

A compromise was reached when two aspects of the design were changed:

1. only two years of data was held as a basis for DSS analysis, not ten years; and
2. activities were summarized by the week.

The net effect of these compromises—which realistically did little to lessen the effect of doing DSS processing—was to lower the cost of DSS processing and storage by almost two orders of magnitude.

The third issue facing the DSS analyst wishing to build an effective DSS environment is that of cost.

IN SUMMARY

There are three major issues which separate the DSS environment from the effective DSS environment. Those issues are:

- credibility;
- timeliness; and
- cost.

Credibility is a function of the number of people doing DSS processing and the timing, algorithmic content, number of levels of extract, and the extraneous data that gets in the analysis stream. Timeliness and ease of access of DSS processing relates to the amount and consolidation of DSS data, and to the length of the information cycle. The cost of DSS processing relates to who pays for DSS processing and the level of detail that is stored.

QUESTIONS: CHAPTER 2

1. The first technology associated with DSS processing was ________ and ______________.
2. The DSS/ORACLE environment MAY/MAY NOT draw data from the IMS, VSAM, or other environments.
3. IMS IS/IS NOT a good tool to use for DSS processing.
4. The three major issues of DSS/ORACLE data are: ___________, , and ______________.
5. A "time basis" of data is one requirement for reconciliation. T/F
6. External data SHOULD/SHOULD NOT fit into the DSS environment.
7. Because data already exists in a shop's systems it IS/MIGHT BE/ IS NOT easy to access.
8. The flow from operational to DSS systems to the business back to the operational environment is called the ______________
9. END USER/DP should pay for DSS processing.

CHAPTER 3

An Architecture for Effective DSS/ORACLE Systems

Recognizing the issues that must be resolved for an effective DSS/ORACLE environment is the first step toward the creation of that environment. But mere recognition of the issues is not enough. The next, necessary step is the creation of an architecture that can be used to address the issues of effective DSS/ORACLE processing.

Part of the architecture is technical and part of the architecture is application-oriented. Both components—the technical and the application—are required. Either aspect without the other is insufficient.

There is a standard architecture that has evolved that addresses the needs of effective DSS/ORACLE processing. The architecture is generic across many types of businesses—airlines, banks, insurance companies, government institutions, retailers, manufacturers, and *many* others. In fact, what is surprising is not the number and types of businesses the architecture is applicable to, but the number and types of business that the architecture is not applicable to. There are very few types of enterprise to which the effective DSS architecture is not applicable.

The effective DSS architecture is described in great detail in *DATA ARCHITECTURE: THE INFORMATION PARADIGM*, QED Information Sciences, Inc., 1989. The description of the DSS architecture here will be cursory and will focus on the DSS and ORACLE aspects of the architecture. The reader is invited to read the book above for more detail than can be presented here.

THE EVOLUTION OF THE ARCHITECTURE

The origins of the architecture for effective DSS processing began long ago. ORACLE and relational technology were not born when the seeds for the effective DSS architecture were sown. In the early 1960's there sprang up master files with the first attempts at automation. Master files were almost exclusively found on magnetic tapes. The master files were a standard part of the data processing milieu which included punched cards, paper tape, COBOL, and many reports. Figure 3.1 is a simple depiction of the world of automation of the 1960's.

The automated processing of the 1960's exploded, and the number of master files grew at a geometric rate. Soon the few master files that a shop had begun with had increased into many, many (in the largest case the author has seen—up to 180,000) master files, as shown by Figure 3.2.

The explosion and proliferation of master files was such that oftentimes the number of tape drives that could be hung off of the computer became a limiting operational and design factor.

The massive explosion of tape drives carried with it an interesting

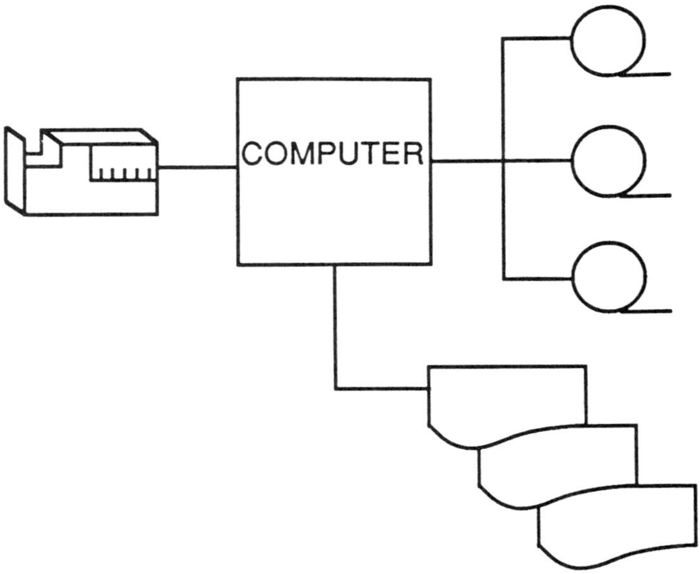

FIGURE 3.1 The world of 1960's data processing.

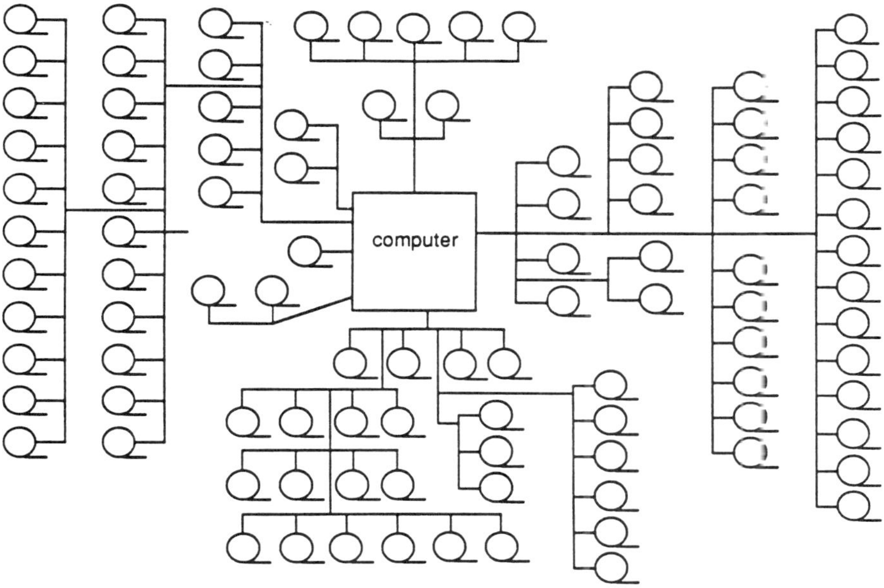

FIGURE 3.2 The explosion of master files.

implication. On one hand, the number of master files were exploding but the master files were not—after a point—covering and containing new ground. The same data was beginning to appear on master file after master file. Redundancy of data across the master file environment became one of the largest problems facing the data processing manager. The problems of redundancy showed up in many guises—maintenance problems, synchronization problems, development problems, and so forth. Figure 3.3 illustrates the redundant data that came with master files.

An interesting phenomenon is that, after a point, the more master files that were built, the more redundancy of data there was. In other words, the more new development that was completed, the more redundancy became a problem. At some point it actually became self-defeating to build new systems in the face of master files.

The wholesale problems of redundancy of data that arose with master files did not go unnoticed. With the advent of the widespread availability of direct access storage devices (DASD) arose the notion of the database.

Database and DASD offered some technological advantages, such

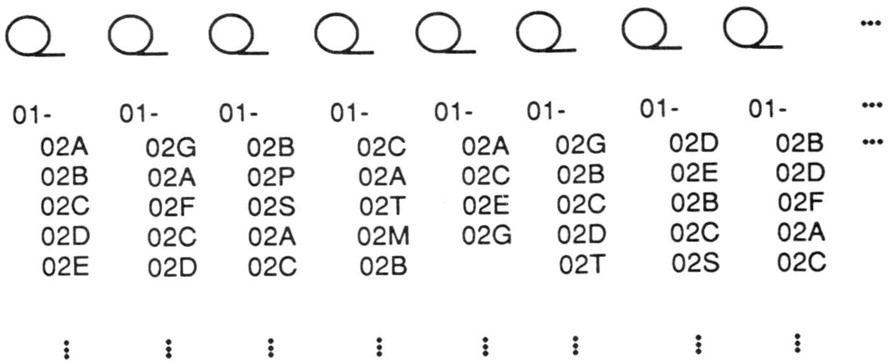

FIGURE 3.3 Taken collectively, the master files contained tremendous amounts of redundant data.

as the ability to directly access data (unlike master files, which could only be sequentially accessed). But, database also offered the means by which data could be consolidated; and, with the consolidation of data, the removal of the redundancy of data. Figure 3.4 shows the consolidation of data and the advent of data base and DASD.

Because master files had produced so much redundancy of data, and because redundancy of data truly was one of the worst problems facing the data processing department, one of the basic tenets of database became

- Databases contain no redundancy of data.

For a world in 1970 that was reeling from the master files that were engulfing it, the notion of reducing or eliminating redundancy of data was welcome relief.

Soon after data began to find its way onto DASD and data-bases, on-line processing began to emerge. Since there was no longer a need to sequentially pass massive amounts of data to get to a single record, it became possible to access data directly and efficiently. This new-found capability of being able to efficiently access a single record of data allowed an entirely new way of processing data to be born. On-line processing is processing that can occur quickly enough for the user to respond interactively. A two to three second response is the norm for online processing. With the emergence of on-line processing came a whole new way of using the computer. Soon the computer was closely

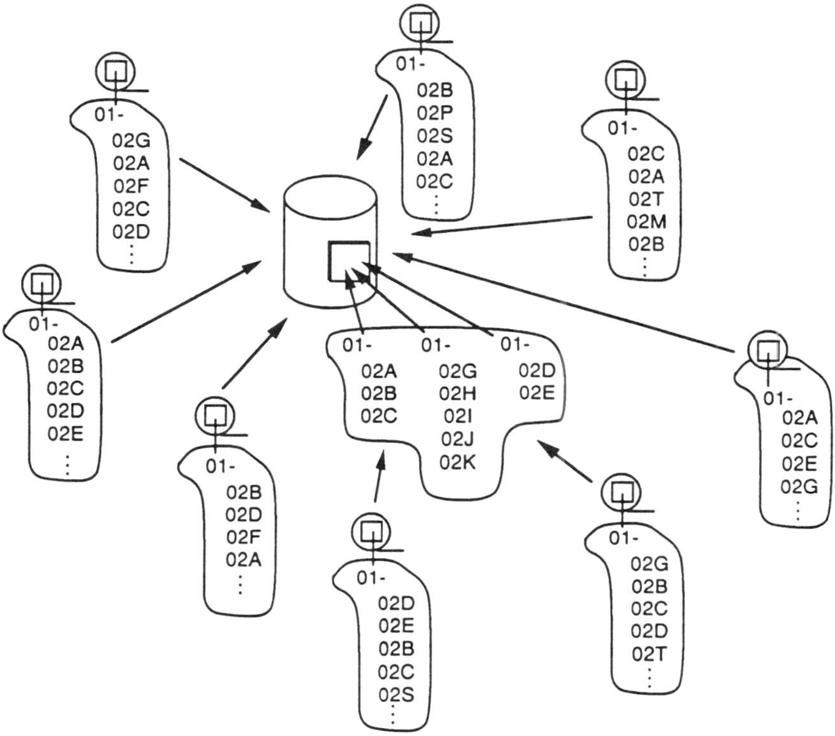

FIGURE 3.4 Database offered the hope of consolidating the many master files that had arisen and reducing the redundancy of data.

linked to the day-to-day business of the enterprise through the transaction processing possible with the online access of data. Figure 3.5 shows the *standard* configuration that applied to the 1970–1980 time period.

While on-line processing made possible entirely new ways to do business, it also demanded a discipline of design and operation in order to give consistent, good response time. In fact, because on-line processing was so closely tied to the business, good response time became essential.

At the same time that online transaction processing was occurring and large, detailed databases were beginning to be built, there arose the notion that the data collected and the database operations in place

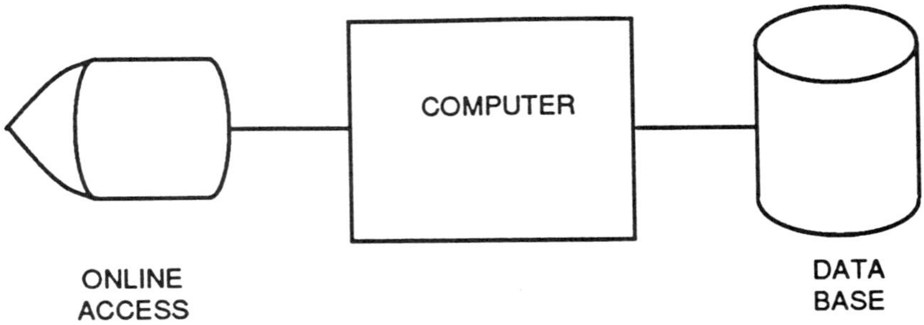

FIGURE 3.5 The standard operating configuration of the 1970–1980 time frame.

could be used for more than operational processing. There arose the notion that DSS processing could also be done with databases. (In the earliest days, DSS processing was known as MIS, or Management Information Systems.)

Because the database concept that arose with the redundancy of master files called for a single database to serve all purposes, the first attempts at DSS processing were simply to use operational, on-line databases for DSS processing, as shown in Figure 3.6.

In the first efforts at DSS processing there was little or no attempt

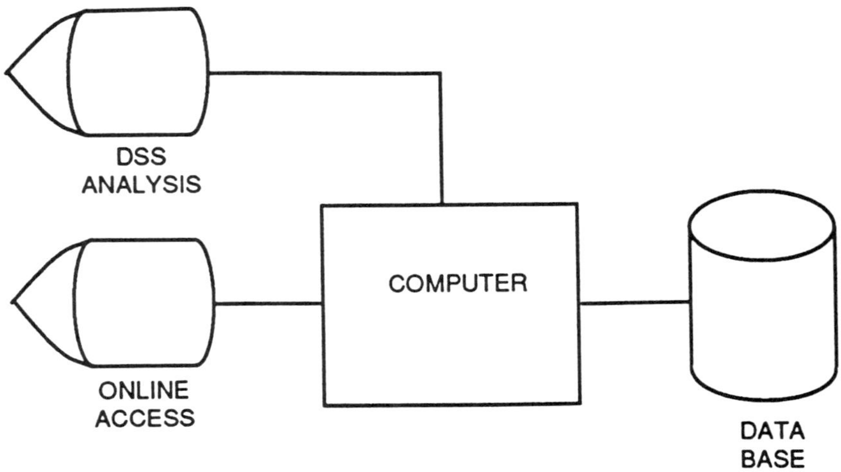

FIGURE 3.6 The first attempts at using database for DSS processing.

made to distinguish between the two types of processing—on-line operational processing and DSS, analytical processing. This strategy presented no problem as long as:

- There were plenty of hardware resources to go around;
- there were no massive DSS processes that had to be run during the on-line day (i.e., as long as DSS processing looked like just another form of operational processing); and
- the level of DSS processing remained stable.

But in short order, one or more of these conditions were violated. The very nature of DSS processing ran contrary to these conditions, and in short order the operations staff had two choices:

- run no DSS processing and maintain good online, operational response time; or
- try to run DSS processing with operational on-line processing and buy a lot more hardware.

Some shops actually tried to buy hardware as a solution to the problems of doing operational and analytical processing together, but they soon found it was a futile approach for a variety of reasons. Buying more hardware was like trying to build on shifting sand. The purchase of more hardware for one component created other hardware bottlenecks elsewhere. Buying more DASD led to a demand for more and larger communications lines. Larger communication lines led to the request for more buffers. More buffers led to the request for more regions. Larger regions led to the request for different software. And so forth. It was like a dog chasing its tail—a very expensive tail at that. The next strategy was to *duplex* the computer, as shown in Figure 3.7.

In Figure 3.7 it is seen that on-line, operational processing is done from 8:00 a.m. to 5:00 p.m., the normal working hours of the corporation. DSS processing is done from 7:00 p.m. to 6:00 a.m., when the machine resources become available. While the tools the DSS analyst used may have been very *user friendly*, the fact that the DSS analyst had to work the graveyard shift was decidedly unfriendly, and the duplexing strategy soon ground to a halt.

The next approach in the evolution of DSS processing occurred as data was *extracted* from the operational data-base, as shown by Figure 3.8.

The extraction of data solved all sorts of problems. It allowed data

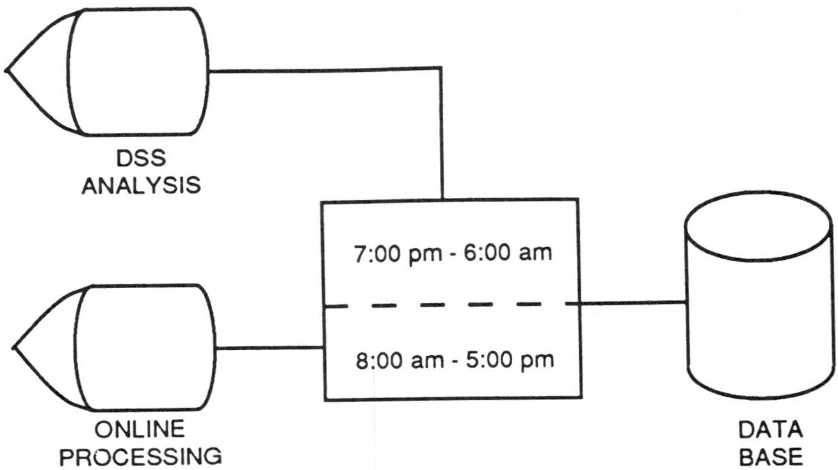

FIGURE 3.7 A duplexed processing exvironment.

to be pulled into other environments where there was no conflict of resources. Once the data was extracted, it could be accessed anytime, night or day.

No one seemed to notice that extraction of data was violating the principle of nonredundancy of data that had been so hard won in the 1970's. Extraction of data as a solution to the conflicts of DSS and operational processing directly and immediately led to redundancy of data.

As data was extracted, it was transported to a variety of machines for processing. Some data was sent back to the same machine on which on-line processing was done. Other data was sent to other processors.

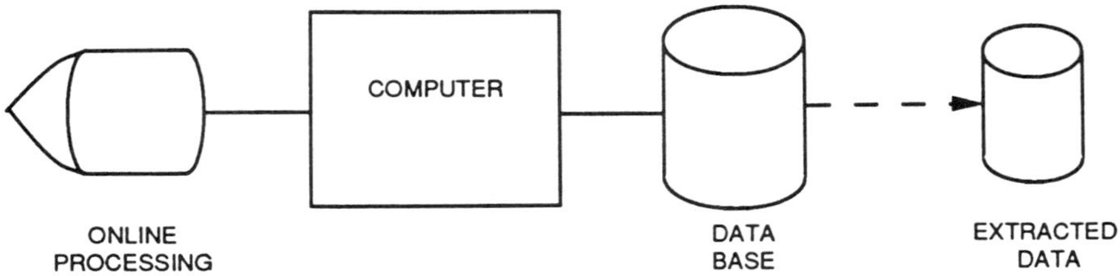

FIGURE 3.8 The extraction of data.

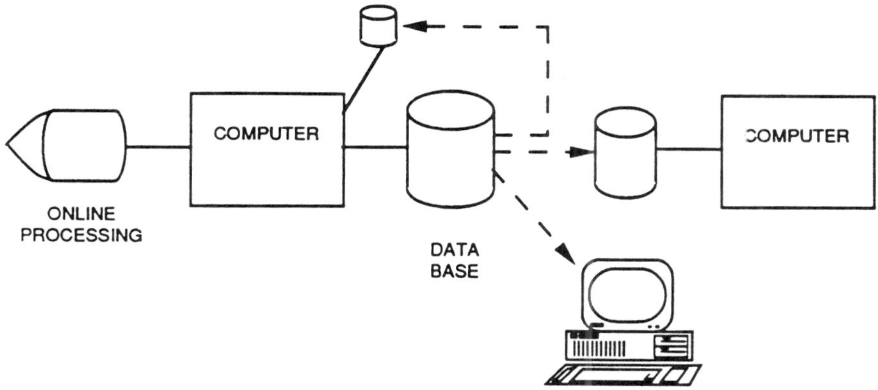

FIGURE 3.9 The extracted data was sent to a variety of processors.

Still other data was sent to smaller microprocessors. Figure 3.9 shows the wide variety of processors to which extracted data was sent.

After a while, not much extracted data was sent back to the processor that was originally doing the on-line processing, and more extracted data was sent elsewhere. There were increasingly fewer resources available for on-line operational processing. What resources were available were dedicated to the on-line operational processing, not to DSS processing.

The demand for extract processing grew quickly, much like the explosive growth of master files that had occurred almost two decades earlier. In short order, a massive amount of extract processing grew up overnight. But the extract processing did not grow in an orderly fashion. Instead it grew in a random fashion. And extracts soon grew from other extracts, not just from the operational source of data. These *second level* extracts quickly grew into *third level*, then *fourth level* extracts, and so forth. In addition, external sources of data were introduced into the stream of analysis. The explosive growth of extract processing is depicted by Figure 3.10.

In due time organizations found that the scenario in Figure 3.10 was grossly wasteful of resources and, among other things, led to a lack of credibility of DSS processing (as discussed in Chapter 2). As soon as the organization became serious about DSS processing, the evolution toward a centralized, foundation DSS database began. Such a foundation is termed an *atomic* level DSS database due to the very

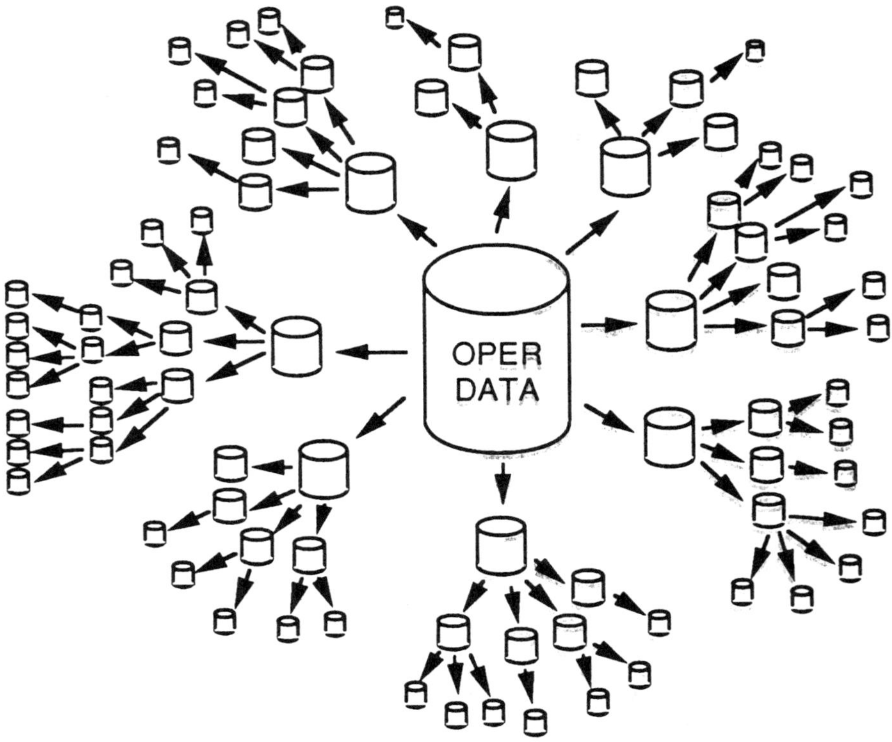

FIGURE 3.10 The explosion of extract processing.

granular nature of the data. The migration to an atomic DSS database from the chaos created by the explosion of extract processing is shown by Figure 3.11.

In Figure 3.11 it is seen that DSS processing migrates to an atomic foundation when the pressures for credibility and productivity grow strong enough. (As long as an organization does not recognize and/or care about the issues of credibility and productivity, there is little incentive to migrate to the atomic-centered environment.)

The final stage of the migration to the atomic-centered environment occurs as the DSS environment beyond the atomic level formalizes. Two types of DSS processing emerge from the chaos beyond the atomic level. One type of DSS processing that emerges is departmental processing, which usually involves large, scheduled reports.

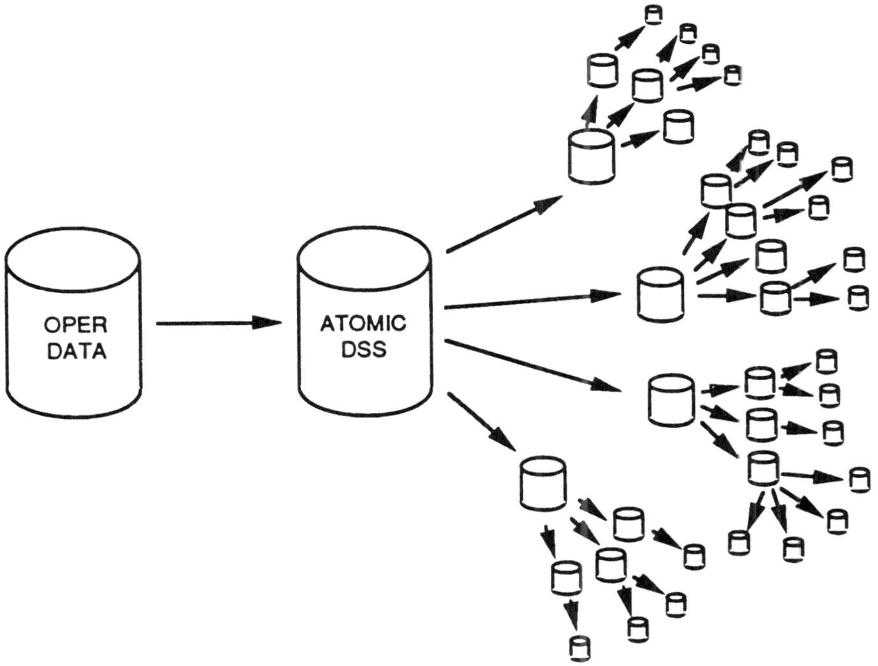

FIGURE 3.11 The consolidation of DSS processing around an atomic (foundation) DSS database.

The other type of DSS processing which emerges is individual processing, which is a smaller scale of departmental processing and is usually done on a nonscheduled, non-repetitive basis. Figure 3.12 depicts the fully-mature DSS environment.

The different phases of evolution of the DSS architecture are depicted by Figure 3.13.

The length of time for full evolution is years in most shops. Major changes do not happen overnight. And, in fact, the evolution seldom takes place as cleanly as depicted. But the evolution does occur and is the product of very powerful forces.

The architecture that has been presented is useful as a paradigm. The different components of the architecture are worthy of examination. In later chapters the components of the architecture will be discussed in depth.

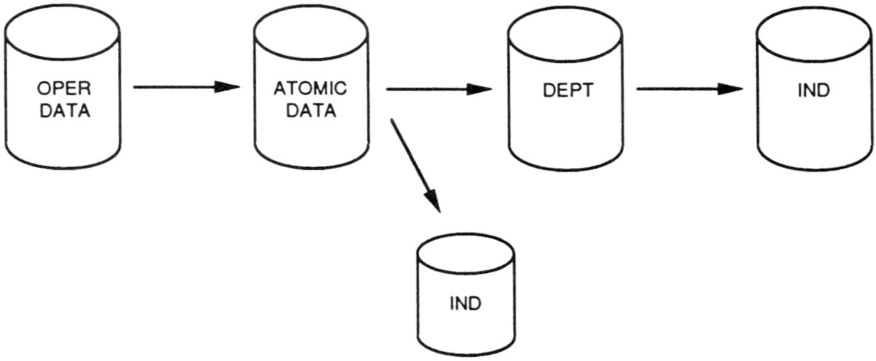

FIGURE 3.12 The fully matured DSS environment.

The four major components of the architecture are:

- operational data and processing—IMS and VSAM and other standard pieces of software usually fill this niche, for no other reason than historically they were the first on-line, operational systems built;
- atomic data and processing—ORACLE fills this niche in many shops;
- departmental data and processing—a wide variety of software, such as SAS, FOCUS, ORACLE, M204, etc. fill this niche; and
- individual data and processing—PC-oriented software such as Lotus 1-2-3, dBASEIV, etc. fill this niche.

The DSS components of the architecture include:

- atomic data and processing;
- departmental data and processing; and
- individual data and processing.

From the technology of ORACLE, a typical, fully-matured environment might look like that shown in Figure 3.13.1

Operational VSAM and IMS databases feed atomic level ORACLE databases. The ORACLE atomic databases feed a wide variety of data bases, such as M204, FOCUS, SAS, etc. The departmental databases feed a variety of individual data-bases.

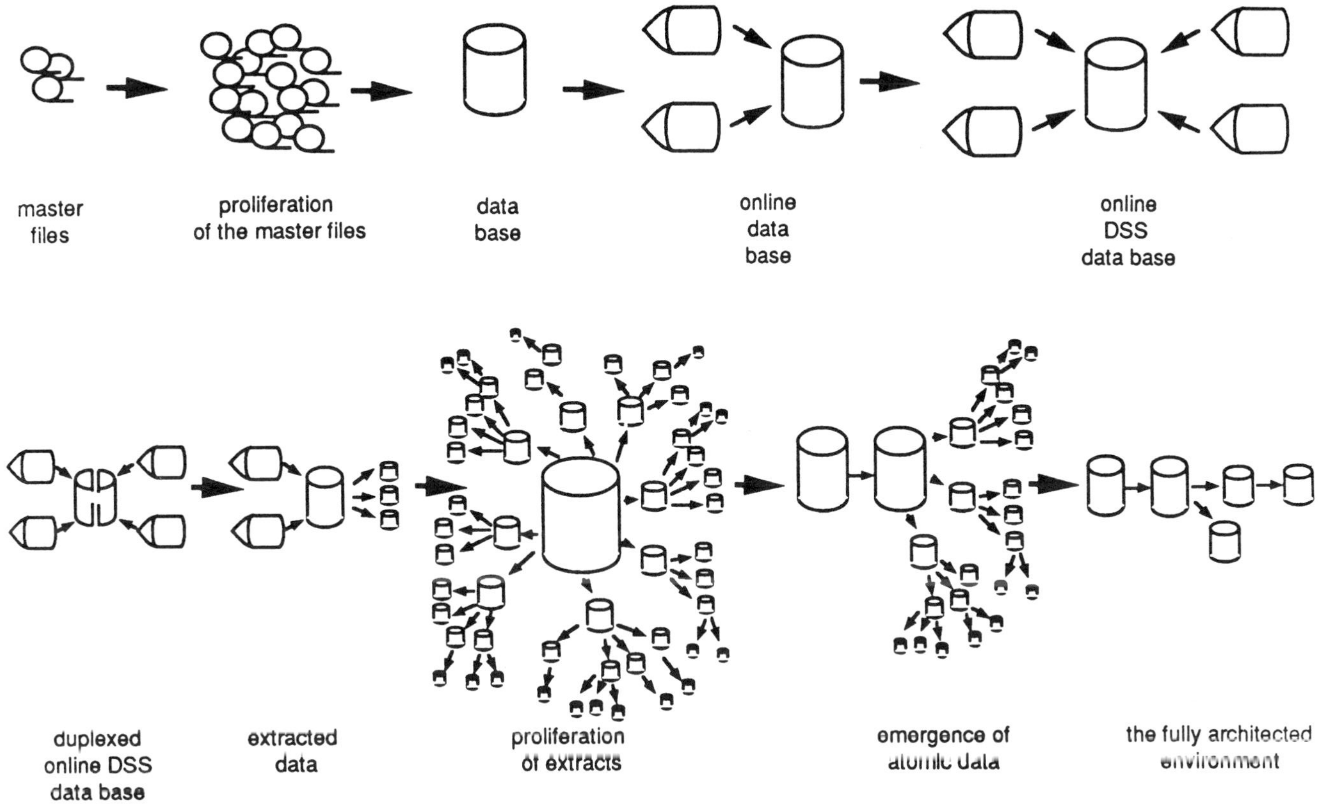

FIGURE 3.13 The different stages of the evolution of the atomic-centered environment.

Operational Data

Operational data is data that is required to run the day-to-day business of the corporation. As such, the probability of access of operational data is high. Indeed, the single most defining characteristic of operational data is its high probability of access. In general, operational data is very detailed, and is accurate up to the second. Operational data is featured in high-performance, high-availability systems.

Atomic Data

Atomic data is the most granular data that a corporation has. Every element of atomic level data is associated with some moment in time (i.e., all atomic level data is archival). There is a modest to low probability of access of atomic data. Atomic level data is available for use as the foundation for all DSS processing. Indeed, no DSS processing is done using official data that does not have as its origin atomic level data. The atomic level may contain summary data when the summary data needs to be available to the corporation (sometimes called *public* summary data). The source of atomic level data is operational data and, occasionally, external sources of data. Atomic data is organized according to the main subject areas of the corporation.

Atomic Data and Redundancy

At first glance it appears that when an organization builds an atomic level database it is introducing massive amounts of redundancy into the atomic-centered environment. A closer inspection of what is happening reveals that quite the opposite is true. By going to an atomic-centered environment, an organization is actually greatly reducing data redundancy.

This point is not easy to see, and requires a deeper explanation. Consider the classical production database, built under the approach that a single database should serve all purposes (a popular notion as database emerged from the era of master files.) Consider the data found in the production database. Figure Insert 1 shows a representation of the classical production environment.

Now compare the atomic-centered operational and the atomic environment to the classical production environment. A comparison is shown by Figure Insert 2.

The figure shows that, from a functional perspective, there is no net gain or loss of data between the classical production environment

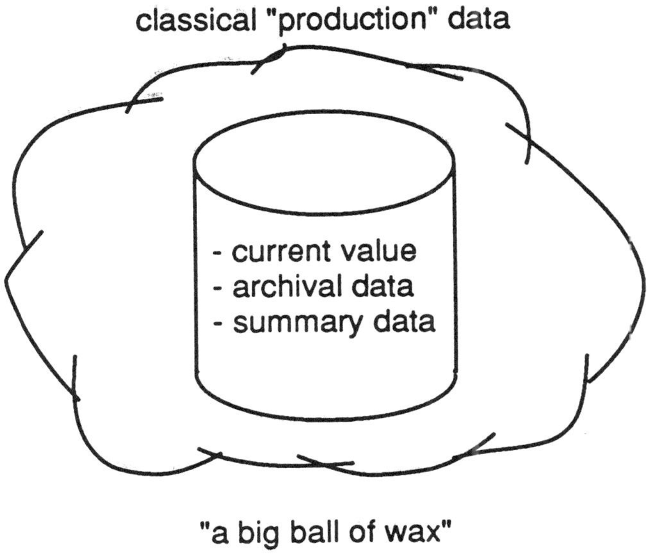

FIGURE 1 All types of data are found in the classical "production" environment. Of course, there are often many physical databases that make up the environment.

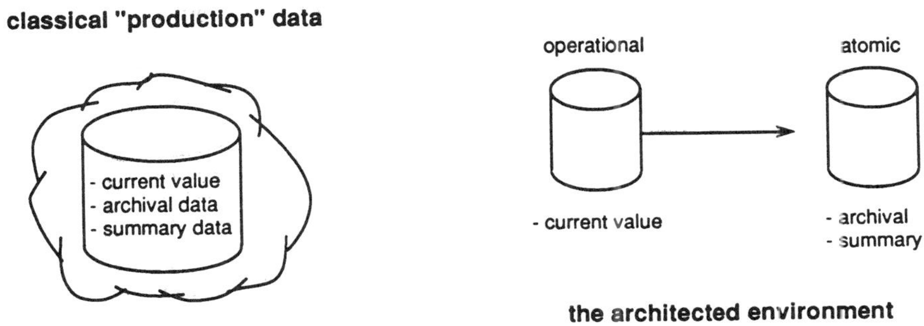

FIGURE 2 From a functional perspective, there is no difference—no net gain or loss—in the amount of data in the atomic centered environment and the classical production environment.

and the atomic-centered environment. Both the classical production environments and the atomic-centered environments have:

- current value data;
- archival data; and
- summary data.

The real difference then between the classical production environment and the atomic-centered environment is not in the quantity of data but in the structuring of the data. The atomic-centered approach recognizes the fundamental difference in usage of data and separates data accordingly, while the classical production environment recognizes no such differences.

An argument can be made that the atomic-centered environment actually saves storage. This argument is made in light of the DSS processing done against a classical production database. Consider how DSS processing is done against a classical production database environment. DSS processing inevitably begins with extract processing. Over time there are not a few extracts done. Instead, many extracts are done. Given the competition to get at classical production data, soon second, third, fourth, and so on generations of extracts are done. Figure Insert 3 shows the normal state of affairs for DSS processing against the classical production environment.

Without a doubt, as DSS processing grows there is *much* redundancy of data among the extracted files. Just how much redundancy is suggested by Figure Insert 4.

The figure shows that there is *much* redundant data stored and processed throughout the classical production environment. A redundancy factor of 500% to 1,000% is not unheard of. There is a certain mindset in this environment that if you can get hold of data, grab as much as you can and hold onto it for a long as you can.

Now consider the atomic-centered environment. How much redundant data exists between the operational and the atomic environment? Figure Insert 5 shows that there is a redundancy factor of not more than 10% between the operational and the atomic levels of data.

What about the remainder of the architected environment—the departmental and the individual levels of processing. There is redundancy of data from one department to the next, and from one individual DSS analyst to the next, as shown by Figure Insert 6.

Most of the data stored and created at the departmental level is summarized data which is unique to the department. While there is

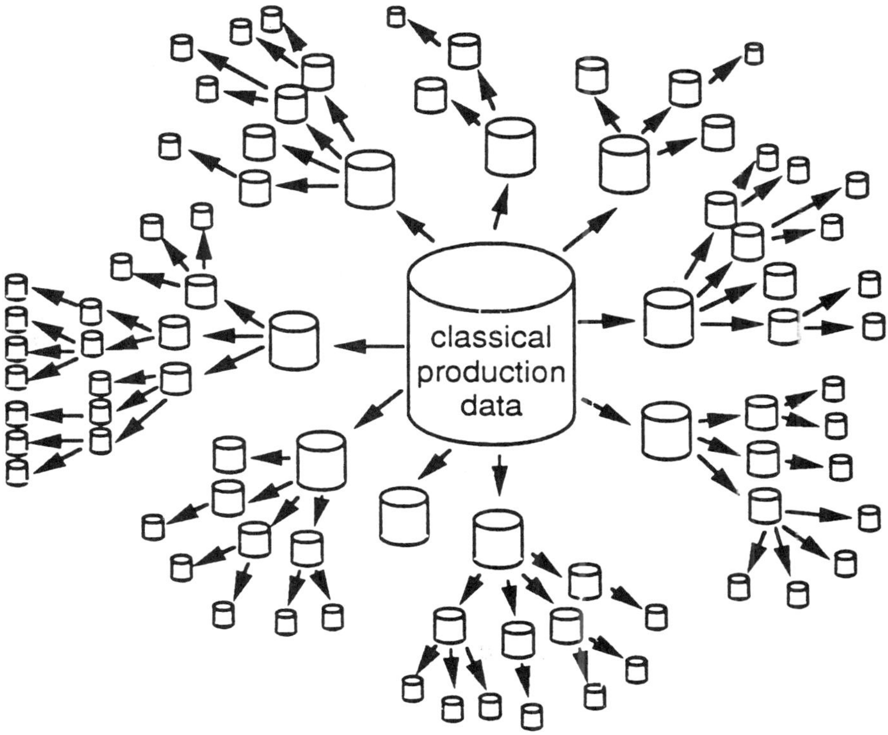

FIGURE 3 A typical classical production environment surrounded by extracts required for DSS processing.

some amount of detailed data stored at the departmental level (that data is certainly redundant among all the other departmental level data), there is only a modicum of data stored there. There is a psychological motivation for not transferring massive amounts of data from the atomic level, and that is the easy availability and easy accessibility of atomic level data. Unlike classical production data where there is a mindset of grabbing as much as you can as often as you can, with the atomic level data there is no need to adopt such a stance.

Furthermore, when data and processing are organized according to departments and budgeting occurs along the lines of the department, the departmental analyst stores as little data as possible because of the costs of storage and manipulation. Thus, in the architected environment there is a psychological freedom that allows the de-

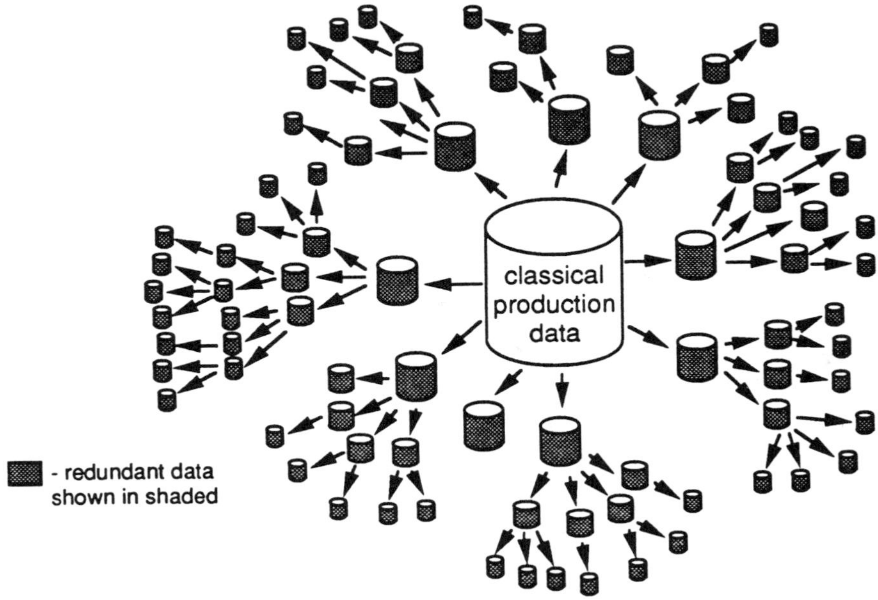

FIGURE 4 The amount of redundant data shown by shaded areas. There is *much* redundant data in the classical DSS extract from "production" data environment.

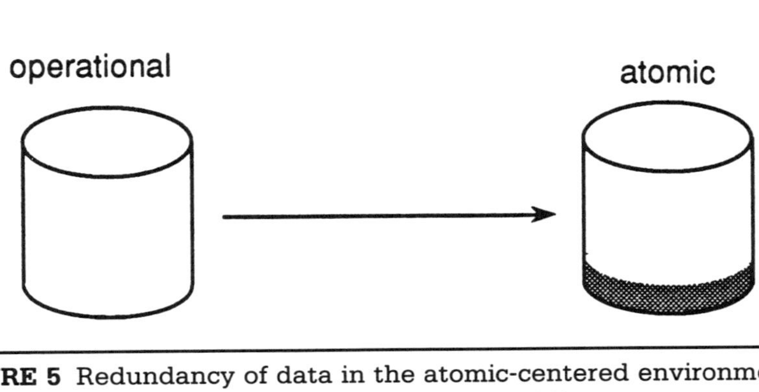

FIGURE 5 Redundancy of data in the atomic-centered environment. A redundancy factor of no more than 10% between operational and the atomic level of data is normal.

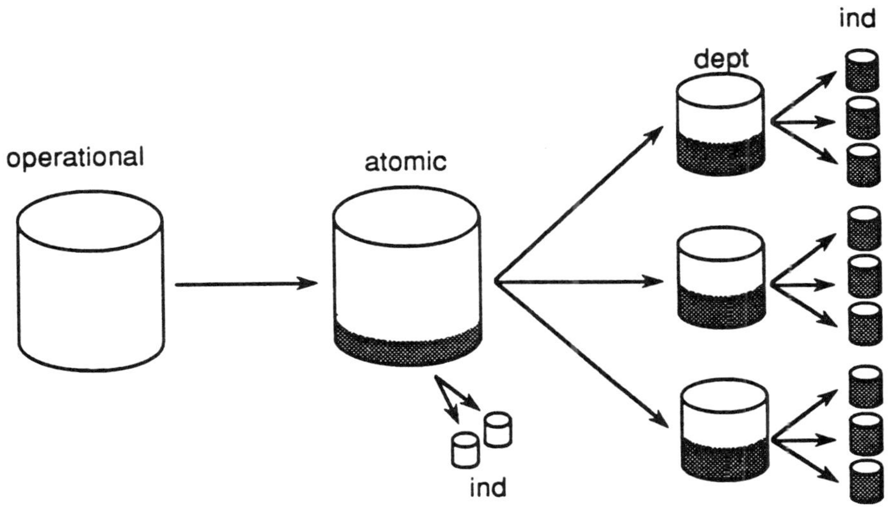

FIGURE 6 There is some data redundancy within the atomic-centered environment.

partmental DSS analyst to grab only what data is needed and no more, as well as a financial incentive.

There is another reason why less total data storage is needed in the atomic-centered environment. The discipline imposed on departmental and individual DSS processing encourages (enforces!) the notion that the DSS analyst use what extracts and what data are already in place. In the classical production environment where there is no discipline in DSS processing at all, the DSS analyst does whatever he or she can do whenever he or she can do it. The mere formalization of the flow of data and processing in the architected environment and the notion that the usage of existing facilities already in place is the proper stance encourages a minimization of redundancy of data.

In the final analysis, the issue of redundancy of data for DSS processing boils down to the comparison made in Figure Insert 7.

In a word, the architected environment is an orderly environment that can be used as a building block for future DSS processing. In doing so, the minimum amount of data redundancy is introduced into the system in the architected environment. On the other hand, the classical production environment with its random extract processing

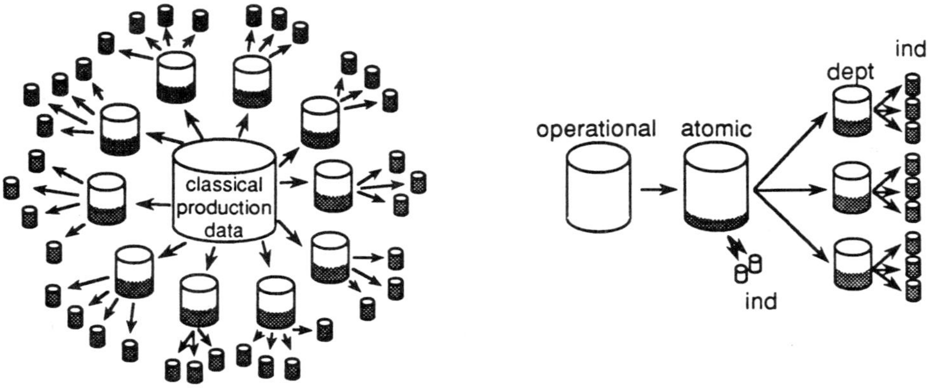

FIGURE 7 Redundancy in the two environments.

encourages massive amounts of redundancy because it does not serve as a foundation on which to build. As a result, every new DSS system must *reinvent* the wheel and, in doing so, create massive amounts of redundancy of data.

Departmental Data

Departmental data is data that is useful and relevant to a department (or a functional area) of the corporation. Departmental data is a combination of both summarized (or derived) data and detailed data, although most departmental data is summarized. There is a great deal of data redundancy from one department to the next. All official data that is fed into the departmental level of processing comes from the atomic level. Private (external) data may be fed into the departmental level if there is absolutely no chance the private data will not be needed anywhere else in the corporation.

Departmental data is characterized by data that is analyzed and used on a scheduled basis, usually involving some large amounts of processing. Typical departmental processing includes such processing as trend analysis, scheduled monthly/quarterly reports, demographic analysis, and so forth.

Individual Levels of Data

Individual processing shares many of the characteristics of departmental processing. The two primary differences between individual and departmental processing are that individual processing is not done on a scheduled basis, and that individual processing usually involves much less data than departmental processing. Other than that, individual level DSS processing is the same, for all practical purposes as departmental processing.

The source of individual processing is atomic level data or departmental level data. In general, the preferred source is the departmental level. On occasion, individual level DSS processing involves using private (external) sources of data when there is absolutely no chance that the private data will be needed anywhere else in the organization.

The flow of data in the architecture has been depicted as a unidirectional flow, as seen in Figure 3.12. But the flow depicted in that figure is only a part of a larger picture. Instead the complete flow of data is as shown in Figure 3.14.

Figure 3.14 shows that data flows from the operational to the DSS world, as has been discussed. But decisions are made using the DSS data. Those decisions in turn affect the business of the organization. And the business of the organization is measured by the operational systems of the organization, which restarts the cycle again.

As an example of the complete cycle of the flow of information, consider a bank. The banking teller and the banking ATM systems

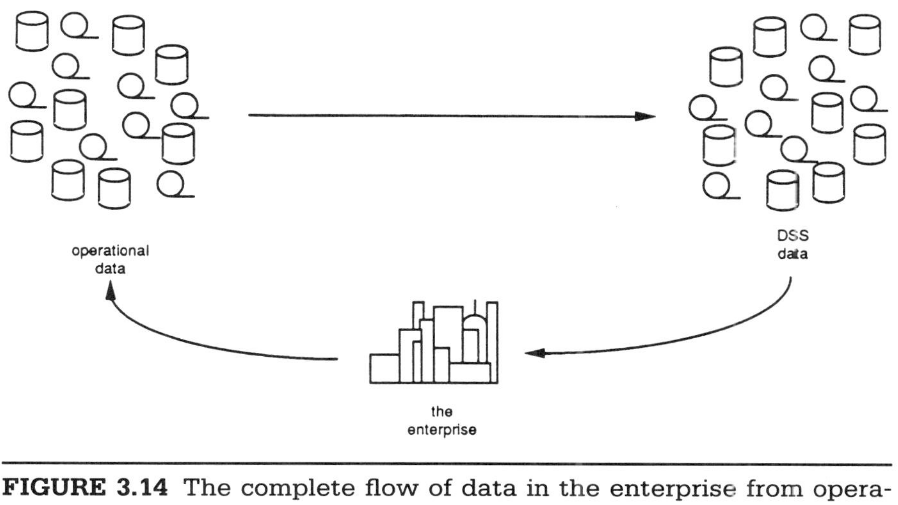

FIGURE 3.14 The complete flow of data in the enterprise from operational to DSS. Decisions made at the DSS level affect the enterprise, which is measured by operational processing.

(operational systems) measure and interact with the business of the bank on a regular and detailed basis. DSS data is taken from the operational processing. Based upon the DSS data that is taken (and other sources of data as well, such as long-range interest forecasts, the Federal Reserve's action, and so forth,) decisions are made. Some of the decisions made include those that relate to interest rates that the bank charges its customers. Should the bank lower interest rates? Raise them? Keep them the same? One way or the other, the rates are set. The setting of the rates has a big effect on the business of the bank. If the rates are lowered, more customers apply for loans. If the rates are raised, fewer customers apply for loans. The effect the raising or lowering of the rates has on the business is measured by operational systems.

It is a mistake to think of the architected DSS environment in terms of the simple uni-directional flow of data depicted in Figure 3.14, even though the flow is accurate as depicted. Instead the analyst must keep in mind the full flow of the information cycle, as portrayed in Figure 3.14.

In a sense, even the simple cycle portrayed by Figure 3.14 is inaccurate because it portrays the manager making decisions that influence the business as receiving input only from the DSS processing that occurs. In fact, the manager who is making business decisions that influence the enterprise is making decisions on much more than just the information generated internally by the organization's own DSS systems.

The larger perspective of how the manager makes decisions is shown by Figure 3.15.

The manager who directs the business of the enterprise uses a wide variety of information in order to make decisions. The DSS input—as important as it is—only serves as input in regards to the internal operation of the enterprise. Other input into the manager includes external information about such topics as:

- the existing marketplace;
- the potential marketplace;
- the consumers;
- the patterns of consumption;
- other external topics, such as the general state of the economy; and
- the competition.

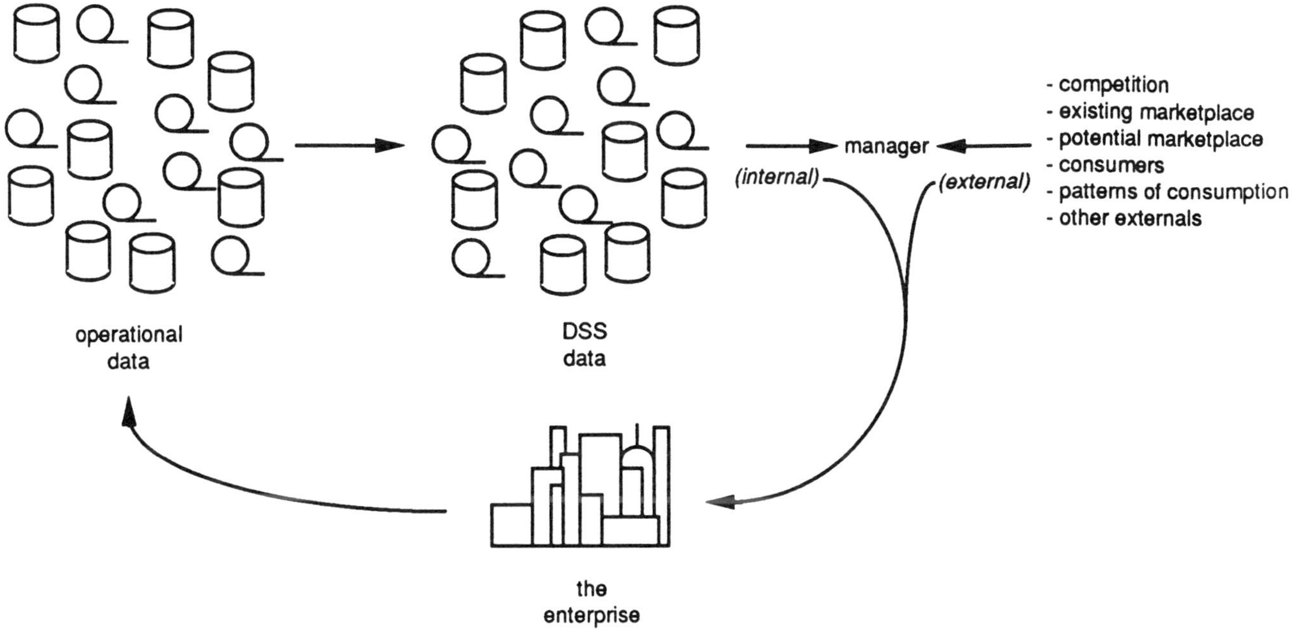

FIGURE 3.15 A more realistic portrayal of the input used by the manager to make decisions that will affect the running of the enterprise.

The manager uses both external and internal input to make decisions. There are (at least!) three aspects to the effective DSS environment as far as supplying management with information. These three critical aspects are:

- timeliness;
- consistency; and
- accuracy.

Each of these aspects will be addressed.

Timeliness is important. It does no good for a manufacturer to find out that orders are dropping off by 10% a month if it takes half of a year to calculate the information. Whenever orders are falling or rising the sooner the manufacturer can have the information, the better.

In most organizations there really isn't one manager who makes decisions that direct the enterprise. It is much more normal for many managers to collectively determine decisions that direct the enterprise. It then becomes important to supply *each* of the managers with consistent information, so that the response to business conditions across the organization will also be consistent.

And finally, accuracy of information is mandatory. If management is being fed incorrect DSS analysis, there is no chance of making the best or consistent business response.

Using the Architecture

The architecture that evolves from operational systems is one that addresses the issues of timeliness, consistency and accuracy, although at first glance it is not immediately obvious how those issues are addressed. Each of these issues will be considered in the context of the architecture.

TIMELINESS. There are two aspects to timeliness—getting the data to flow through the system in a timely manner and delivery of data to the DSS analyst so that each unit of data has the time to which it is relevant as an integral part of the analysis.

The very essence of the atomic level data is timeliness. Each unit of data at the atomic level has the moment in time to which it is relevant *stamped* onto the data. Some examples of atomic level time stamping are:

```
ATM TRANSACTION ID          CHAR (6)
    DATE                    CHAR (6)
    TIME                    CHAR (8)
    AMOUNT                  DECIMALS (5)
    LOCATION                CHAR (2)
    ACCOUNT ID              CHAR (16)
    LINKED TRANSACTION      CHAR (6)
    BALANCE VERIFIED        CHAR (1)
```

or an annual account balance record for a bank's customer:

```
YEAR END                    CHAR (2)
ACCOUNT                     CHAR (10
YEAR BEGINNING BALANCE      DECIMAL (9)
YEAR ENDING BALANCE         DECIMAL (9)
AVERAGE BALANCE             DECIMAL (9)
NUMBER OF OVERDRAFTS        DECIMAL (3)
MAXIMUM BALANCE             DECIMAL (9)
NUMBER OF DEPOSITS          DECIMAL (3)
NUMBER OF WITHDRAWALS       DECIMAL (5)
```

The two types of data layouts shown are typical of what might be found in an atomic database. One data layout—that for ATM transactions—is created whenever an ATM transaction occurs. The time of the activity is prominently featured in the record. Each element of data is relevant to only one activity which in turn is tied to some moment in time.

Another type of activity is the annual account record for a bank's account holder. The record is relevant to the year for which the account has been measured. Interesting information about the account as the account was used throughout the year is stored. Again, all data in the atomic environment is relevant to some moment in time.

The two simple examples of data that might be found in an atomic level data base show ways in which time variancy can be captured or measured in the atomic environment. In some cases as an event occurs; i.e., as an ATM transaction is made, the moment at which the transaction is selected is used to tie the data about the transaction to a moment in time. In the other case, where an annual snapshot of an account's activity is made, the periodicity of the passing of time is used to mark the data. In any case, the data found in either store of data is relevant to some moment in time. All atomic data has this distinction.

Atomic data needs to be tied to some moment in time at the detailed level because of the wide audience using atomic level data. If there ever is to be reconcilability of DSS processing, it must come within the context of time. For example, it is not enough for the accounting DSS analyst to say monthly revenues were $25,651,320, and the marketing analyst to say that revenues were $28,792,434. Either one or the other is right. What is meant by a month must be carefully couched in the context of time, and, with atomic level data that is oriented towards time, such an orientation is easily possible. For example, the accountant, more precisely, should say that monthly revenues for the accounting month—from the 28th of February to the 27th of March are $25,651,320. And marketing, more precisely, should say that for the calendar month of March—from the 1st to the 31st—that revenues are $28,792,434. Now—with the time frames precisely identified—it is clear what the differences between the data are. But without the careful time stamping of detailed data at the atomic level, these distinctions are not possible.

While the emphasis on time stamping of atomic data may appear to be very picky, such attention to detail is necessary if the reconciliation data is to be done. Not all discrepancies of data are solved as easily as the example presented.

Consider another case. The DSS analyst from marketing analyses data in response to a request from management to determine how sales in the West Coast have been going for a new product line. The marketing analyst reports that, to date, $5,000,000 in sales have been counted. Management asks the same question of accounting and accounting states that $7,200,000 in sales have occurred. Who does management believe? And more to the point, who has the correct data?

After close examination, it is determined that marketing has used numbers as of the 15th of the month, and accounting has used more recent numbers as of the 1st of the month. Both analysts are right, but they have not agreed on the right time frame for analysis. Without detailed time stamping of data at the atomic level, it is not possible to reconcile the differences.

It should be pointed out that if reconciliation were never needed between more than two or three parties, the attention to the detail of the time variancy of data at the atomic level would not be necessary. But where there are hundreds, and in some cases thousands of analysts doing work, reconciliation of data becomes a very large, very complex task that can only be accomplished by careful definition of what the DSS analysis entails and what data goes into the DSS analysis.

But reconciliation of the time basis of data is only one issue of timeliness. The other issue is how fast the data flows through the architecture, from the point of becoming electronically known to the operational systems to the point of being available to DSS processing.

Contrast the flow of data required in the architected environment to that required in the classical *production* environment, where many extracts of data are done, as shown in Figure 3.16.

The length of time to go from the operational environment to the departmental environment is absolutely the minimal amount of time. The flow in the architected environment is direct, and the only extracts that exist are those that must exist.

CONSISTENCY. The next major issue of DSS processing is the issue of consistency. Consistency in DSS processing refers to the consistency of the data delivered to each DSS analyst who needs to use the data. When the same data is not delivered to the DSS analyst (or more correctly, when each DSS analyst does not have the opportunity for data to be delivered to it), there could be no consistency and compatibility of data in the DSS environment.

Consider the path data must follow in the classical production environment, as depicted by Figure 3.17.

Figure 3.17 shows only three of the paths that DSS data must follow in order for DSS consistency to be achieved. It is worthy of note that there are *many* other paths that must be followed that are not shown by Figure 3.17. In order for DSS consistency to be achieved, two conditions must be satisfied.

- the flow of data must occur; and
- the flow of data must be synchronized.

Given the very large number of DSS extract processes that must be run and synchronized in the classical production environment, it is no wonder that the world of DSS processing is *never* in synch and, as a result, is *never* consistent.

Now consider the same issues of data flow in the architected DSS environment, as shown by Figure 3.18.

In Figure 3.18, the flow of data shows that there is a single, one-time-only flow of data from the operational to the atomic level. So the flow of data and the consistency of the flow of data from the operational to the atomic level is a non-issue. What about the flow of data from the atomic to the departmental and then on to the individual level? The flow occurs on a sporadic basis. The flow may be sporadic, but since each data element in the atomic environment is time-related and

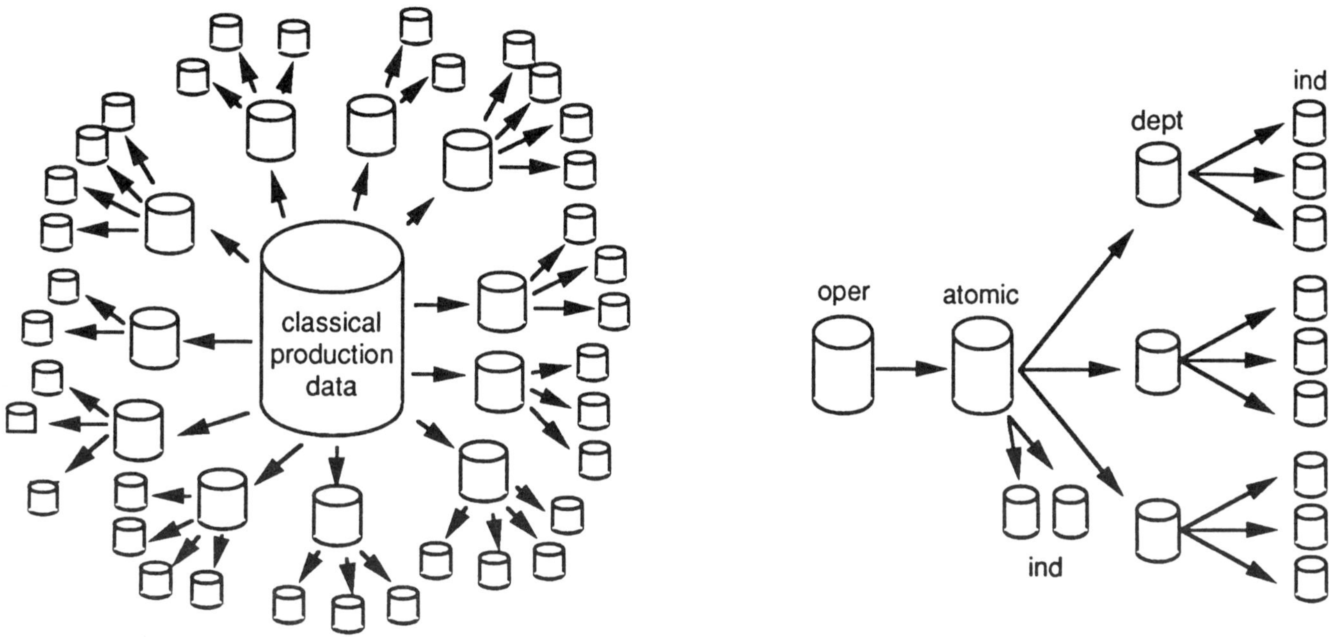

FIGURE 3.16 The flow through the classical production environment is uneven and very costly because so many extracts have to be run. The flow through the atomic-centered environment is direct and simple. To get from the operational to the atomic requires the execution of a simple program.

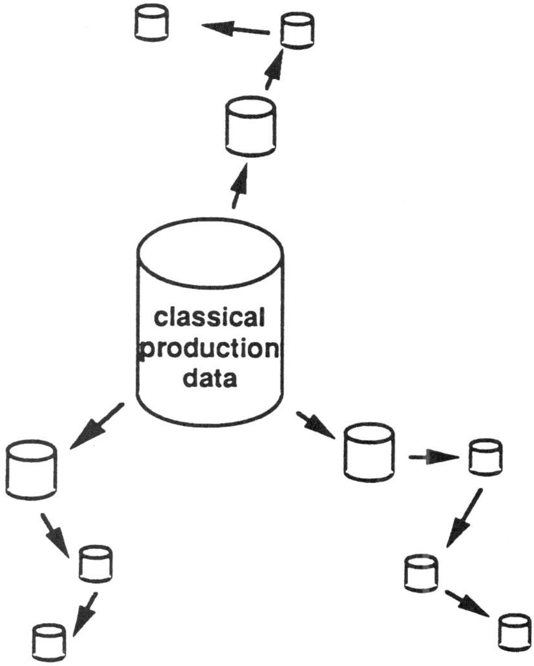

FIGURE 3.17 Three of the paths (of potentially many) that DSS data must take in the classical production environment.

since the DSS processing done at the departmental level and the individual level is tightly controlled as far as time is concerned, there is no problem with consistency. If two consistent DSS reports are desired, it is simply a matter of referencing the same time-oriented data at the atomic level.

But consistency is an issue beyond the timeliness of data. There is another way that inconsistent DSS processing can be done. Consider the marketing analyst that does DSS analysis against all accounts that have been active since 1975. The marketing analyst is asked to determine what the average annual sales per account has been. The same sort of request is made of the accounting DSS analyst, except the accounting DSS analyst chooses as a base for analysis all accounts domiciled on the East Coast. Is there any necessary correlation between the accounts on the East Coast and the accounts who have been active since 1975? It would be surprising if in fact there *were* a signifi-

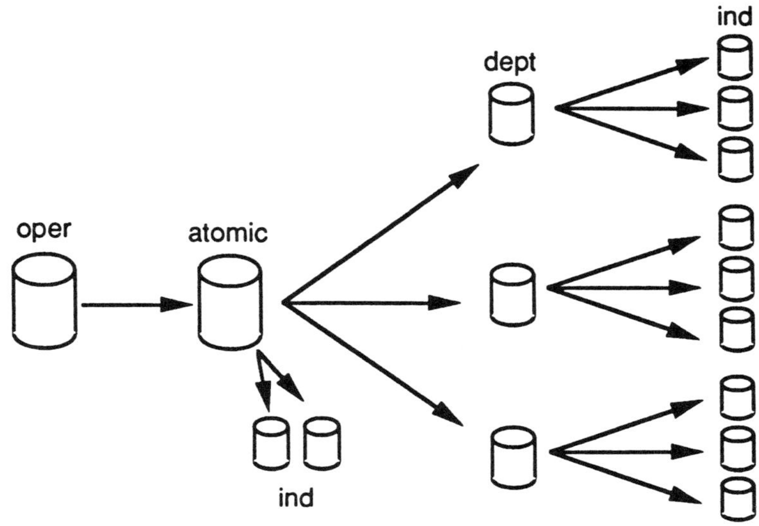

FIGURE 3.18 The flow of data in the atomic-centered environment.

cant correlation between the two criteria. Why then is it surprising when the marketing DSS analyst states that the average sales per account is $752.00 and the accounting DSS analyst states that the average sale per account if $1,152.00? Since the marketing and the accounting DSS analyst were using very different data for analysis, the inconsistency of the results is not surprising.

How does the DSS architecture enhance the chances of success for consistency of processing? The DSS architecture allows DSS processing to occur much closer to a common source. Contrast the two environments shown in Figure 3.19.

In the classical production environment, there is a long, tenuous stream of DSS analysis as data is passed from one level of extract to the next. The processing that occurs at every level is very individual, and the data passed from one level to the next tends to be unique to each extract. Furthermore, in the stream of analysis new, external sources of data make their appearance. At the end of the stream of analysis the results are very inconsistent. Furthermore, reconciling the data is a difficult thing to do.

Now consider the same analysis done in the atomic-centered environment. The data used in the analysis is done very close to the

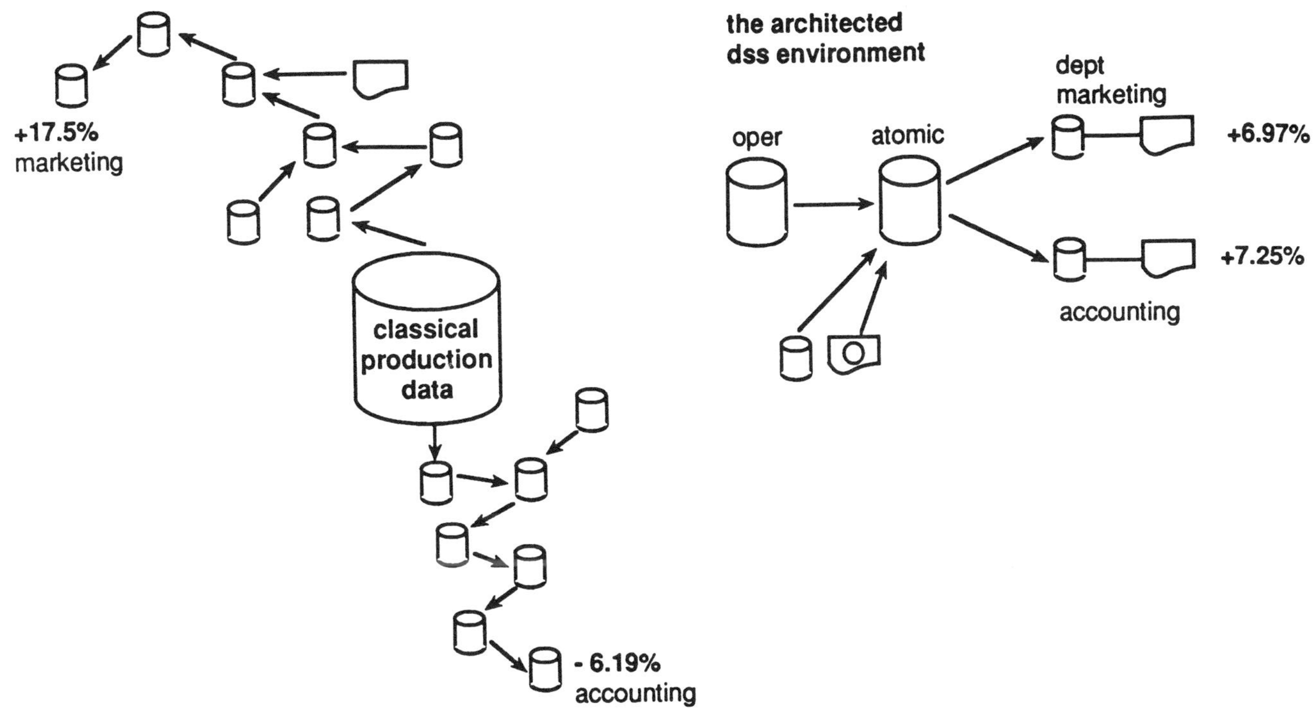

FIGURE 3.19 In the atomic-centered DSS environment, DSS analysis takes place close to a common source, and it does not in the classical environment. Furthermore, external data, if it enters the stream of analysis at all, enters so that *all* DSS analysis has access to the data.

source of the data. When there is a significant discrepancy between the results achieved, it is a simple matter to go to the basic source of data and determine why the discrepancy occurred. Furthermore, when there is a need to introduce extraneous data in the stream of analysis, it is introduced at the atomic level where *all* DSS analysis has an opportunity to use the external data, something not possible in the classical production environment.

Another perspective—a more global one—of this same issue is to look at where the DSS analysis is done. Figure 3.20 illustrates this perspective.

Figure 3.20 shows that DSS reporting and analysis is done much closer to the source of data in the atomic-centered environment than in the classical production environment. It is worth noting that the diagram for the classical production environment shown in Figure 3.20 shows a simplified version of what happens. In actuality, DSS analysis and reporting is usually much further removed from the data of its origin than shown.

The closer to the data of origin, the better the data is and, as a consequence, the more consistent the DSS analysis is.

ACCURACY. The third issue of effective DSS processing is that of accuracy of data. It is in this arena that the usefulness of the architecture best shows its strength. The classical production environment has been depicted as a single source of data. The DSS extracts that emanate from the production environment have done so under the assumption that the data emanating from the center was accurate and consistent. That is usually anything but the case. In fact, the classical production environment is normally made up of a lot of databases, usually containing redundant data. A more realistic portrayal of the DSS extract process in the classical production environment is shown by Figure 3.21.

Figure 3.21 shows that there are usually multiple physical sources of data that serve as a basis for DSS extract processing in the classical production environment. In one case extract A may show that Kathy Allan's account has $562.32 in it and extract B may show that Kathy's account has $956.45 in it. If the DSS processing cannot even begin with the same data, it is no wonder that it cannot be reconciled. If the DSS data is inaccurate at the start of the extract process, it will be inaccurate throughout. Operating from a diverse, random source of data is absolutely normal for the classical production environment's DSS processing.

A feature of the atomic-centered DSS environment is that data is

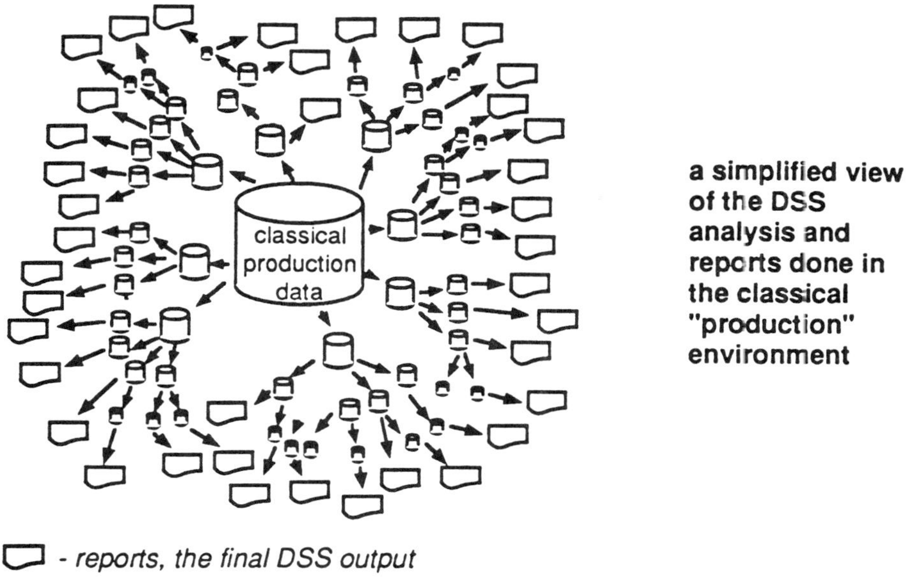

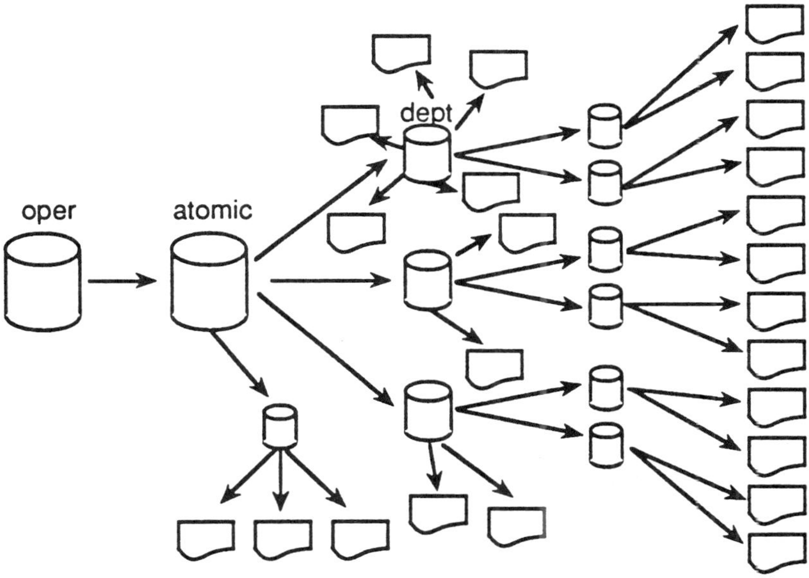

FIGURE 3.20 DSS analysis and reporting in the atomic-centered DSS environment are much closer to the source than in the classical production environment.

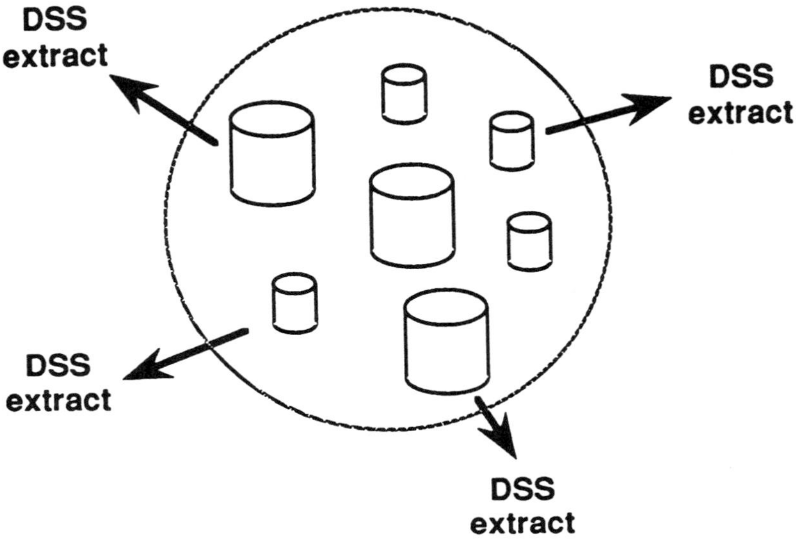

FIGURE 3.21 The classical production environment.

drawn from a single unified source. Accuracy is established in that there is a single source of data in the operational environment that is determined to be the *system of record*. Consider how the atomic level of data is built in the first place.

The first step in the building of the atomic level data is the identification of a system of record in the current operational environment.

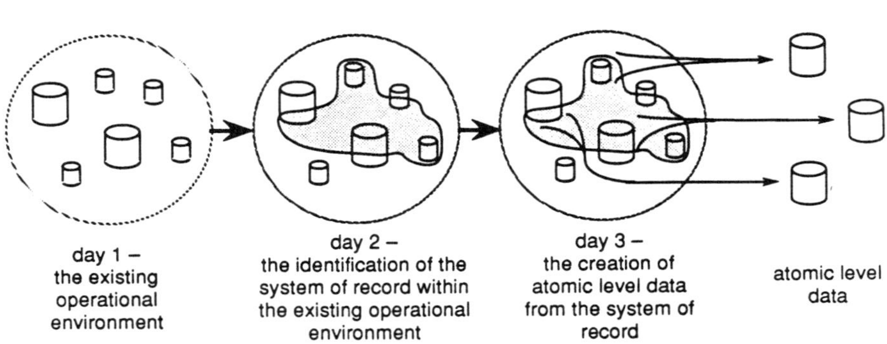

FIGURE 3.22 The classical production envirnoment.

Figure 3.22 shows a typical progression of the development steps in building an atomic level of data.

On day 1 there exists an operational environment. It is normal for the operational environment to contain a wide variety of data. On day 2, the system of record within the operational environment is identified. On day 3, the atomic level data is created from the system of record. Then, on day 4 (and on all days thereafter), DSS processing and analysis is done from the atomic level data. Consistency and accuracy of data ceases to be an issue because of multiple operational sources of data in the face of atomic level data.

The salient features of the atomic-centered DSS environment that addresses timeliness, consistency, and accuracy of data are:

- each atomic level data element has some moment in time associated with it;
- there is a short, singular flow of data through the architected DSS environment;
- DSS analysis and reporting are done close to the source data in the architected DSS environment;
- there is a disciplined flow of data which can be reconstructed if necessary and can be built upon in the architected DSS environment;
- there is a place for external data to enter the stream of analysis where the external data is consistently made available to all DSS analysts who need to use the data;
- there is a single source of operational data—the system of record—which accurately identifies the value of data in the atomic-centered DSS environment.

In short, the atomic-centered DSS environment is a vehicle for addressing the major issues of DSS processing.

SOME EXAMPLES

As an example of a classical DSS architecture, consider a bank. The bank has an operational environment where loans, dda (demand deposit accounts—checking accounts), cds (certificates of deposit), and other operational processes are serviced. The operational environment has been established for many years and contains a wide variety of processing. The system of record has been established and, from that, several atomic data bases have been created. Among other atomic databases, an account activity and a customer activity data base are established at the atomic level, being fed by operational data. Departmental—scheduled DSS processing—is done on a regular basis, and individual DSS processing is done on a non-scheduled basis. Figure 3.23 shows the simple banking DSS architecture.

Now consider a variation of the classical atomic-centered DSS environment. The next example is of a telephone company, shown by Figure 3.24.

The operational data of the telephone company contains billing data and data relating to a customer's phone calls. There is normally about one month's worth of billing data in the operational database. Because the phone company handles *many* telephone calls, and be-

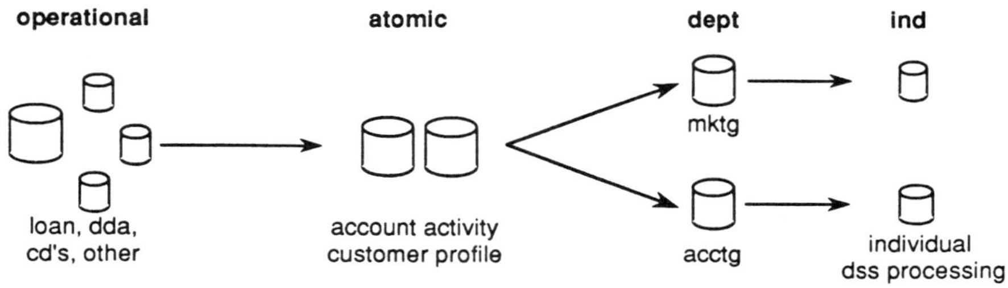

FIGURE 3.23 A variation of the standard DSS environment.

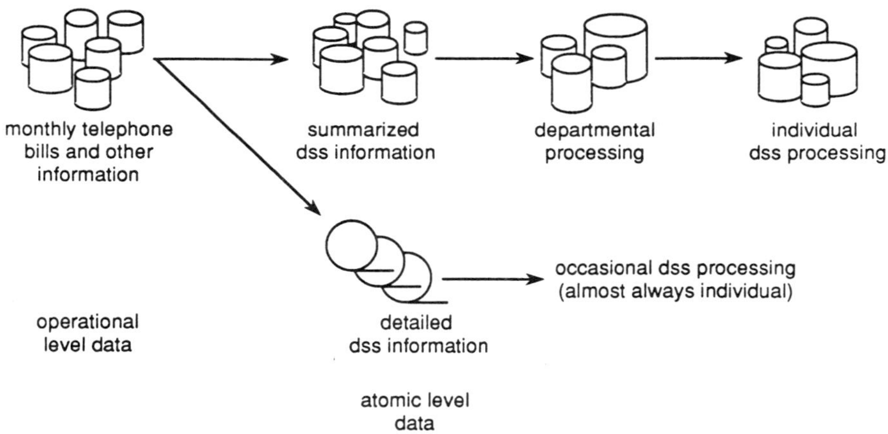

FIGURE 3.24 A variation of the standard DSS environment.

cause there is a substantial amount of data required for each phone call, keeping track of even a month's worth of detailed operational data is a challenge.

There is other data in the operational data base as well, such as the number of new customers gained (or lost) throughout the month, the status of lines, the promotions and activities carried on by marketing, and so forth. From the standpoint of the bulk of data, the operational environment is dominated by the volume of detailed phone call information gathered and billed each month.

The atomic environment is broken into two types of data in the DSS architecture of the telephone company. There is the summary atomic DSS data and the true detailed *archival* data. In the summary atomic DSS data there is up to three year's worth of detail. If one month's worth of detail is bulky, then three year's worth of detail is overwhelming. There simply is too much detailed data to even consider keeping all of it for regular DSS use. So the atomic level DSS data is summarized. Typical summaries at the atomic level look like:

average length of phone calls started from 1:00 a.m. to 2:00 a.m.
average length of phone calls started from 2:00 a.m. to 3:00 a.m.
average length of phone calls started from 3:00 a.m. to 4:00 a.m.
| | | and so forth | |

or,

number of phone calls from 12:00 p.m. to 1:00 p.m.
number of phone calls from 1:00 p.m. to 2:00 p.m.
number of phone calls from 2:00 p.m. to 3:00 p.m.
| | | and so forth | |

The specific detail of each phone call is lost in the atomic DSS summarized data base, but each piece of detail contributes to its appropriate category(s) of summation.

Over time the summarized data "rolls" forward into larger time slots. After the most recent week's detailed hourly history is kept, the week's hourly history is rolled into a daily history. And, after a period of time, daily history is rolled into weekly history, and so forth, under the assumption that the most detailed DSS analysis needs to be done on the most recent data. Figure 3.25 shows the compacting of summarized data based upon the timeliness of the data.

The older the data gets, the more detail is lost.

There is a second *tier* to the atomic DSS level data, however. The actual detail of telephone conversations is stored in a separate *true*

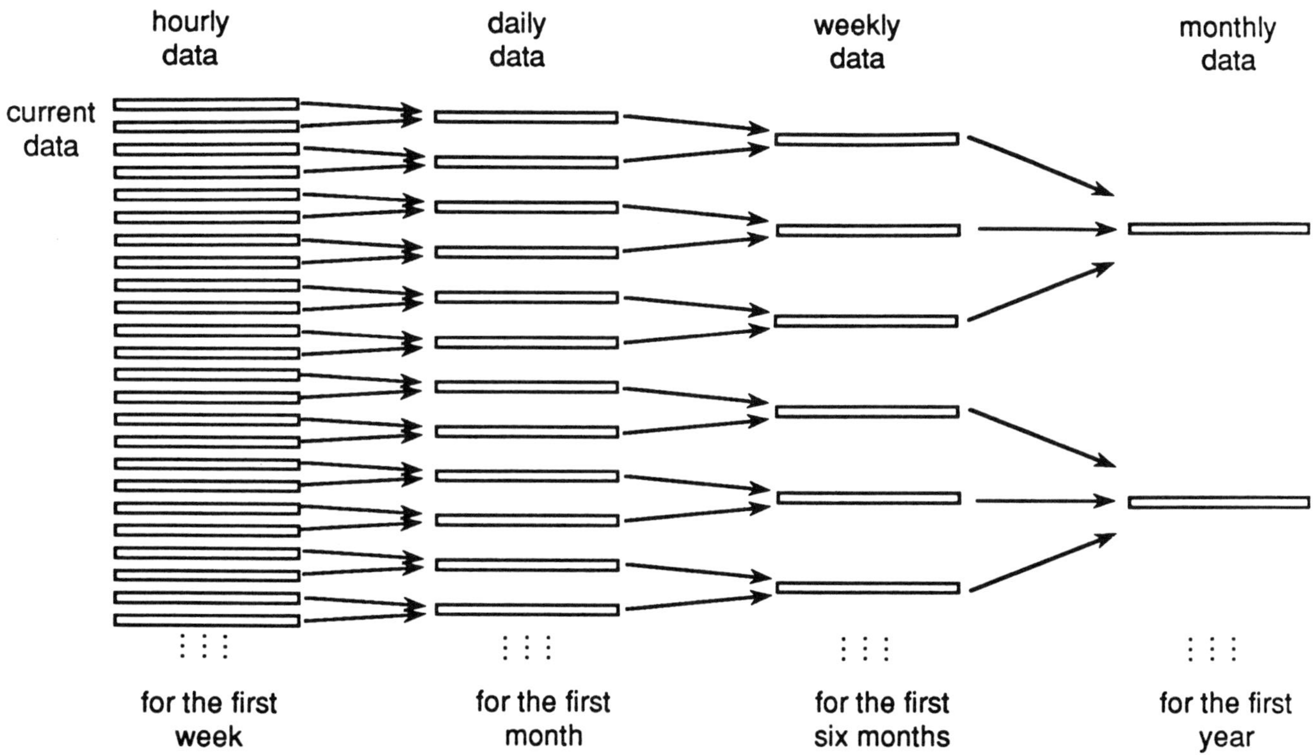

FIGURE 3.25 The compaction of atomic DSS summarized data based upon the timeliness of the data. The older the data gets, the more it becomes compacted.

archival file. Over time these files grow to contain *MUCH!* data. All the detail that ever exists about phone calls is, in fact, stored at the true archival level.

The true archival level exists because the following argument is made. What if an end-user wishes to process against data in the atomic level summarized level, and the desired data is not there? By summarizing data at the atomic level, the DSS analyst has changed the degree of granularity of the data. The atomic DSS database, when summarized, *is not* the most granular data the corporation has.

Instead, the true archival data is the most granular data the corporation has. So the true archival data exists and is available for DSS processing. But there are strong incentives for the DSS analyst not to use the true archival data unless absolutely necessary. Figure 3.26 illustrates those incentives.

The bulk of data that is passed, the length of time to pass the true archival data, and the inability to process against the true archival data all work against doing regular DSS processing against the true archival database.

The reasons why DSS analysts do not process against true archival data on a regular basis is because processing takes a lot of time and costs a lot of money. The DSS analyst is strongly encouraged, on all occasions, to do analysis against the atomic DSS summarized database. If the DSS analyst starts to do regular processing against the true

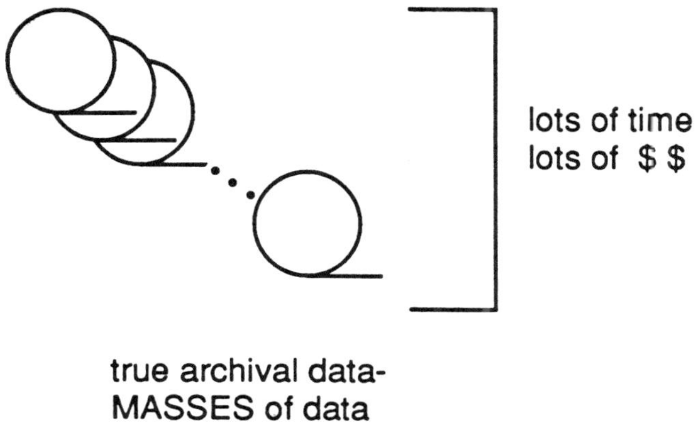

FIGURE 3.26 The incentives to not process against the true archival data.

archival data base, then a new portion of the atomic DSS summarized data base may be created to accommodate the regular processing.

A third variation in the atomic architecture is illustrated by an insurance company, as shown by Figure 3.27.

Figure 3.27 shows the standard architectural features. Claims, policies, and expenses are handled by the architecture in a standard fashion. But emanating from the atomic level data is a unique type of data called *living sample* data.

Living sample data is nothing more than a subset of atomic level data. Typically there is a ratio from 100:1 to 10,000:1 between atomic level data and living sample data. In other words, living sample data is much smaller than the actual data by a factor of up to 10,000 to 1.

Living sample data is used for a very special purpose, but for a purpose which is frequently practiced by actuaries and a few other DSS analysts. Living sample data is used for statistical sampling. For example, you would not use living sample data to find out whether Jeanne Friedman had made a home owner's claim on her policy in 1988. It could well be that Jeanne Friedman had made such a claim but that the information about her claim simply had not been selected for inclusion into the living sample.

Instead, living sample data is used to answer statistical analysis queries such as:

- Are there more serious car accidents in February than there are in October?
- What is the average cost of a settlement for claims settled in court?
- At what point does the safe driving record of men begin to equal that of women?

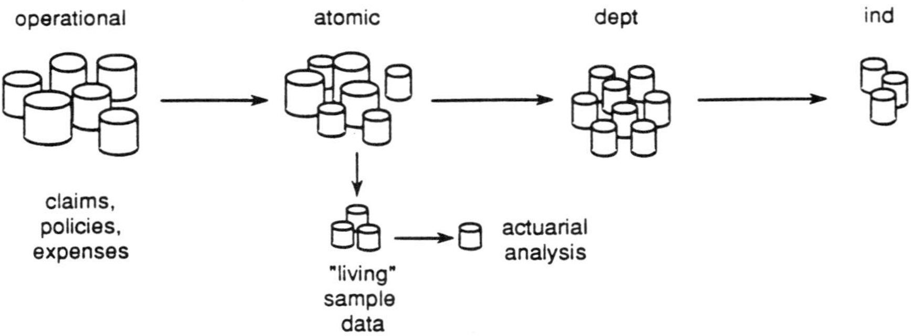

FIGURE 3.27 Another variation of the atomic-centered environment.

Living sample data is always much more efficient to process against and, if built properly, yields very adequate results.

As an example of the effectiveness of using living sample data, consider the following query run against two data bases—a regular atomic data base and a living sample data base.

"Are there more serious accidents in February than in October?"

The query is first run against 50,000,000 claims gathered across the insurance industry and put into an atomic database. The processing requires 48 hours of dedicated computer time. The results obtained are:

- February usually brings about 8.5% of the total serious claims;
- October usually brings about 4.24% of the total serious claims.

Now, suppose the DSS analyst chooses to run the same statistical analyses against a living sample database. The living sample database contains information about 500,000 claims, about 1/100th of the claims in the larger atomic data-base.

The results of the queries come back:

- February usually brings about 8.35% of the total serious claims;
- October usually brings about 5.1% of the total serious claims.

Given the extreme similarity of the results, it has cost the DSS analyst a great deal in hardware to have a finely-tuned answer.

There simply is no question that the analysis done from the larger data base is more accurate. There also simply is no doubt that it cost much, much more to achieve the more accurate results.

The very nature of much statistical analysis is heuristic processing. Where the analyst is working with very large databases, the iterations that he or she can run are limited. But working with a living sample database, the DSS analyst may do many iterations of analysis. In fact, if the DSS analyst demands to go against a fullfledged large atomic database, a rational strategy is to do as much iterative analysis as possible against the living sample data and do the final analysis against the large atomic data base.

One of the problems with living sample data is the bias that is automatically introduced into the database. Because the living sample database is a subset of a larger data-base, there is the very real chance that the living sample database will overrepresent some classes of data and under-represent other classes of data. When the living sample is biased, of course any processing done against it is also biased.

But the potential savings in processing that are possible with living sample data is well worth dealing with the problems of biased data.

Living Sample Data

The term *living sample* data stems from the fact that:

- living sample data is always a subset of a larger database, as such it is a *sample*;
- living sample data must be periodically refreshed. Because it is constant by being refreshed, it is—in a sense—living.

The term living sample data was first used (to the best of the author's knowledge) by USAA, in San Antonio, Texas, for much of their actuarial analysis.

IN SUMMARY

There is an evolution toward a DSS architecture. The evolution is toward four levels of data:

- operational;
- atomic;
- departmental;
- individual.

The evolution occurs over a period of years and occurs as a result of several strong forces interacting.

Atomic level data positions the organization to solve many of its classical DSS problems. In particular, the existence and usage of atomic level data:

- solves the problem of time reconciliation of data by forcing each occurrence of data in the environment to have a moment in time associated with it;
- minimizes the problems of the flow of data by streamlining the flow from the operational to the individual level;
- enhances the consistency of DSS processing by allowing DSS analysis and reporting to be done close to the source;

- creates a flow of data that can be built upon easily;
- creates structuring of data where there is a natural place for external data to enter the stream of analysis;
- addresses the issue of accuracy of data by causing all operational data to flow from a single *system of record.*

And finally, there are many variations of atomic level data. Four forms of atomic level data are:

- standard atomic level data—detailed, archival;
- *living sample*;
- very detailed archival (i.e., "true archival"); and
- summarized atomic.

QUESTIONS: CHAPTER 3

1. Master files were typically placed on ______________.
2. The method in which master files were accessed was __________
3. On a master file, to get at 5% of the data, 100% of the data had to be accessed. T/F
4. The explosion of master files led to an explosion of __________ of data.
5. Data placed on DASD could be accessed ______________.
6. To get at data on DASD required that MUCH/SOME/NO extraneous data be accessed.
7. Data placed on DASD could be accessed either by __________ or by ______________.
8. The norm for response time for online processing is __________ seconds.
9. Online processing entails UPDATE/ACCESS and UPDATE/ACCESS only of data.
10. An early name for DSS processing was ______________.
11. Mixing online and DSS processing in the face of much data and/or much processing required ______________ or ____________.
12. Even with very user friendly software, making the end-user run HIS/HER processes at 3:00 a.m. is very user ______________.

13. _____________ processing alleviated much of the conflict of mixing online processing and DSS processing.
14. Once data was extracted, it could be _____________, _________, or _____________.
15. The growth of extract processing was EXPLOSIVE/ANEMIC/UNEXCITING.
16. An atomic database contains nuclear data. T/F
17. Another name for an atomic database is _____________.
18. Atomic data is fed by _____________ and _____________.
19. Every unit of atomic data is relevant to a single moment in time. T/F
20. Atomic data serves as a basis for _____________ and _________.
21. The atomic level MUST BE/SHOULD BE/CAN BE an ORACLE-based environment.
22. Atomic databases contain detailed data and _____________ data.
23. Private data CAN/CANNOT be fed into the departmental level.
24. Individual data CAN BE/SHOULD BE/CANNOT BE on a personal computer.
25. The two types of decision makers are _____________ and ____.
26. The three typical forms of time stamping are , _____________, and _____________.
27. The atomic-centered environment ELIMINATES THE NEED FOR/MAKES MANAGEABLE the process of reconciliation of data.
28. The single operational source for atomic data is called the _____.
29. All external data should be placed in the *atomic* data base. T/F
30. The level of detail of atomic data is referred to as its _________.
31. The finer the level of granularity, the MORE/LESS data at the atomic level.
32. The finer the level of granularity, the MORE/LESS analysis can be done.
33. The tradeoff of granularity of data is between volume of data and the ability to conduct many analyses and _____________.

34. Living sample data is only good for statistical analysis. T/F
35. Choosing every 1/100th record to go into a living sample data base MAY/MAY NOT/USUALLY produce a statistically significant sample.
36. Heuristic processing is very EFFICIENT/INEFFICIENT on a living sample database.

CHAPTER 4

Operational Data/External Data In Support of the DSS/ORACLE Environment

Operational data is not of itself DSS data in the sense that has been discussed in this book. But operational data forms the foundation for most of DSS data and, as such, is an appropriate topic for discussion.

ORACLE can be used either operationally or in a DSS mode, as has been discussed. When ORACLE is used operationally, it is still extracted to form a DSS basis. But most DSS/ORACLE data does not come from another ORACLE source. Instead, most DSS/ORACLE data comes from IMS, CICS/VSAM, IDMS, or other sources. Operational systems historically were the first systems built, and they were built in one of the early DBMS. When shops start to build DSS/ORACLE systems, the first systems are fed from existing operational systems.

In most shops, operational data already exists by the time the DSS effort gets underway. (Although in a few shops where all systems must be built from the ground floor up, such is not the case. However, very few shops have the luxury of building all systems from the ground up.) In those shops where operational systems were built first, there usually has been little or no thought given to DSS processing. It is up to the DSS analyst to transform that operational base to the needs of the DSS processing.

It is no wonder that the operational designer has paid little or no attention to the DSS needs. The operational designer faces the task of achieving high performance or throughput, of satisfying many business rules, of achieving a high degree of availability, and doing all this on a stringent timetable. It is no wonder, then, that operational systems usually are not built with future DSS processing in mind.

In addition, some or much of the operational environment usually is already in place and has been for a long while. It is not unusual to encounter operational systems that have been up and running for as long as twenty years. These older systems are run on very mature technology; the programs are patched to the point they can be patched no more; and the users' requirements that were used as a basis for the system so long ago are not even relevant today. However, no one wants to change the programs or replace them.

INPUT/OUTPUT

The input to the operational environment is either the measurement of some external stimuli or the input from some other operational system, as shown by Figure 4.1.

The output of an operational program is either a response, usually to the stimulating party and/or the recording of the event. The DSS analyst is seldom interested in many of the details of operational processing. Instead, the DSS analyst is interested in much of the data that resides at the operational level and what data is fit (and relevant) for usage in DSS processing.

Some data is clearly only fit for or applicable to the operational level of processing. For example, a bank's operational systems record the teller transaction number for each activity a teller does, or an ATM transaction has its electronic id appended to the record of the transaction.

There simply is no use at all for that level or type of detail in any DSS/ORACLE processing. And there is no point in carrying that level

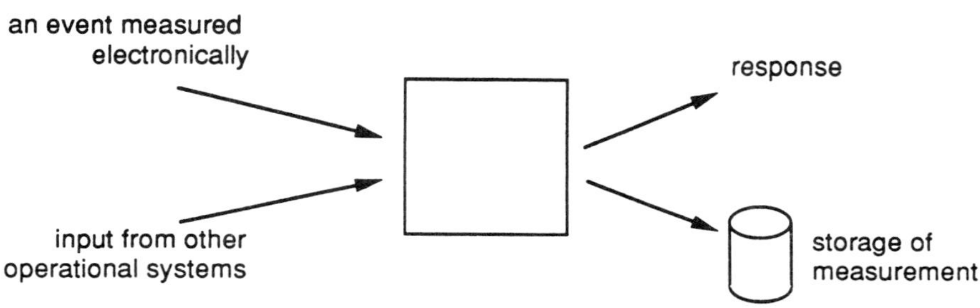

FIGURE 4.1 Operational system.

of detail forward in the DSS environment. But the biggest challenge facing the DSS analyst does not lie in what operational data elements are to be excluded because of their inapplicability to the DSS environment. Instead, the DSS/ORACLE analyst faces the problem of massively unintegrated data that exists in the current operational environment.

The lack of integration in the operational environment shows up in several ways:

- the incompatibility of key structures across operational systems;
- the incompatibility of encoding/decoding structures across operational systems;
- redundant data and processing across operational systems; and
- the mixture of different kinds of processing across existing operational systems.

An example of each of these instances of unintegrated data will be given with an explanation of how it affects the DSS analyst.

Key Structure Incompatibility

In one operational system a customer has a key structure of 25 bytes, which is hashed from the customer's name and address In another operational system the customer has a key structure of 15 bytes which is merely the first fifteen bytes of the customer's name. The problem is that there is not a clear, clean-cut relationship between the key structures of the two customer files. In most cases, the same customer will end up with compatible keys in both systems, but, not in all cases. If the DSS analyst pushes data into the DSS environment using one or the other or *both* structures, some customers will end up being misrepresented. The quality of the DSS analysis that occurs depends upon the accuracy of the data at the outset. If data fed into the DSS/ORACLE environment is not accurate at the outset, how can the DSS/ORACLE analyst be blamed for later inaccuracies?

Encoding Incompatibility

A second issue of the lack of integration of the operational environment is that of encoding/decoding incompatibility. In general, encoding incompatibility is not the order or magnitude of problem as that of key incompatibility from the perspective that key incompatibility is at the very root of data relationships and coding structures of data are relatively less profound. As an example of encoding incompatibility, suppose one system has encoded overhead charges as O, direct charges as D, and indirect charges as I. Another accounting system encodes supplies as a 1, monthly fixed expenses as a 2, monthly variable expenses as a 3, and so forth. Not only are the codes themselves at odds with each other, but even the categories of codes are askew. Trying to merge data from both systems into a single DSS/ORACLE system with a meaningful, unified coding structure is a complex, arduous task.

The DSS analyst needs to establish either one or two categorizations of codes (preferably one category, unless it is mandatory to have two) and to establish a single valid set of codes for each category. Then, as the data is transformed to the atomic level, the uniform encoding structure is put into force.

Key Conversion

Suppose there is a system—System A—that is a *smart* system. System A can convert keys that are compatible based on a sophisticated formula. Some of the conversions it can make are:

```
INTERNATIONAL BUSINESS MACHINE        ----    INBUMAC
IBM                                   ----    INBUMAC
BIGBLUE                               ----    INBUMAC
MINNESOTA MINING, MANUFACTURING       ----    MIMIMAN
3M                                    ----    MIMIMAN
SIMON AND SCHUSTER                    ----    SISCCOM
PRENTICE-HALL                         ----    SISCCOM
P-H                                   ----    SISCCOM
```

By using the sophisticated key algorithm, the system is able to maintain customer information.

Now consider System B, a much less sophisticated system. Some of the transformations made by System B are:

```
INTERNATIONAL BUSINESS MACHINE        ----    INTERNA
IBM                                   ----    IBM
BIGBLUE                               ----    BIGBLUE
MINNESOTA MINING, MANUFACTURING       ----    MINNESO
3M                                    ----    MMM
SIMON AND SCHUSTER                    ----    SIMONAN
PRENTICE-HALL                         ----    PRENTIC
P-H                                   ----    P-H
and so forth.
```

System B is unable to make sophisticated distinctions. Trying to integrate System A and System B is very difficult because data at a very fundamental level is incompatible.

A typical approach is to create an index that can be used to translate a key from one table to the next. This approach is expensive in terms of time needed for conversion and complexity of programming. A second approach is to apply the more sophisticated algorithm to both databases, and convert the simpler data-base. A third approach is to convert the databases into a single system. Whichever approach is used, machine resources and complexity of processing are required.

Redundant Operational Data and Processing

Another manifestation of unintegrated operational data and processing which the DSS/ORACLE analyst is likely to encounter is redundant operational data and processing. Redundant operational data and processing is the result of the long-standing practice of building (or otherwise acquiring) operational systems an application at a time. Over time, the same ground is covered first by one application, then another, and so forth. As a simple example of redundant processing, a bank has a loans system, a credit card system, and a line of credit system. Each of the applications has the facility for checking credit. Each facility wants to know such things as:

- income;
- outstanding debt;
- monthly payments;
- arrests,
- other credit;
- payment history;
- past problems with payment;
- referencing history

In short, the same credit application (or subapplication) is built in three places. In order for the DSS analyst to accurately portray the data, the DSS analyst must identify and organize the commonality of data across the different applications while preserving the uniqueness of the applications. As the operational data enters the DSS/ORACLE environment, a single image of credit processing is presented even though

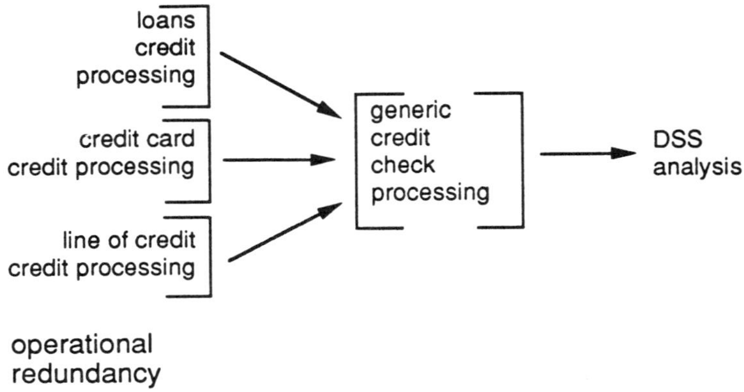

FIGURE 4.2 Atomic level data.

the underlying operational data is gleaned from three systems. Figure 4.2 shows the work the DSS analyst must do to achieve accuracy and credibility of DSS/ORACLE processing when there is an underlying operational environment that contains redundant data and processing.

Extracting Data into the DSS/ORACLE Environment

There are (at least!) two ways data is transported into the DSS/ORACLE environment—through system utilities or through common COBOL or application written programs.

It is usually most expedient to write a simple system utility transporting data into the ORACLE environment. As long as the source is simple and well-structured and as long as complex program logic is not required, system utilities serve well. But in some cases, the source of data is complex or in an environment not easily suited for system utilities. In this case system supplied utilities will not suffice. Even if the source of the data is simple, the selection logic or the logic required in the scanning of the data is sufficiently complex to the point where a standard programming approach makes sense. A *dual* extract strategy is probably the best generic strategy there is.

Mixture of Operational and Other Kinds of Processing

The world of applications development for database began with the notion that a single database should serve all purposes. But, for reasons well documented elsewhere, a whole cadre of processing grew up around the *single data base*. It is no surprise that the early database applications contain a mixture of every type of processing known.

For example, a manufacturing database application keeps track of how many parts are shipped and received, on a detailed basis. Each shipment and each deposit of parts is marked by the system as the transaction occurs. In addition, on-line query as to the status of a given part is allowed. In that regard, the application is a purely operational application. But the application, as originally designed, does quite a few other functions as well. The application also:

- produces monthly reports, showing total shipments and total receipts;
- produces variance reports. When a part is stocked longer than a month and the quantity on hand is greater than a one-month supply, a report is issued;
- changes the lead time when the outage period is greater than a month for whole classes of parts;
- creates an inventory stock list when total inventory rises more than 10% in a week's time;
- determines historical usage of a part, and by classes of parts.

In short, much analytical work well beyond the mere stocking of a part is built into the application, making the application a very complicated one.

The DSS/ORACLE analyst needs to determine what parts of the application are better left in the operational world and what parts of the applications are better moved to atomic and departmental processing into ORACLE.

As a rule, data and processing that are:

- historically oriented;
- summation oriented;
- oriented toward a large volume of data;
- not update oriented;
- oriented towards analytical processing;

are much better relocated to the DSS environment. Other functions may well remain in the operational environment.

THE SYSTEM OF RECORD

The job of the DSS analyst is to define, within the confines of the existing operational environment, the system of record. The system of record is the definitive, nonredundant detailed source of operational data, valid up to the second, for each data element in the operational environment.

The system of record must be defined prior to the writing of the extract programs to pull data from the operational to the DSS/ORACLE arena. Trying to build the DSS/ORACLE environment without a firm definition of the system of record is not recommended.

At any moment, there is one and only one valid occurrence of data in the system of record in the operational environment.

As previously suggested, it is the job of the DSS analyst to wade through the:

- incompatible keys;
- incompatible codes;
- redundant data; and
- myriad uses of data

found in the operational environment to define the system of record which, in turn, is the foundation of the design of the atomic level data.

The DSS/ORACLE analyst will find useful, where it has been created, a data model in defining the system of record. (Refer to *INFORMATION ENGINEERING FOR THE PRACTITIONER: FROM THEORY INTO PRACTICE*, Yourdon Press, 1988 for a detailed discussion of the building of the data model). The data model, which centers around the primitive data of the corporation, is the definitive source as to what should and should not be in the system of record.

Supporting Technology

The technology that supports the operational environment is oriented to three things:

- response time;
- throughput; and
- availability.

Only after these major criteria are satisfied do other criteria, such as ease of use, portability, speed of development, and so forth begin to matter.

In addition, the DSS/ORACLE analyst needs to be aware that there is strong motivation to leave existing systems untouched. Regardless of the quality of the existing system, regardless of the underlying technology (IMS, VSAM, etc.), and regardless of the age of the system, if it works, there is tremendous incentive not to make major changes to the existing applications.

The DSS analyst should be aware of the priorities that underlie operational systems because it is inevitable that the DSS analyst will, to a larger or smaller extent, run afoul of classical operational technology. The extract processing that the DSS/ORACLE analyst needs to have done requires considerable resources. However it is designed, a large amount of operational data must be periodically scanned and a portion of the operational data placed in a queue to be transported to the atomic environment. And while the operational data is being scanned and extracted, machine resources are not available for other processing. Therefore, the DSS/ORACLE analyst places his or her own resource demands on the operational environment. The DSS/ORACLE analyst should be sensitive to the disruptions that will be made in the existing operational world. As a rule, the DSS analyst will cause as little disturbance as possible to the existing operational world.

There are a few occasions when existing application code needs to be touched. If there is a massive amount of operational data, each time an extract is necessary, the entire database must be scanned. On these occasions it may make sense to go into the existing application code and, at the moment of update, place the appropriate DSS data into a *holding tank*. When a refreshment of DSS data is done, it is done by emptying the holding tank rather than by scanning the entire database. At the expense of the interruption of code, great savings can be made in the scanning of data.

Of course, when there is not much operational data, or when the data subject to DSS scrutiny can be easily isolated, there is no need to go into existing code. The periodic refreshment of data can be done efficiently in this case, with no need to siphon data off at the moment of update.

External Data

To the DSS analyst, external data shares many of the characteristics of operational data. External data is data that enters the DSS environment in ways other than the world of operational systems. Purchased databases, public databases, and the entry of data manually through Lotus 1-2-3 are all forms of external data. Both operational and external data are candidates for extraction into the atomic environment—both are detailed (usually!), both are beyond the direct control of the DSS/ORACLE analyst, and both require editing before usage in the DSS/ORACLE environment.

There are differences between operational and external as well. If major problems are found with operational data, the DSS analyst may alert the in-house maintenance staff to make needed changes. But, if there are changes that need to be made to external data, not much can be done except to delete the offending external data. In any case, external data and operational level data form the basis of all atomic DSS/ORACLE data, as shown by Figure 4.3

As the DSS analyst creates the designs for the atomic level of data, and identifies and formalizes the system of record, he or she usually cannot escape the temptation to comment on the integration (or the lack thereof!) of the existing operational environment. It is a real temptation to use the analysis done for atomic level data as a basis for modifying or restructuring the operational environment into a more integrated whole.

In almost every case it is patently a mistake to do so!

When the DSS analyst recognizes the degree of unintegration in the existing operational environment, the analyst will recognize just

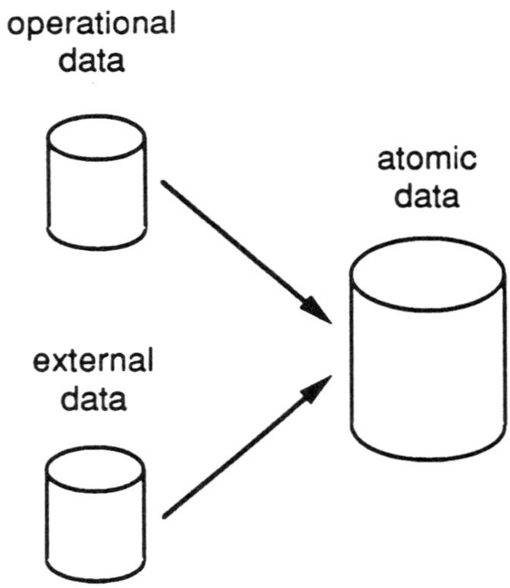

FIGURE 4.3 Operational and atomic level data form the basis of all atomic data.

how much is to be gained by restructuring the existing operational environment. What the DSS analyst does not see is just how intransigent the existing operational environment really is. In a word, organizations simply do not change existing systems, once the systems are built. For whatever reasons, management would rather die than restructure existing systems, however poorly those systems were written or however poorly they form a cohesive environment.

The DSS/ORACLE analyst then is forewarned. It is an extremely dangerous diversion of the DSS effort to try to use the unifying, integrating design of the atomic database as a basis for integration and restructuring of the existing environment. The danger is that the momentum of the DSS effort will become sidetracked, then derailed, by the awesome forces of inertia that exist in the existing operational environment.

The same line of thinking is applicable to technology. It is a temptation to look at the newness of ORACLE technology and attempt to replace existing, older technology, such as IMS, VSAM, etc. It is almost always a mistake to try to supplant existing technologies. The world of DP is *change aversive*, whether it be for reasons of technology, integration, or practically anything else. The effort to move new DSS projects to ORACLE is diluted when the attempt is made to replace older technologies with ORACLE.

IN SUMMARY

The basis of all atomic data is operational and external data. The DSS analyst needs to form a conceptual *system of record* and then determine what operational data meets the criteria. Having built the system or record, the next step is to identify extract processes to transport the data out of the operational environment into the DSS/ORACLE environment. Some of the issues of this transformation are frequency of refreshment, complexity of refreshment, and resources needed for refreshment.

A major issue the DSS/ORACLE analyst faces is that of the intransigencies of existing systems. As a rule, it is more productive to build new systems than it is to try to replace older systems.

QUESTIONS: CHAPTER 4

1. Operational data is the foundation for ALL/MOST OF/SOME OF/NONE of atomic data.
2. Most operational data IS/IS NOT in ORACLE.

3. Name four typical technologies where operational data is found.
4. ALL/SOME/MOST/NONE of the data at the operational environment is transported to the atomic environment.
5. When two or more operational systems serve as a basis for atomic level data, the following (name 5) ______________ must be integrated.
6. All archival data is found in the atomic level. T/F
7. All data in the atomic environment is archived. T/F
8. The source of operational data that serves as a basis for atomic data is the ______________.
9. External data is placed in the atomic level data. T/F
10. The high-level data model serves as a map for integration of operational data. T/F
11. It is almost always a mistake to try to restructure the operational environment because it differs from the data model. T/F
12. Making massive changes to the operational environment IS/IS NOT an easy thing to accomplish.

CHAPTER 5

Atomic Level DSS/ ORACLE Data

The atomic level is, in many ways, the center of the DSS/ORACLE universe. Certainly the atomic level data forms the foundation on which all DSS processing—at any level—rests. Unless there are extenuating circumstances, ORACLE serves as the technical foundation on which the atomic data is built. The atomic level contains the most data in terms of volume and contains the most granular data in terms of content. The atomic level data is nonredundant at the nonkey level and, where foreign key data relationships exist, is redundant at the key level. Figure 5.1 illustrates the difference between redundancy and nonredundancy of key and nonkey data.

What's In A Name—Atomic Level Data

Atomic level data is so named because of its granularity. In general the corporation has no more detailed data than that found in the atomic database.

There is, however, nothing *atomic* about an atomic database from the standpoint of physics. An atomic database does not mimic the shape of atoms (or what we think of atoms to be). And an atomic database has no neutrons, protons, or psi mesons, that we know of. Some organizations use other terms for atomic level databases. Some of those terms are:

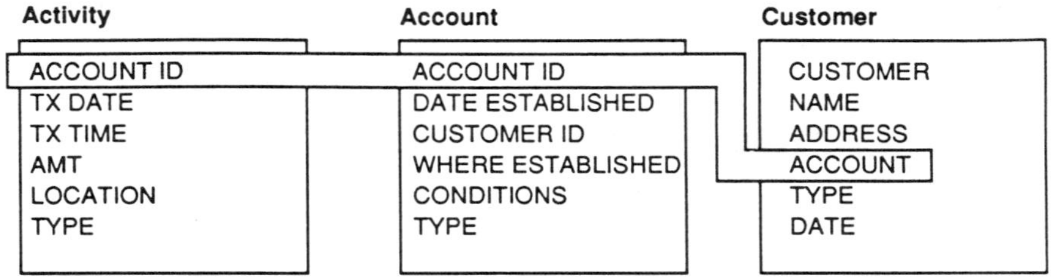

FIGURE 5.1 Account data, a form of key data, is redundant across different atomic structures. It serves to relate different types of data together. Often non-key data is non-redundant. Note that *type* is not redundant even though it appears in more than one place. In the activity data, type refers to the type of activity. In the account data, type refers to the type of account. In the customer data, type refers to the type of customer.

- reports database;
- foundation database;
- DSS database;
- extracts database;
- historical database;
- informational warehouse.

Many organizations use some functionality or content of the atomic database. If the organization builds and uses the atomic database properly, it can use any term it likes.

The input to the atomic level is from operational data, and, to a smaller extent, from external data. The output of atomic level data serves departmental DSS processing and, on occasion, serves the individual DSS processing. Figure 5.2 shows the input and output of data to and from the atomic level.

The atomic level of data is made up of multiple physical tables of data. Atomic level data is generally detailed data. In fact, it is the *most* detailed data the organization has. The very low level of detail found in this level of data gives atomic level data its name. Each data element at the atomic level is associated with, or is relevant to, some moment

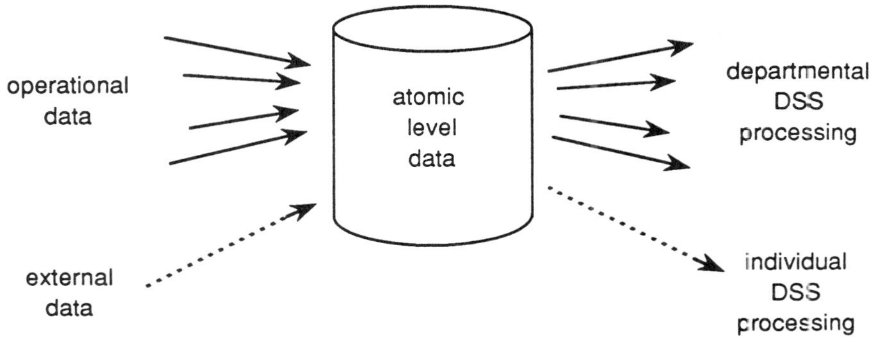

FIGURE 5.2 The input and the output to the atomic level data.

in time. One of the distinguishing features of atomic level data is its emphasis on the time value of data. There are, generally speaking, three classifications of time value data, as shown by Figure 5.3

Figure 5.3 shows that there are three general classifications of time variancy—continuous, event discrete, and periodic discrete. In actuality, there are many variations of the different forms of time variance. (Some forms are continuous, some have *implicit* endings, and so forth.) Continuous data is that data that is defined over a span of time. Discrete data is that data that is defined only for a single moment in time. A discrete measurement of data may be taken because of the occurrence of an event, or a discrete measurement of data may be taken because of the periodic passing of time. An example of each of these types of time variant data that are typically found at the atomic level will be given.

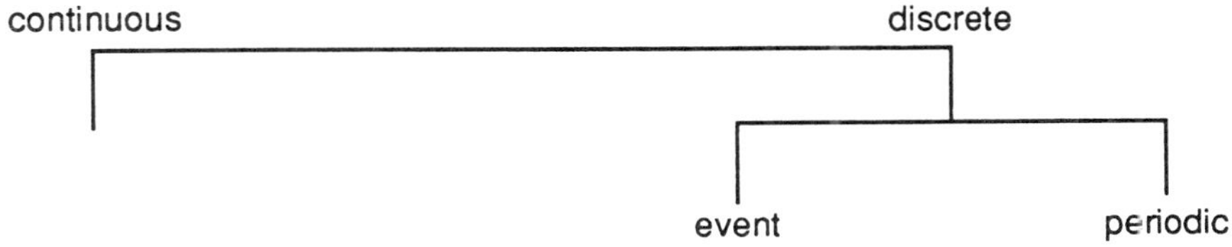

FIGURE 5.3 The classification of time variance of atomic level data—
—continuous
—event discrete
—periodic discrete.

When ORACLE is not a Good Choice for Atomic Level Data

Although ORACLE is usually a good choice for atomic level data, there are occasions where ORACLE is not a proper choice. These exceptional circumstances occasions include:

- when much heuristic processing is being done;
- when there is a need to update individual atomic records (which occasionally happens);
- when there is a truly massive amount of data;
- when there is not a clear division between operational and DSS processing;
- when large collections of data cannot be partitioned at either the ORACLE or the application level;
- when more than two indexes are mandatory for tables.

CONTINUOUS DATA

The history of a customer's relationship with the enterprise, especially the status of a customer's credit, may be measured continuously. For example, suppose a record is created as shown:

```
CUSTOMER ID
FROM DATE
TO DATE
STATUS
LIMIT
```

This record shows who the customer is, the status of the customer's credit, the limit of the customer's credit, and the beginning and ending date of the status. Typical status states are: A = abeyance states—the status of a customer as an account is being established and credit is not yet granted; O = OK—credit is granted, up to the limit; I = inactive—credit is suspended because of lack of activity.

The different status states and the use of continuous time span data are illustrated in terms of an example, for customer—AJAX Warehousing.

The history of the credit limit of AJAX Warehousing is described by the series of continuous records shown in the example. On January 1, AJAX Warehousing filed an application for credit. On January 1,

	Record1	*Record2*	*Record3*	*Record4*	*Record5*
CUSTOMER	AJAX	AJAX	AJAX	AJAX	AJAX
FROM DATE	JAN1	JAN6	FEB11	APRIL25	AUG16
TO DATE	JAN5	FEB10	APRIL24	AUG15	NOV16
STATUS	A	O	O	O	I
LIMIT	—	100	500	250	—

AJAX became a customer even though credit was granted a few days later. On January 6 AJAX's credit limit was established at 100. The continuous record of AJAX's credit limit is reflected by the record in that at any moment in time from January 6 to February 10, the credit limit of AJAX was 100. On February 11, a credit raise to AJAX was granted raising AJAX's limit to 500. On April 24, AJAX's limit was lowered to 250. Finally, because of inactivity, AJAX's credit limit was disapproved on August 16. Finally, three months later, AJAX was disallowed as a customer.

At any moment in time, from the FROM DATE to the TO DATE, the value of the limit of credit and the status of credit is defined. In addition, when the records are taken together, a continuous definition of data is formed from the first FROM DATE to the last TO DATE. The product of the structure is a continuous definition of data and is typical of that found in a ORACLE atomic data base.

How does this continuous definition of data as found at the DSS/ORACLE atomic level differ from similar data that might be found at the operational level? At the operational level, a similar structure of data might be:

- CUSTOMER
- CREDIT STATUS
- LIMIT

The data in the operational level is essentially the same as that found at the atomic level except for the FROM DATE and the TO DATE which is not present in the operational data. At any moment in time the customer's current status and limit can be determined by using the operational data. To find out the history of a customer's status and limit requires that the records in the atomic level be searched. In other words, in operational processing it is assumed that only the current status and credit limit of a customer are of concern. In atomic processing, *all* history is of concern. Figure 5.4 highlights the difference between operational and atomic data and processing.

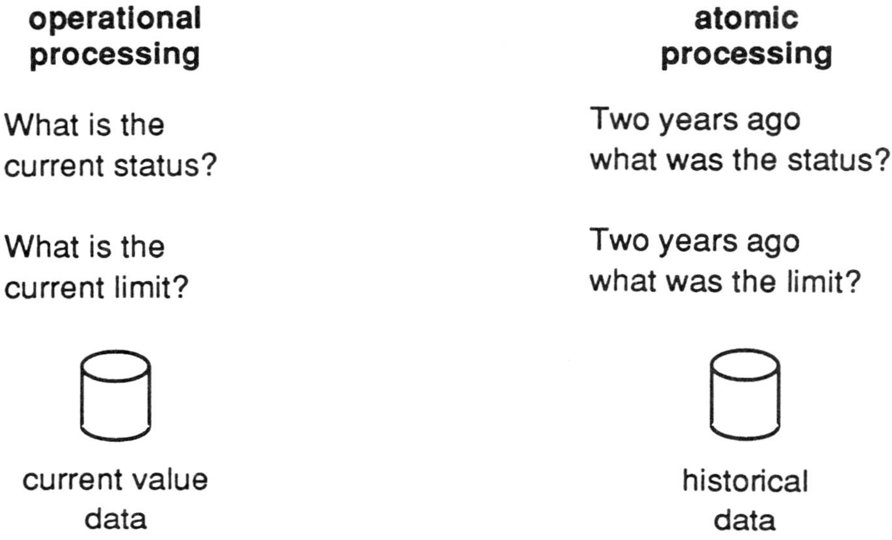

FIGURE 5.4 The difference between operational and atomic processing.

EVENT DISCRETE DATA

Discrete data in DSS/ORACLE atomic level databases is data whose value is measured as of some single moment in time. For example, suppose a banking activity—a payment, a withdrawal, etc.—causes an activity record to be written. An event—the execution of a transaction—causes a record—a discrete recording of one or more variables—to be written. The data layout for the measurement of the variables involved in the transaction might look like:

```
ACCOUNT ID
DATE
TIME
TYPE OF TRANSACTION
AMT
LOCATION
BALANCE UPON COMPLETION
```

The activity record keeps track of the date and the time that the transaction occurred, what type of transaction transpired, the amount of the transaction, where the transaction occurred, and the ending balance of the account at completion of the transaction. The key of the record likely would be account id, date, and time.

What is the difference between this type of data stored at the atomic level and the corresponding type of data stored at the operational level? At first glance there is very little difference. But a closer look reveals quite a few major differences. Some of them are:

- operational activity typically includes only the last few weeks of transactions; atomic activity typically includes many years of activity. The sheer volume of activity at the atomic level is greater by one or two orders of magnitude than the data found at the operational level.
- content of data. The atomic level data is nearly always a subset of operational data as far as content of data elements is concerned. Figure 5.5 shows that only data elements useful to DSS analysis are passed from the operational level to the atomic level.
- granularity of data. Operational data, on occasion, may be more granular than atomic data when there is a very large amount of data, as demonstrated in Chapter 3 by the telephone company that had more than one type of atomic data.
- probability of access. Operational data enjoys a relatively high probability of access. Atomic level data enjoys a low to moderate probability of access.

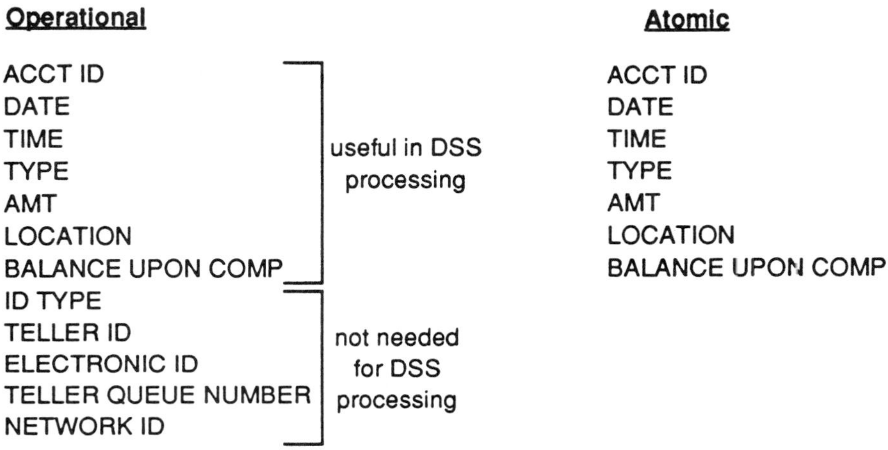

FIGURE 5.5 Only some types of data are passed to the atomic level.

- units of access. Operational data is accessed a single unit at a time. Atomic level data is accessed by sets and subsets.

PERIODIC DISCRETE ATOMIC DATA

Atomic level data on occasions may take a third form of time variancy—periodic discrete time variant data. Periodic discrete atomic data varies from event discrete atomic data in that in periodic discrete atomic data the regular passage of time triggers a snapshot of data to be taken, whereas, with event discrete data, the passage of an event causes the discrete snapshot of data to be taken.

As an example of periodic discrete data, consider the daily measurement of the Dow-Jones Industrial average. At the closing bell each day the Dow-Jones average is measured. The Dow-Jones Industrial average is a composite average of stock trades that have taken place throughout the day for the stocks which make up the Dow-Jones Average. There is, practically speaking, no way the average can be measured every time a share of stock is bought or sold. If the Dow Jones Average were measured that way, there would be millions and tens of millions of records created for a day's activity. In fact, so much data would be created that getting through the data itself would be its own nightmare.

Instead, the value of the Dow Jones Average is measured at the same time each day, usually at the closing bell. This is an example of discrete measurements of data based upon the periodic passage of time.

How does periodic discrete data found at the atomic level differ from similar data found at the operational level? For all practical purposes periodic discrete data is not found at the operational level. (Strictly speaking, it is possible to find periodic discrete data at the operational level, but it is so rare that it is an anomaly.) There is no comparison then between periodic discrete data found at the two levels.

Figure 5.6 shows how the two environments compare.

REFRESHING THE ATOMIC DATA

One of the major issues of the atomic-centered DSS/ORACLE environment is how often atomic data is refreshed from operational data. Given the volume of data that normally flows from the operational to the atomic, it is not realistic to refresh atomic data any more often than once every 24 hours in the most stringent of conditions. Indeed, if processing against the atomic database is specified so that data fresher than 24 hours is required, the question must be asked of the processing,

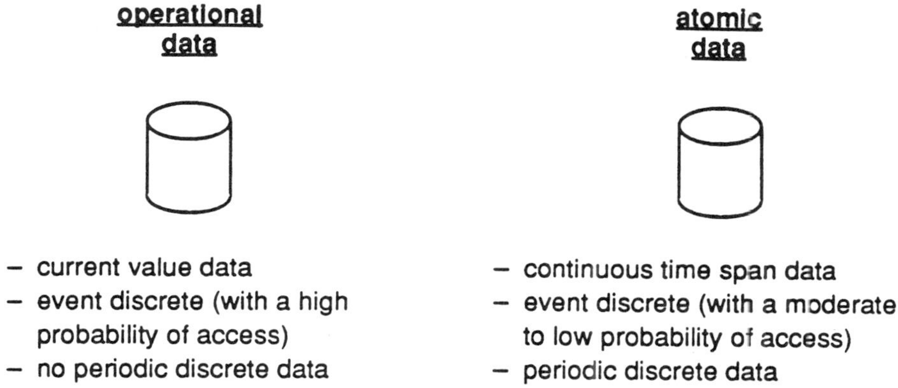

FIGURE 5.6 How the two environments compare.

"Isn't that type of processing better placed in the operational environment?" Figure 5.7 illustrates this point.

Of course, a period longer than 24 hours may (in fact, usually is) be chosen for refreshing the data. If the data from the operational environment is not needed at the atomic level more than monthly, for example, it is wasteful to extract operational data more often than that.

Data extraction can be done in (at least!) two ways. One way is to scan the entire operational database, looking for data that needs to be

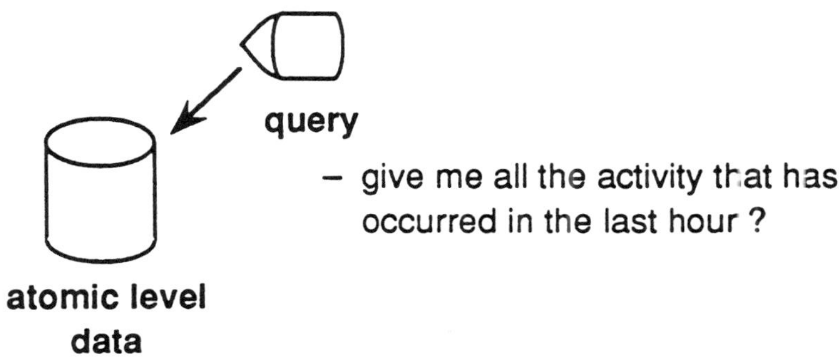

FIGURE 5.7 Processing that requires data to be fresher than 24 hours old is best placed in the operational environment, not the atomic or DSS environment.

moved over to the atomic level data-base. This approach is often used when the operational update programs have long been in place and there is a desire not to disturb them, or when there are very many and/or very complex operational update programs in place. The full data-base scan approach can be put in place then with no impact whatsoever on existing operational code. The problem with the full database scan approach is that much unnecessary data must be scanned. From a global perspective, scanning entire large databases to locate a fraction of the data is wasteful.

A second approach for refreshment of data at the atomic level is that of requiring the operational update programs to keep track of what data needs and does not need to be sent to the atomic level while update is occurring. There are many ways update programs can do this. One way is to *mark* operational data that has been updated. Another way is to create a *delta* file. The delta file is nothing more than a collection of the successful updates which are relevant to the atomic DSS level. There are, undoubtedly, many more ways of using the update program to collect the data that needs to be passed to the atomic level. The advantage of using update programs for this task is that it is very efficient to do so. There is no need to scan large databases

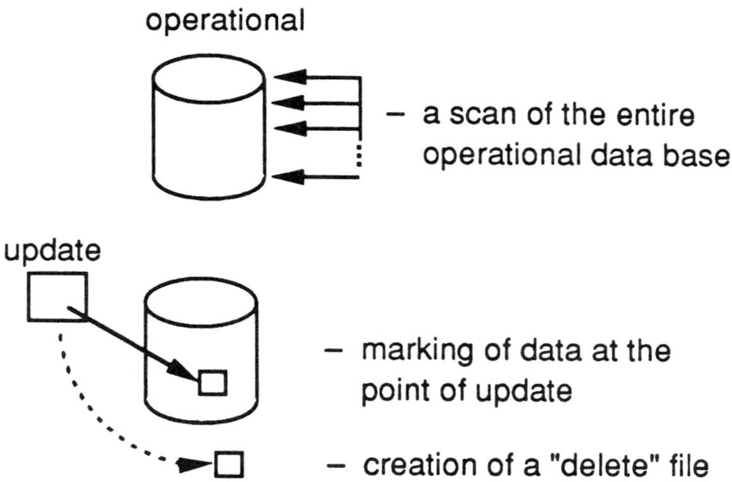

FIGURE 5.8 Two approaches to determine what operational data is passed to the atomic environment.

looking for a fraction of the data in the database. But the disadvantage of using update programs to prepare for the extract of operational data to the atomic level is that it necessarily involves altering the program logic that has been built for the update of operational data. Some of the many reasons why the managers do not want to change that update logic are:

- a lot of update programs may need to be changed;
- update logic is complex as it is;
- update code is older code that has already been patched and maintained enough as it is.

The tradeoff in the refreshment of atomic level data is between the inefficiency of massive scans of operational data and the modification of operational update logic.

It should be stated that wholesale replacement of operational data to atomic data is almost never done. Such a strategy is inevitably wasteful and, in light of the time variant nature of atomic level data, defeats much of the purpose of atomic data.

ACCESSING ATOMIC DATA

The atomic environment, when viewed from the perspective of the types of processing done within the atomic environment, is peculiar in that nearly all of the processing done at the atomic level can be described as:

- sequential loading of data from an operational extract;
- sequential scanning of data in preparation for DSS departmental extract.

These very simple types of processing represent, practically speaking, *all* of the processing done at the atomic level. There is no:

- direct access of a single record;
- update of a single record;
- online access of data;
- high response time processing;
- high availability processing, and so forth.

The types of processing—such as online access of data—common to many other parts of the world of data processing simply are not found in the DSS atomic environment.

The need for accessing data is such that indexed access of data is the one way that data should be organized in the atomic environment. Figure 5.9 shows the indexed organization of atomic data.

Given the large amount of data found at the atomic level, however, means that not many indexes will be used to access atomic data. The amount of time required to load the data and the space required preclude the usage of more than a few indexes. It is possible that an atomic database may require two indexes. It is unlikely that three indexes would ever be used, and it is practically out of the realm of imagination that as many as four indexes on an atomic data base would ever be required. As a rule of thumb then:

- An atomic data base will have a single index on its primary key. An option, where applicable, is one or more sparse indexes. A sparse index is merely an index which exists for some values of the table being indexed. Sparse indexes are not implemented as a component of ORACLE. Instead they have to be implemented as a component of the database management system or as a part of the atomic level infrastructure application.

Because of the amount of data found in the atomic level, it is often wise to partition the atomic level data. A partition of atomic level data is merely a physical subset of data. Partitioning can be done at the ORACLE level or at the application level. Unless there are overwhelming reasons to do so, partitioning at the application level functionally accomplishes everything possible at the ORACLE level and has many more options. Figure 5.10 shows an example of atomic level data which has been partitioned by year.

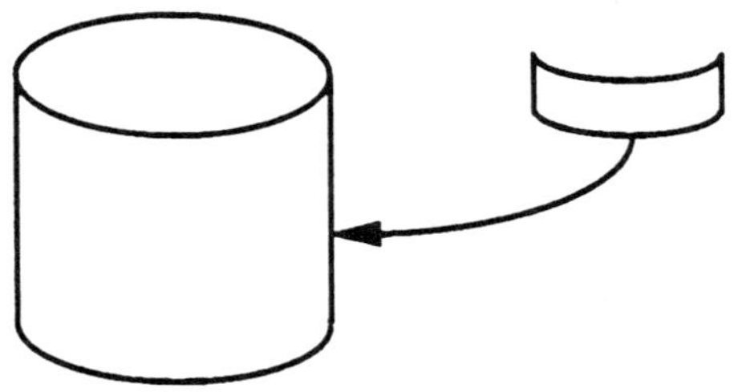

FIGURE 5.9 Atomic level data—accessed through an index.

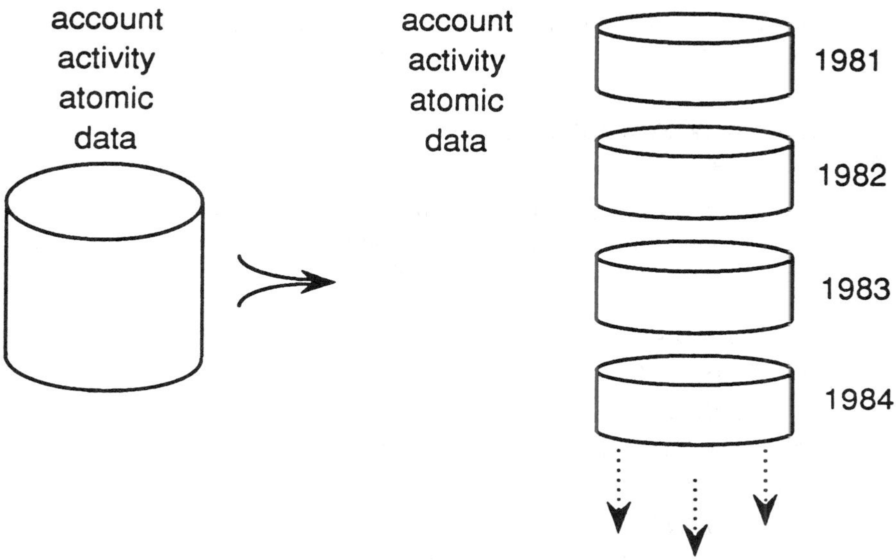

FIGURE 5.10 Atomic level data which has been partitioned by year.

On one hand there is a large collection of data. But once the data is partitioned there are physically more databases (i.e., tables), but each database is much smaller than the original collection of data. Accessing and recovering a small amount of data is a much more pleasing prospect than accessing and recovering a large amount of data.

Note that in the example there is exactly the same amount of data whether it is partitioned or not. Partitioning has not added or subtracted any data from the atomic level. Instead, partitioning has organized data so that it is much more easily managed.

PURGING ATOMIC DATA

At some point atomic level data must be purged. It is not desirable or even possible to continue to add data to a database endlessly. Even though the DSS analyst may postpone the actual writing and execution of purge programs, the criteria for purging should be determined at the outset.

There are two choices (at least!) for the DSS analyst upon purging the data. Once choice is to simply discard the purged data—literally throwing it away. The other choice is to push the purged data off onto yet another medium, such as tape or microfiche, and to save the tapes or microfiche for undefined future processing.

SUBJECT ORIENTATION OF ATOMIC LEVEL DATA

Atomic level data, from a design perspective, has a strong subject orientation. For example, it is common to see atomic level data organized around the following typical subjects:

- SHIPMENT
- CUSTOMER
- SUPPLIER
- ACTIVITY/TRANSACTION
- ORDER
- ACCOUNT
- PART/PRODUCT, and so forth.

The subject orientation of data means that data does not appear (usually!) as a single physical database or table at the atomic level. Instead the subject orientation takes the form of multiple physical databases or tables related by a common key. Figure 5.11 shows an example of physically separate data at the atomic level linked by their key to form part of a subject area.

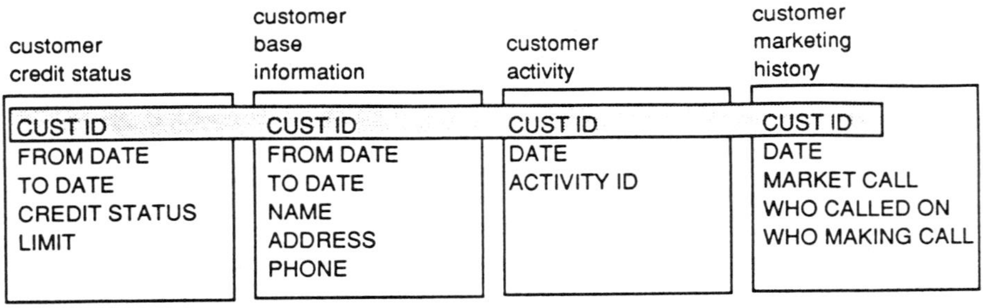

FIGURE 5.11 Four physically related tables at the atomic level that comprise part of a subject area.

SUPPORTING TECHNOLOGY

There are two distinctive characteristics for technology that are used successfully at the atomic level. Those characteristics are:

- the ability to support large-scale sequential access loading/scanning of data efficiently;
- the ability to interface with more than a few types of software for the access and loading of data.

The first technical requirement—the efficient sequential loading of data and the efficient sequential access of data—should be obvious. ORACLE meets these technical requirements nicely. What may not be obvious is the second requirement. Figure 5.12 shows the importance of the second set of technical requirements. The second set of requirements fits very well with ORACLE as well. Along with VSAM, ORACLE is widely used and enjoys an interface with many products.

It is anticipated that the atomic level will receive data from a wide variety of operational sources. It is anticipated that the atomic level will pass data to an even wider variety of sources of data for further DSS processing. If technology is chosen that does not have a wide variety of interfaces, then the technology itself will become a limiting factor as to what can be done at the atomic level. The DSS analyst should choose a technology for atomic processing which is as widely

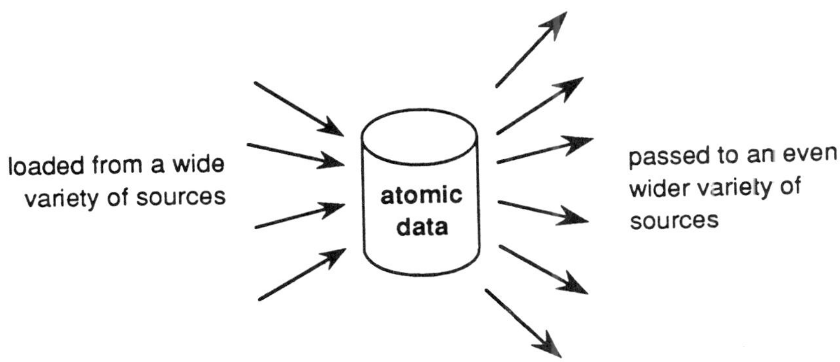

FIGURE 5.12 The second set of technical requirements.

used as possible, and ORACLE fits nicely with the technical requirements for atomic level processing.

There are two aspects of technological interface between two products which the DSS analyst should know. The ability of one technology to interface to another technology should be judged on:

- the existence of a standard interface between the technologies
- the maturity of the standard interface between the technologies

There is a big difference between merely having an interface and having a mature interface.

SUMMARIZED ATOMIC DATA

While the vast majority of the data found at the atomic level is granular and detailed, there is some small amount of atomic DSS data that is summarized. That data is public summarized data that has common usage throughout the DSS environment. For example, accounting produces as part of its regular processing the quarterly corporate totals for:

- revenues
- costs
- net profit, and so forth.

These summarized figures become the *official* corporate figures, and many other departments use these quarterly figures in their analyses. In order to make those public summarized figures available, they are put into the atomic database. Figure 5.13 illustrates the flow of data.

Note that only *public* or corporate *official* summary data is put into the atomic database. There will be much summary corporate data that will not be placed into the atomic database because there is not a widespread corporate use of the summary data.

DIFFERENT LEVELS OF ATOMIC DATA

In a large, sophisticated DSS environment, it is not uncommon to have multiple levels of DSS atomic data. A typical environment might have:

- a standard atomic environment where data was lightly summarized;

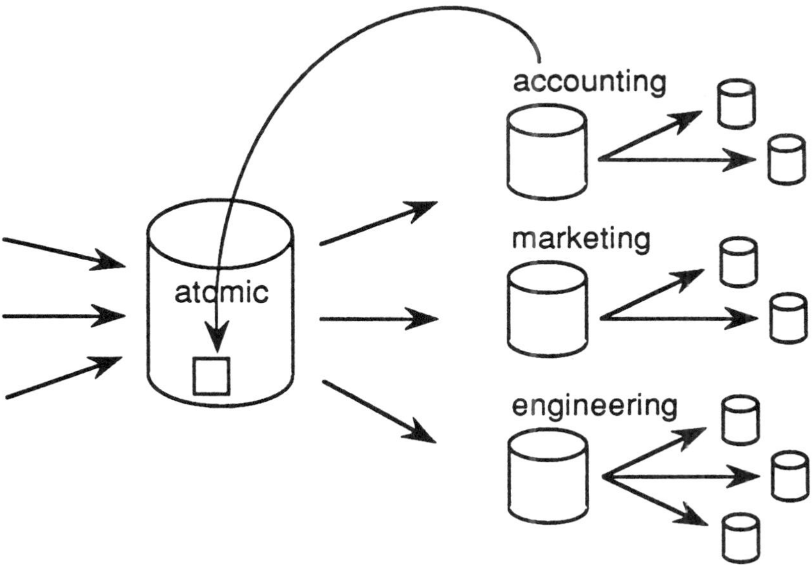

FIGURE 5.13 The feedback loop from accounting. Accounting calculates certain official figures which are then made available to the corporation by placing the figures in the atomic database.

- a *living sample* atomic database from which sampling could be done quite efficiently;
- a *true archival* environment where all detailed information is stored.

These different levels of atomic level data have been discussed at length in earlier chapters.

Breaking the atomic environment into different levels greatly enhances the efficiency of processing that is possible. More than any tuning or technical *wizardry*, designing the atomic environment strategically sets the stage for performance.

What effect does creating multiple levels of atomic data have on processing? The net effect is to manage large amounts of data efficiently. Instead of doing many massive queries and scans of large amounts of data, the queries and scans operate against smaller amounts of data. In doing so, the queries and scans can be run more quickly using less resources.

It is noteworthy that the different levels of data within the atomic environment may or may not be managed by ORACLE. For example, the true archival environment contains huge amounts of data and most likely is found on magnetic tape or microfiche. And the living sample environment may be managed by SAS or Model 204, for example. The very different processing characteristics of the different levels of data may well be managed by separate technologies.

IN SUMMARY

Atomic level data forms the backbone of DSS processing. The source of atomic level data is operational data and external data. Most atomic level data is detailed, granular data, although corporate summary data is stored at the atomic level as well.

There are three ways time variancy of atomic data is stored—continuously, event discrete, and periodic discrete. All atomic level data is time variant. Atomic level data is stored according to subjects. In general there is one index per atomic database. When there is a lot of data in an atomic database, the atomic database is partitioned.

Technology such as ORACLE supporting atomic databases has two salient characteristics:

- the technology can handle sequential loading and access of data efficiently; and
- the technology shares a common and mature interface to many other technologies.

QUESTIONS: CHAPTER 5

1. Non-key data is REDUNDANT/NON REDUNDANT at the atomic level.
2. Key data is REDUNDANT/NON REDUNDANT at the atomic level.
3. External data CAN BE/MUST BE placed in the atomic level.
4. The three standard forms of time variance are ______________, ______________, and ______________.
5. Algorithmically, the most difficult type of time variant data to manage is ______________.
6. The most common type of time variant data is ______________.
7. The most predictable type of time variant data is ______________.

8. There is NO/A LITTLE/SOME/A LOT OF/WHOLESALE redundancy of data from the operational level to the atomic level.
9. The soonest that atomic data is refreshed is every __________.
10. Atomic data can be refreshed with no disruption to existing code. T/F
11. If existing code can be disrupted, only updates that affect atomic data can be saved, thus streamlining the __________ process.
12. Wholesale movement of data from the operational to the atomic level is a COMMON/RARE practice.
13. Atomic data access can be characterized as __________.
14. Because of the volume of atomic data, it is mandatory that there be at least __________ indexes.
15. Because of the volume of atomic data, it is mandatory that there be no more than __________ indexes.
16. Units of atomic data, once placed on the atomic data base are NEVER/SELDOM/FREQUENTLY/ALWAYS updated.
17. Breaking up the atomic level of data into __________ physically subdivides the data.
18. Partitioning data ADDS/SUBTRACTS/NEITHER ADDS NOR SUBTRACTS data at the atomic level.
19. Atomic data MUST BE/MAY BE/DOES NOT NEED TO BE purged.
20. The overall organization of atomic level data can be described as a __________ orientation.
21. The two technical criteria for atomic level data are __________ and __________.
22. ALL/SOME/MOST atomic data is detailed.
23. Name some nonstandard levels of atomic data.
24. If there are different levels of atomic data, they MUST/MAY BE/CANNOT BE under the same technology.

CHAPTER 6

Departmental, Individual Level Data in the DSS/ ORACLE Environment

The effective usage and purpose of departmental and individual level data in the DSS/ORACLE environment is best understood in the context of what, where and how data is used. In Chapter 3 the full information cycle was discussed. The cycle that was identified looked very similar to that in Figure 6.1.

In the simplistic discussion that ensued, it was assumed that merely getting DSS data to the manager making the decisions was enough to create the effective DSS/ORACLE environment. Now the discussion will go much more deeply into that role—of the manager and the DSS analyst—and what kind of DSS data and processing is useful.

Two kinds of managerial decisions affect the enterprise—there are continuous operation decisions (i.e., *operational decisions*) and new operations/new market (i.e., *directional*) decisions. Both kinds of decisions have a profound effect on the enterprise, but each requires very different DSS support.

The types of objectives each style of management has are very different.

Operational management

- maintains continuity of the business,
- maintains existing market share,
- minimizes expenses, and
- maximizes existing revenue.

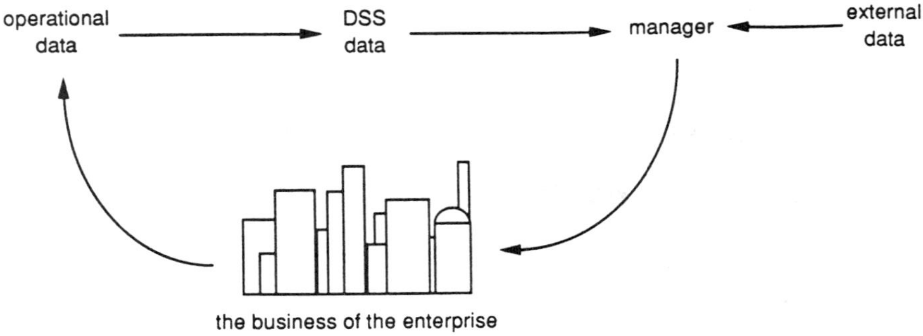

FIGURE 6.1 The full cycle of information.

Directional management

- develops new products,
- develops new markets,
- develops strategic markets, and
- keeps abreast of new technology, new business opportunities.

The objectives of the different managers who affect the business of the enterprise are very different. The objective of the operational manager is to maintain status quo as efficiently as possible. The objective of the directional manager is to remain anything but status quo.

In addition, the frequency of the decisions of the two types of decision makers is quite different. The operational manager often makes small, frequent adjustments to the business, much like a train engineer constantly adjusting the level of pressure inside the engine. The directional manager does not make frequent decisions; however when he or she makes decisions they are momentous. Analogically, the directional manager is like a railroad executive who decides to build a new route. The executive does not decide to build a new route very frequently, but when he or she does, the consequences to the organization are enormous.

To use some day-to-day examples of the different types of managers who affect the business:

Banking	
operational	managers who adjust the rates for money on deposit or for loans being made by the bank
directional	managers who create new banking products or who decide to expand services overseas
Insurance	
operational	managers who determine the premium rates for policy renewals
directional	managers who commit resources to go into new lines of insurance
Manufacturing	
operational	managers who monitor the reject rate of assembly lines or the cost of production
directional	managers who develop new products to be manufactured
Retail	
operational	managers who calculate the restocking formulae for products or determine when sales are to be held
directional	managers who determine where to build the next store or what markets are to be expanded into

Both types of managers are absolutely vital to the health of the organization. But both types of managers need very different types of DSS data in order to function effectively.

The difference in the types of information needed for effective decision making is highlighted by:

As an example of the different interests in DSS data, the operational manager will be quite interested in what the monthly and weekly production levels are, what amount revenues look like, what the backlog of orders looks like, and so forth. While all of this information will be of passing interest to the directional manager, he or she is much more likely to be interested in new technological developments that are relevant to the product line, in new products introduced by the competition, in shifts in the demographics of the marketplace, and so

	Operational	Directional
What	periodic costs - periodic revenues - usage rates - restocking rates - inventory levels	- new product opportunities - demographic analysis - competitive thrusts - risk assessment - new technological advances
Frequency	- regular - cyclical	- irregular - as opportunity arises
Internal, external	- data generated internal to organization is most relevant	- data from outside the organization is probably most relevant

forth. The day-to-day goings on of the enterprise are interesting to the directional manager, but not that interesting.

A somewhat more representative model of the managerial position is shown by Figure 6.2.

Figure 6.2 shows that there are two very different components to the managerial function—the operational component and the directional component. The continuous operations component has regular input from the DSS processing done at the departmental and the atomic level. The operational component regularly makes small adjustments to the day-to-day business of the enterprise.

Input to the directional component comes from two sources. As required, directional management looks at what is going on with the day-to-day operations. And, occasionally, directional management gets

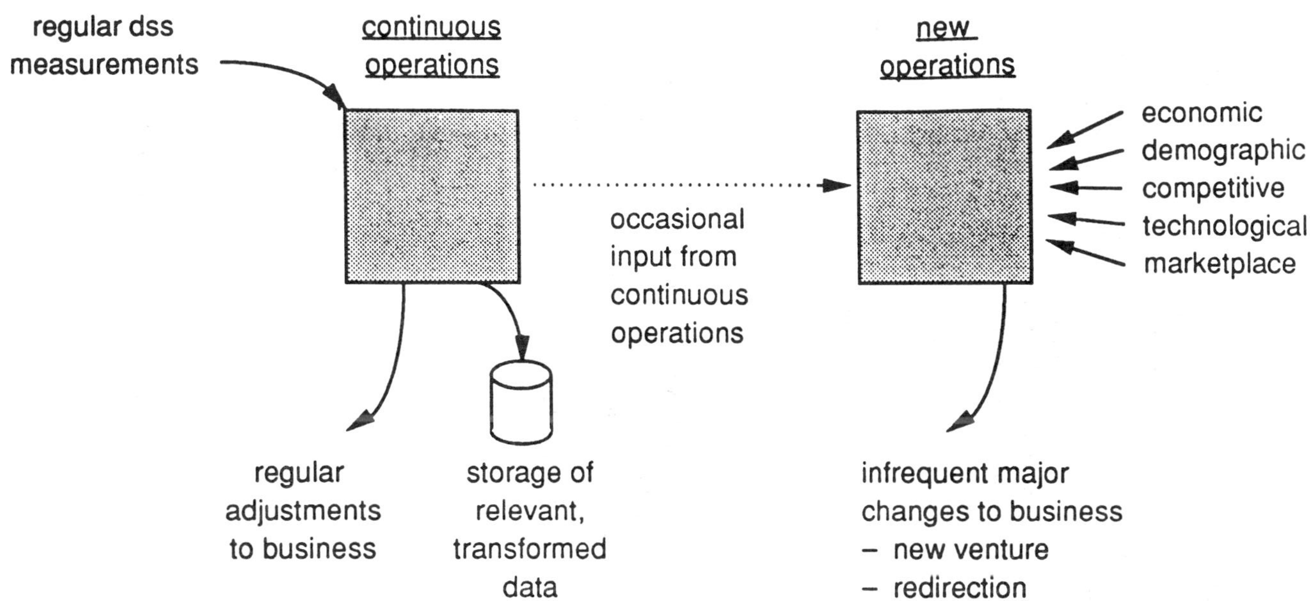

FIGURE 6.2 The managerial function.

input from a wide variety of external sources. The external information covers such diverse areas as economic, demographic, competitive, technological, and marketplace information.

Infrequently, directional management makes changes to the business of the corporation. The changes are sweeping, such as the entering of new ventures, the redirection of existing ventures, the closing of existing ventures, and so forth.

The departmental DSS analysis supports almost entirely the operational business and individual processing supports both operational and directional operations. The different types of DSS processing and how they relate to operational and directional management is shown by Figure 6.3.

Archival Data—DSS Processing

It is a temptation to state that all data that is archived is in the atomic level database. While it is true that all data in the atomic level database is archived, it is not true that all archival data is in the atomic level database.

There are at least two notable exceptions to the rule. Archival data, if it has a high probability of access, is quite naturally found in the operational database. And trend analysis data, almost always calculated and stored at the summary level, is found in the departmental and individual level databases.

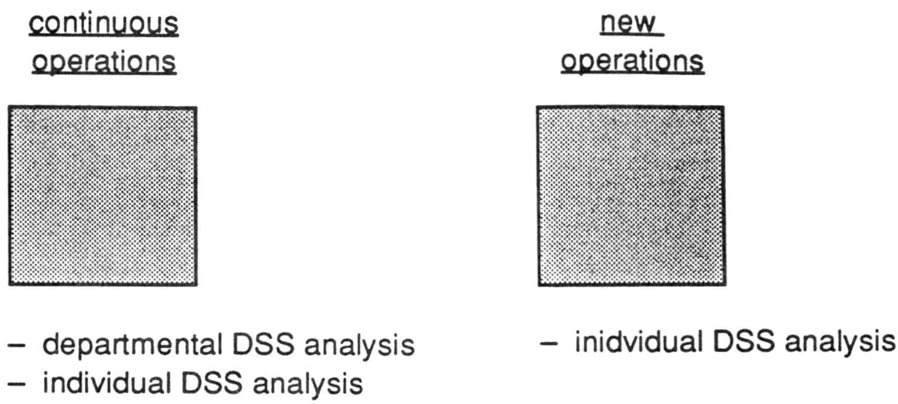

FIGURE 6.3 The environments in which individual and DSS analysis is done.

For example, suppose a bank wishes to keep the last month's checking activity of its customers in its on-line operational environment. Each check, as it is posted, is stored in the online, operational database. This allows the bank to answer very quickly such queries as:

- "Did my check for the rent clear last week?"
- "Did my insurance premium get paid?"

Suppose the bank also wishes to store the last 10 years' checking activity in its atomic database.

There is a big difference between storing one month's worth of data on-line and storing 10 years' data in an atomic database. The essential differences are:

- 1 month's customer activity is a relatively small amount of data and has a high probability of access;
- 10 years' activity is a large amount of data and has a low to moderate probability of access.

But 1 month's activity and 10 years' activity are both archived.

Consider another example. The marketing department stores the monthly sales figures, month-by-month in the marketing departmental data-base. Each month new summary figures for sales are calculated. Over time marketing can track trends using comparison of these figures.

Are these figures that marketing stores, archived? Yes they are, but they are properly stored at the departmental level, because, even if the base atomic data exists for their recalculation, the amount of work required is too much. In other words, it does marketing no good to recreate the monthly numbers each month from the atomic data.

Storing the summary data then, on a month-by-month basis is another manner in which archival data is legitimately found throughout the architecture.

But Figures 6.2 and 6.3 are misleading because they portray the different units of decision making as a unified entity. In fact, they are anything but that, and the actual flow and usage of DSS information for managerial decisions is much more complex than that suggested in Figures 6.2 and 6.3

A more realistic representation of the flow and usage of DSS information is shown by Figure 6.4.

In Figure 6.4 the complex interrelationships of data are shown. Internal input comes from the departmental DSS processing that occurs. Internal input comes on a regular basis, and usually comes from a variety of sources. Typical organizations doing continuous analysis are sales, accounting, production control, and purchasing. The operational decision makers feed the directional decision making function on an as-needed basis. The interface between the decision makers is direct.

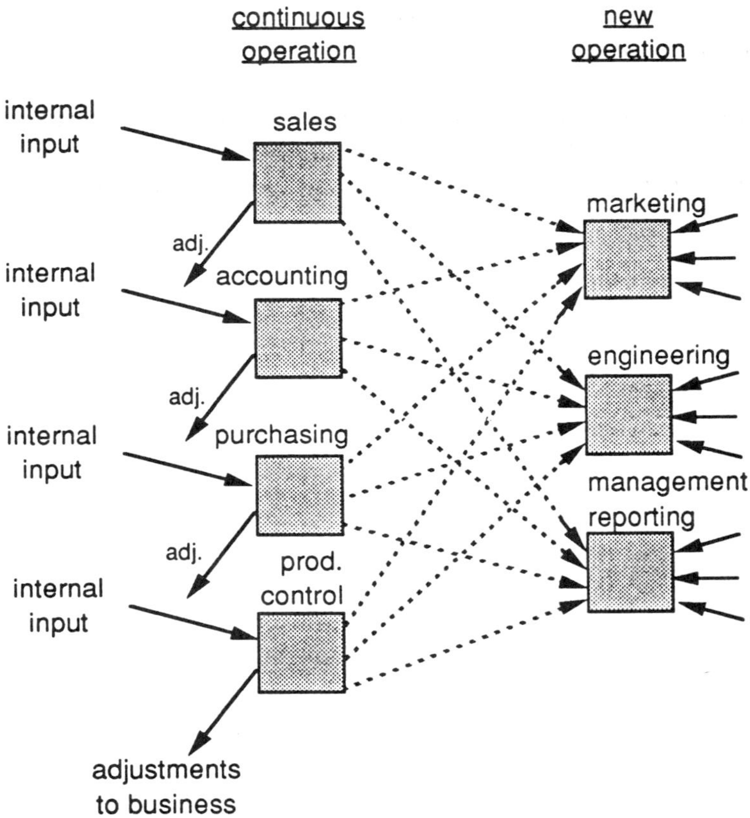

FIGURE 6.4 The more complex picture of DSS data and the complex interrelationships.

Typical organizations that do or influence directional decision making are marketing, engineering, management reporting, and so forth. External input is given to the directional decision analyst on an as-needed basis. In general, the source for external input varies widely.

In other cases, the function of operational and directional analysis is performed in the same organization, such as the actuarial organization, as shown by Figure 6.5.

As a rule of thumb, departmental processing serves the operational community first and individual processing serves the directional decision making community first. Of course, there are exceptions to this.

Some industries align quite strongly with one form of analysis or the other. For example, consider a local utility company supplying electricity to a community. Practically all of the attention of management in this type of company is oriented toward continuous operations and (operational decision making) the periodic monitoring of costs, of levels of service, and so forth. The more stable the business, the more the business becomes monopolistic and the less attention is paid to new operations and directional decision making.

Contrast a local utility company to a semiconductor manufacturer. There is seldom any continuous operations in semiconductors that produces a stable business over the long term. If the semiconductor manufacturer is lucky enough to garner market share, it is predictable

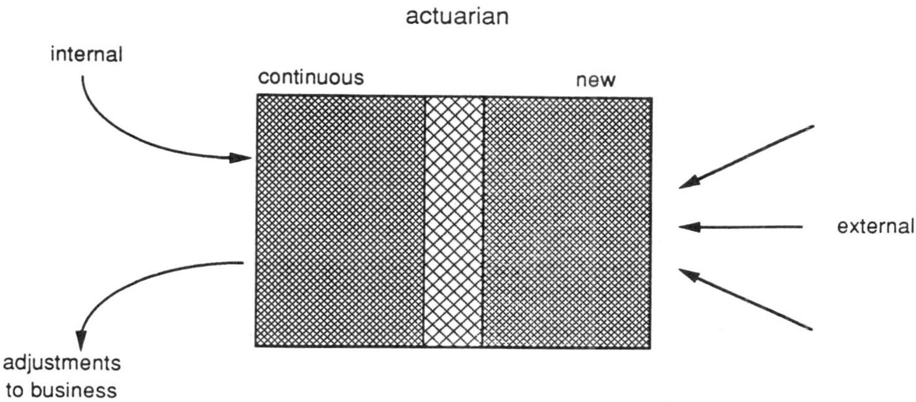

FIGURE 6.5 Some organizations—such as the actuarial organization—perform the entire spectrum of continuous and new operations analysis within the confines of the same department.

that the profitability of the market share will drop in time. Over time, the market will shrink due to new replacement technologies appearing on the horizon. The lifeblood of the semiconductor industry then is new technology, and it is not surprising that new operations and new products are usually at the forefront of the priorities for the semiconductor manager. The directional decision making function is vital to the semiconductor manufacturer. But most organizations are not nearly as stable as electric utilities nor as volatile as semiconductor manufacturers. Most organizations are somewhere in between.

Take, for example, a computer manufacturer. For much of the business of the computer manufacturer there is a need to worry about maintaining or increasing current market share. Support of the computer manufacturer's technology, keeping costs in control, and supplying more of the technology when needed are all characteristics of the continuous operations of the company that manages established products. But management of the computer manufacturer is constantly considering the possibility of new products. The decisions about new products are in the domain of directional decision support analysis. As a new computer product is developed, it passes from new operations to continuous operations. Figure 6.6 shows the normal dynamics of passing products from new operations to old operations.

On day 1, operational decision makers are actively managing products A, B, and C. Input is received on a regular basis and periodic adjustments are made. At the same time, products D and E are being considered by "directional" decision makers.

On day 2, the decision is made to put product D into development and production. In addition, the study of product E goes into full swing at this time. On day 3, the decision is made not to develop product E, and product D goes into sales. Note that product E is not forever rejected as a product for full development. Instead product E merely goes into *back burner* status and may be revisited at a later point in time as market conditions change. On day 4, product D is being managed by continuous operations and new operations begins to consider a new product, product F.

Both departmental and individual levels of DSS analysis are used to support the simple operational/directional model that has been described. From a technical and a functional perspective, there are very few differences between departmental and individual level processing. In general, both types of processing:

- deal with data at a summary level;
- prepare data for managerial consideration;

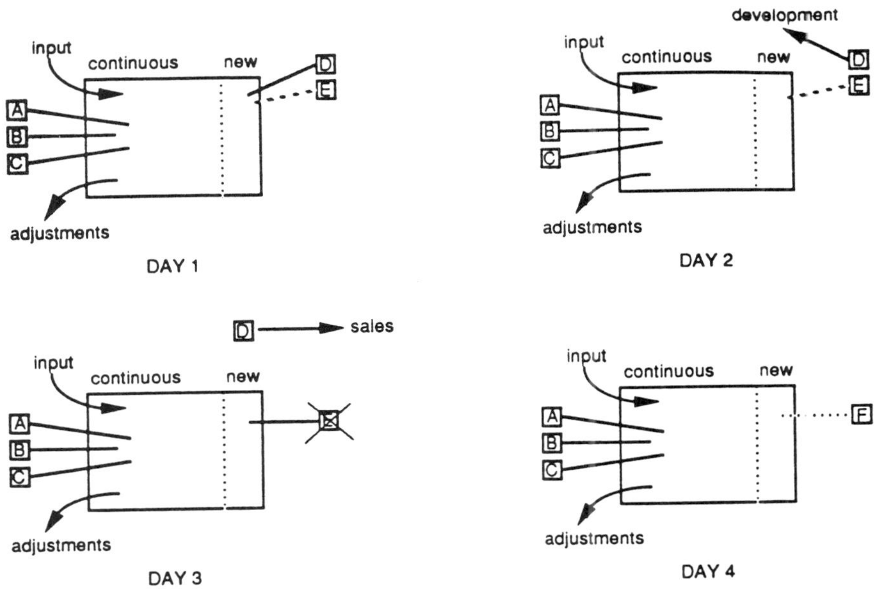

FIGURE 6.6 The dynamics of continuous and new operations in the organization.

- operate primarily from operational data;
- operate on subsets of data;
- are not oriented toward high performance processing, and so forth.

The major differences between departmental and individual processing are:

- departmental processing is regularly scheduled and individual processing is irregularly scheduled, and
- departmental processing normally encompasses much detail and individual processing encompasses (relatively) small amounts of data.

One of the characteristics of both departmental and individual levels of processing is the redundancy of data between different departments, as shown by Figure 6.7.

Figure 6.7 shows that many of the same data elements are found at the departmental level of DSS processing. The concern for the

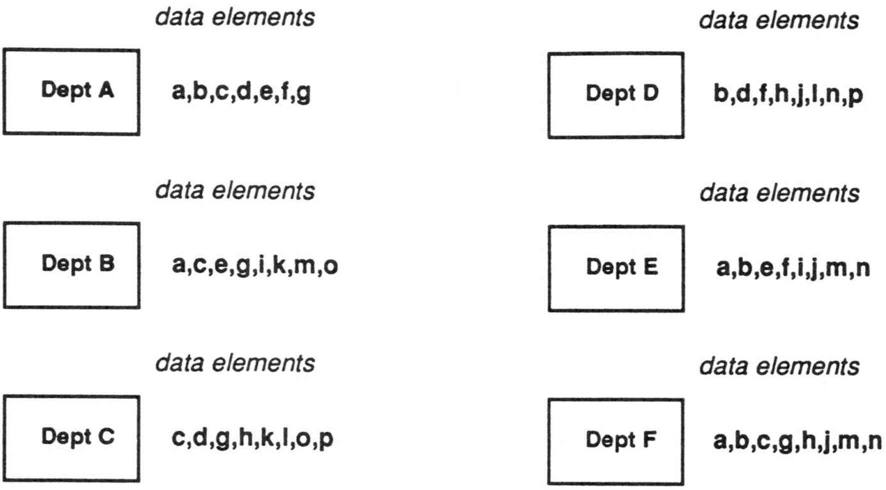

FIGURE 6.7 There is a great deal of redundancy of data among data elements found in the different departments that do departmental DSS processing.

reconcilability of redundant data exists at the departmental level. But the reconciliation is not done directly between departments. Instead, reconcilability occurs at the atomic level where the detailed, time-valued basis of all data resides.

The flow of data to the departmental level is from the atomic level and the flow to the individual level is either from the atomic or the departmental level as shown by Figure 6.8.

As a rule, individual analysis is done from departmental data wherever possible. Widespread individual processing against the atomic level data usually expends gross amounts of resources.

The technology used to support the departmental and individual

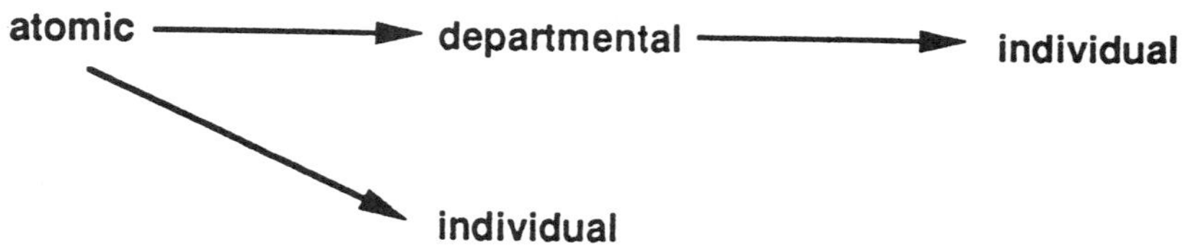

FIGURE 6.8 The flow of data.

levels of processing is oriented toward user-friendliness, speed of development, and speed of change. Issues such as performance and availability—so important in other environments—are secondary issues here.

Most of the data found at the departmental and individual levels is summary, although some detailed data may be transported from the atomic environment. As a rule, no more than 25% of the data found at the departmental or individual level should be detailed.

There are very few ironclad rules as to the usage or passage of data at the atomic level, except that:

- no departmental calculations pass directly to other departments, and
- no individual calculations pass directly to other individuals.

Figure 6.9 shows the types of direct data sharing that are not allowed.

The direct passage of data from one department to the next, however, does not preclude the sharing of data. If there is a need to share data, the sharing is done as shown in Figure 6.10, through the storing

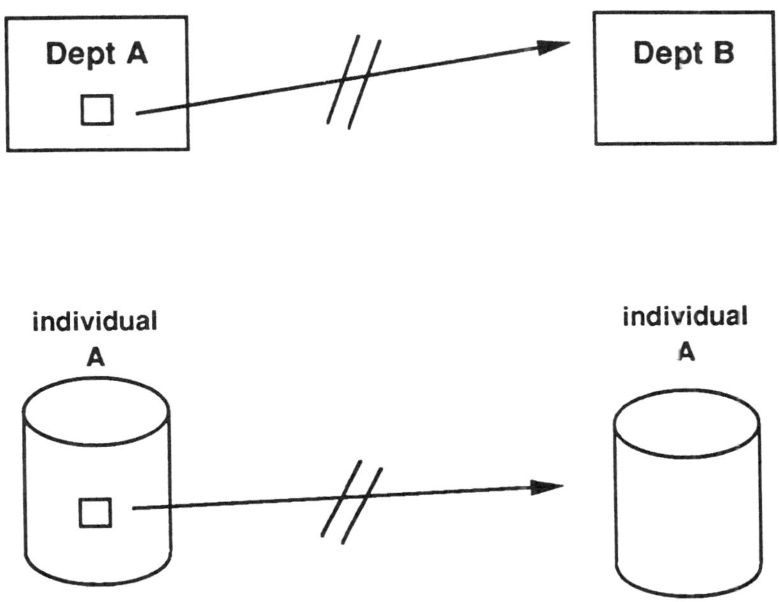

FIGURE 6.9 The types of passage of data that are not allowed.

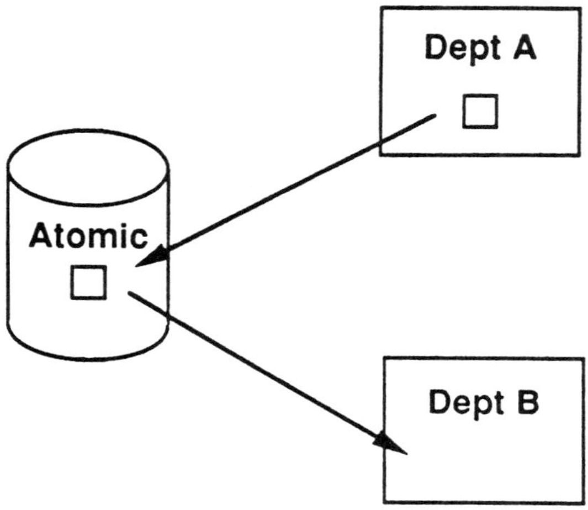

FIGURE 6.10 How dept A and B store data.

of data at the atomic level. When data is placed in the atomic level, it is *public* summary data.

One of the interesting issues of DSS processing is how often DSS departmental and individual data is refreshed. As a rule, the refreshment process is a *pull* process from the atomic level, not a *push* process. In other words, the data is transported to the DSS departmental level or the individual level on an as-needed basis, not on an as-available basis.

Another interesting issue surrounding DSS departmental processing is whether modeling in general and data modeling in particular ought to be done. It is usually faster to simply create the DSS report or system than it is to model it formally and then write it. DSS systems change so rapidly that keeping the model up to date with the system is futile. The types of tools and technologies found in the DSS departmental environment are easily changed. Therefore, producing a formal model of the DSS system is usually not a good practice.

An important consideration in building the departmental/individual DSS environment is whether or not ORACLE is an appropriate technology. As a rule, ORACLE may be appropriate for departmental processing, and PC ORACLE probably is appropriate for individual processing. The underlying technology for the different levels typically looks like:

ATOMIC	DEPARTMENTAL	INDIVIDUAL
ORACLE	ORACLE	Lotus 1-2-3
VSAM	FOCUS	dBASEIII
MODEL204	SAS	QMF
	NOMAD	purchased software
	MODEL204	VISICALC
	RAMIS	ORACLE
	ORACLE	PC ORACLE

IN SUMMARY

There are two kinds of DSS functions that need support—the operational function and the directional decision making functions. The operational function is generally supported by departmental processing. The directional function most closely aligns with individual level processing.

There are many similarities between departmental and individual levels of DSS processing. However, departmental processing is regularly scheduled and individual level processing is not regularly scheduled. In addition, departmental level processing involves much data and individual level processing usually does not involve much data.

There is redundancy of data from one department to the next as well as from one individual to the next. If there is a need for reconcilability of data, it is achieved at the atomic level.

Data does not directly flow from one department to the next. Instead, data flows through the atomic level.

Data is refreshed on an as-needed basis, not on an as-available basis. As a rule, data modeling is not done for DSS processing.

QUESTIONS: CHAPTER 6

1. The source of data for departmental processing is ____________.
2. The source of data for the individual level is ______________ or ______________.
3. The two types of managerial decisions are ____ and ______________
4. Operational management decisions are made ______________.
5. Directional management decisions are made ______________.
6. Operational management is concerned with ____ or ______________ current market.

7. Directional management is concerned with new ____________.
8. The source of most operational management input is ________.
9. The source of most directional management input is ________.
10. In the atomic-centered environment, data is "PUSHED"/ "PULLED".
11. It is LIKELY/UNLIKELY that there will be lots of diverse software packages in the departmental/individual levels of data.

CHAPTER 7

Projection Data/Projection Processing in the DSS/ORACLE Environment

There are two fundamentally different kinds of data—historical data and projection data. The two types of data require very different storage and handling in terms of DSS processing. Far and away, historical data is the most widely used and commonly occurring data.

HISTORICAL DATA

Historical data is data that measures or describes what has happened. Some typical examples of historical data are records of:

- buying an insurance policy;
- cashing a check;
- selling a finished good;
- manufacturing a finished good;
- reserving a seat on an airplane

The world of computing is dominated by measuring or keeping track of events that have occurred. The world of current value data is calculated from historical data. For example:

- A customer's current bank balance is the sum of all historical activity—withdrawals, deposits, interest charges, late charges, and so forth.

- The availability of a seat on an airplane is the result of much historical information—the scheduling of the flight, who has booked which seats, and so forth.
- The current insurance coverage of a client is a function of when the policy was sold, under what terms it was sold, whether premiums were paid, and so forth.

One of the characteristics of historical data and its attendant current value data is that once a historical value is measured or described, as long as the value is correct, it cannot be changed without negatively affecting the accuracy of systems that use the data.

This trait is taken for granted in most systems. For example, once a deposit into an account on January 15 is made for $1,000 and the event is recorded, it is not appropriate to change the value. As long as $1,000 is the correct amount, then the amount would *never* be arbitrarily changed to $750 unless, of course, there were some activity against the account. There exists with historical data the notion of correctness of data as of some moment in time. A value is either correct or it is incorrect; but, in any case, there is only a single value that is correct.

Another trait of historical data is that there is a firm, well-defined algorithmic relationship among the different historical variables. As an example, consider the following simple algorithm to determine the current balance of an account:

```
    Current balance =
    month beginning balance + deposit (1) + deposit (2) +
..
... deposit (n)
    - (withdrawal (1) + withdrawal (2) + ... withdrawal
(n)
    - (monthly charges)
    + (accrued interest)
curr val = deposits - withdrawals - charges + interest
```

At any moment in time there is one and only one correct value for the current account balance based on the specific charges made against the account.

PROJECTION DATA

Projection data is fundamentally different from historical data in that some of the basic assumptions made for historical data do not hold true for projection data. Projection data is that data used for future prediction. Typical of projection data are budget or planning data. Projection data is not based on the measurement or description of events as is historic data and, as such, is a prediction.

The fundamental differences between projection data and historical data are:

- there is no *correct* value for detailed projection data, while there is one and only one correct value for detailed historic data;
- while algorithms may be constructed to show the relationships between elements of projection data, the algorithm often serves as a general guideline and, at any moment, may or may not be correct *with no loss of validity.*

Each of these fundamental differences between projection data and historical data will be explored.

Detailed Content

Projection data does not have a *correct* value at the detailed level. Each detailed variable of data has a best estimate, but each detailed value is open to speculation. For example, suppose the manager of sales estimates that next year's sales by region will be:

```
Region 1—$50,000
Region 2—$150,000
Region 3—$75,000
Region 4—$295,000
```

While the manager may formulate a best estimate, the very nature of the data is an estimate. If a salesperson in region 3 wishes to believe that next year's sales estimate for that region should be $125,000, then the salesperson is quite capable of doing so. There is no loss of credibility of the manager, either. There simply is a difference of opinion and *both* parties may hold valid views.

But with historical data there is one and only one correct value. Detailed data—once the value is established—is not open to speculation and interpretation.

Algorithmic Differences

Projection data often does not balance in terms of algorithmic correctness. For example, suppose division 1 is made up of four regions

—region 1, 2, 3, and 4. Suppose that the sales forecast for next year is as shown:

```
Region 1—        $1,650,000
Region 2—           750,000
Region 3—         2,350,000
Region 4—           600,000
---------------------------
Division 1—      $5,350,000
```

Top management reviews the forecasts and adjusts division 1's forecast to \$5,750,000. When top management rearranges the forecast for the division, the details do not add up to the summary. The forecast is out of synch. But does the status of the forecast being out of synch invalidate the forecast, either at the detailed or the summary level? Not at all. Even though reconciliation needs to be done at some later point in time, there is absolutely nothing wrong with the details of the forecast being out of synch with the summary.

ONE-WAY/TWO-WAY STREET

The forecast process is a two-way street. Historical processing is a "one-way street." In historical processing, the details are determined. Once the historical details are determined, the summary can be created. The calculation process is one way—going from detail to summary.

But the forecast (i.e., projection) process can go either way. The summary can be created from the detail, or the detail can be created from the summary. Thus it is said that forecast data is a two-way street. There are many ways in which summary data may be used as a basis for detailed calculation. One way is simple allocation. If there are four detailed categories, the detailed value equals the sum divided by four.

Another simple way detailed data is recalculated based on summary data is to take the difference between the actual sum and the forecast sum and allocate the difference based on a percentage of the differential. For example, if there are five detailed categories:

```
SUMCAT = CAT1 + CAT2 + CAT3 + CAT4 + CAT5
DIFF = FORECAST - SUMCAT
DELTA = DIFF/5
FORECAST = (CAT1 + DELTA) + (CAT2 + DELTA) +
(CAT3 + DELTA) + (CAT4 + DELTA) + (CAT5 + DELTA)
```

The two simple ways of allocating the difference between the forecasted summary and the actual summary are but a few of the many ways allocation from the summary level to the detailed level can be done.

CONTROLLING UNCONTROLLED DATA

The variability of forecast/projection data leads to all sorts of difficulties, especially when the issue of different views of data is factored into the projection. Suppose a (small!) company has seven departments, a, b, c, d, e, f, and g. Each department does its own forecast for the next year's budget. A corporate budget is created from the detailed departmental budgets. Accounting creates its forecasted budget for the corporation, sales creates its forecasted budget, manufacturing creates its forecasted budget, and engineering creates its forecasted budget, and so forth. The relationship of the budgets is shown in Figure 7.1.

The problems with the budget process come from many directions. Budgets at the detailed level are constantly being changed. Budgets at the summary level are also being changed and a backward allocation strategy is being implemented. And, to top matters off, the accounting (corporate) budget does not total with the sales budget plus the manufacturing budget plus the engineering budget. It is no wonder that the budgetary process is misunderstood and dreaded.

To bring a projection (i.e., a budgeting, a forecast, etc.) process into control requires laying down some ground rules.

The first ground rule is that there can be only one organization controlling each detailed budget line item. This implies that summary allocation and adjustment of budgetary changes can be made at a high level but that actual line item changes are controlled at a lower level. Some amount of negotiation must occur when background summary allocation occurs, but a projection process cannot be controlled if more than one organization can control a given line item number.

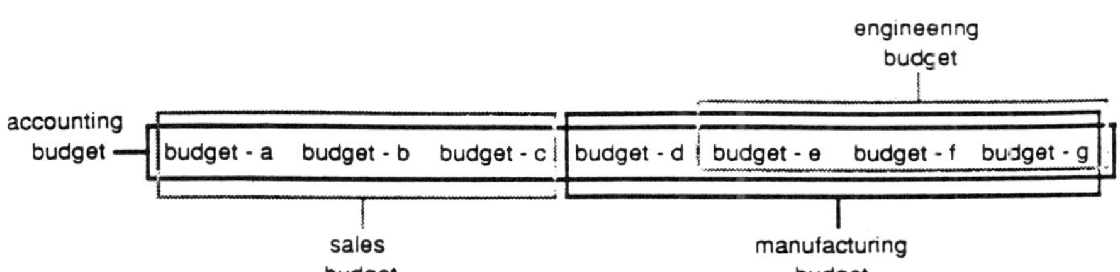

FIGURE 7.1 How the different budgets are created.

There often are three sets of budgetary numbers:

- a *working* budgetary number;
- a *baseline* budgetary number;
- a *most current* budgetary number.

The working budgetary number is a trial number—like a balloon. It is unofficial and can be created and changed by anyone, but it cannot be used *officially*. No time basis information is kept for the working budget.

The baseline budgetary number is an official budgetary number and is controlled only by the single responsible organization. There is an official baseline specification and all detailed entries—actively or by default will have a value. The summary of a baseline budget equals the value of the individual components added together.

The *most current* budgetary number is the number that is changed from moment by moment by the responsible organization (the organization controlling the line item). The most current budgetary number contains time basis information (time stamped).

To show how the three types of budgetary numbers can be used, consider the following simple example. Army headquarters asks its cost centers (i.e., the organization controlling the line item) to submit a budget. The budget has an official title of **19xx Forecasts** and is officially in place as of the 5th of the month. Figure 7.2 shows the baseline figures.

The forecast figures are calculated and are in balance. Headquarters sees that the total is $2,231,000 and adjusts the total to $2,750,000. The $2,750,000 is noted as the forecast of the 17th of the month. In the meantime, another headquarters analyst privately adjusts the cat-

19XX Forecast

	Dept 125	Dept 256	Dept 941	
Category 1	125,000	394,000	27,000	
Category 2	275,000	--	465,000	
Category 3	455,000	195,000	295,000	
TOTAL	855,000	589,000	787,000	Forecast 2,231,000

FIGURE 7.2 The baseline figures.

egory 2 figure for each of the departments. The headquarters view of the budget is shown in Figure 7.3.

The forecast in Figure 7.3 shows all three types of data. Baseline data is in the state as it was originally specified. The most current budgetary numbers are shown by the total adjustment made by headquarters staff, and working budgetary numbers are shown by the estimates made for category 2 numbers.

At the same time, using the baseline data, Department 256 has made their own adjustments to the forecast. Figure 7.4 shows that Dept 256 has adjusted category 1 to $415,000 on the 18th of the month; has adjusted category 2 to $25,000 as of the 16th; and, once again, to $17,500 as of the 19th of the month.

There are two kinds of data shown in Figure 7.4—baseline data and most current data. The usefulness of most current data is illustrated by an example. Suppose both baseline and most current data are shown, as in Figure 7.5.

Now, suppose management wants a most current budget created and balanced. Such a budget is created using the most current budget figures or the baseline figures, if there is no most current figure. Figure 7.6 shows a most current budget.

Of course, every time a new most current figure is added, the most current budget must be changed. One way to freeze the most current process is to select a moment in time as the cutoff point for the most current data. For example, suppose the baseline and most current data

19XX Forecast
(as seen by headquarters after adjustments)

	Dept 125	Dept 256	Dept 941	
Category 1	125,000	394,000	27,000	
Category 2	345,000 (a)	55,000 (a)	275,000 (a)	
Category 3	455,000	195,000	295,000	
TOTAL	855,000	589,000	787,000	(b) Forecast 2,231,000 (17th)

FIGURE 7.3 The budget as viewed by headquarters.
—It is out of balance.
—Items marked (a) are all working figures created by headquarters analysts.
—Item marked (b) is the total forecast as of the 17th of the month.

19XX Forecast - Dept 256

	Baseline		
Category 1	394,000	415,000 (18th)	
Category 2	--	25,000 (16th)	17,000 (19th)
Category 3	195,000		
TOTAL	589,000		

FIGURE 7.4 Dept. 256 makes its own adjustments to the budget. The time each adjustment was made is noted.

19XX Forecast

	Dept 125 Baseline		Dept 256 Baseline			Dept 941 Baseline	
Category 1	125,000	145,000 (17th)	394,000	415,000 (18th)		27,000	
Category 2	275,000		--	25,000 (16th)	17,000 (19th)	465,000	
Category 3	455,000	515,000 (20th)	195,000			295,000	327,000 (21st)
TOTAL	855,000		589,000			787,000	

FIGURE 7.5 Baseline and most current for the 19XX forecast.

19XX Forecast - Most Current Budget

	Dept 125	Dept 256	Dept 941	
Category 1	145,000	415,000	27,000	
Category 2	275,000	17,500	465,000	
Category 3	455,000	195,000	327,000	
TOTAL	875,000	627,500	819,000	Forecast 2,231,500

FIGURE 7.6 The most current forecast created using either baseline or most current data.

found in figure 7.5 are used to create a budget as of the 18th of the month. The result would be the budget shown in Figure 7.7.

After all the budget adjustments are made, headquarters once again announces that a baseline budget will be created as of the 30th of the month. Each category can be reestimated and a baseline version created. If a department has no update to the estimate that was created for the first baseline, then the first baseline numbers will be used. On the 30th of the month another official baseline estimate will be created.

The baseline and the most current forecasts are stored at the atomic level. The working data—which can be created by anyone—can be created anywhere. Figure 7.8 shows the location of the different kinds of data.

19XX Forecast - As of the 18th of the month

	Dept 125	Dept 256	Dept 941	
Category 1	145,000	415,000	27,000	
Category 2	275,000	25,000	465,000	
Category 3	455,000	195,000	295,000	
TOTAL	875,000	635,500	797,000	Forecast 2,307,000

FIGURE 7.7 Baseline and most current numbers as of the 18th of the month are used in this budget.

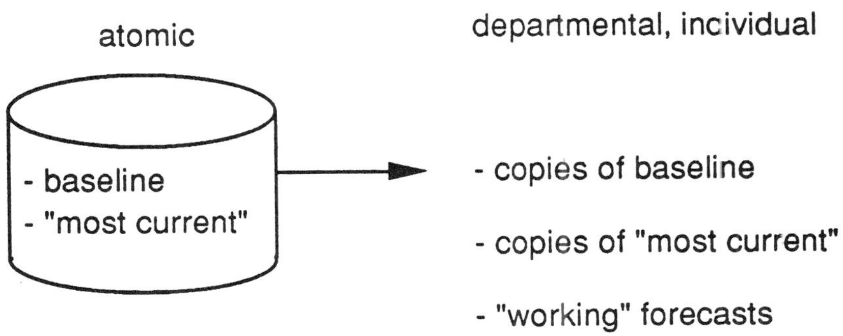

FIGURE 7.8 Where the different types of data are located.

Classical operational data has a very small role in projected or forecast type processing other than as the starting point for forecasts. Of course, as time passes, it is usually interesting to see how the projection data matches to operational data. There is a lesson to be learned both when projections match reality and when projections differ very widely from reality.

IN SUMMARY

There are two different kinds of data—historical data and projection data. Historical data is the classical type of data that is a measurement of an event that has already happened. Projection data is data that is a forecast for events to occur. Projection data differs from historical data in that there is no correct value for any given detail and the summary of any given set of details may not actually be equal to the sum of the parts.

Projection data at the detailed level can have three states:

- it may be working data;
- it may be baseline data; or
- it may be most current data.

QUESTIONS: CHAPTER 7

1. The two most fundamental classifications of data are ____________ and ______________.
2. Historical data has a single correct value. T/F
3. Projection data is data that is used for ______________.
4. There IS/IS NOT an accurate or correct value for projection data.
5. In projection data, details MAY/MAY NOT/MUST/CANNOT add up to their summary.
6. Details MAY/MAY NOT be calculated from summary data in projection data.
7. Name three types of budgetary numbers.

CHAPTER 8

Migration to the DSS/ ORACLE Architecture

Shops usually have large, complex, disorganized arrays of all sorts of data, processing, systems and technology (in other words, a *mess*) on their hands by the time the realization dawns that an architecture is the appropriate direction for the future. Indeed, the *mess* that usually is typical of the collection of existing systems is called the *production* environment.

THE PRODUCTION ENVIRONMENT

All sorts of data and processing are found in the production environment, such as:

- current value data;
- archived data;
- summary data;
- projection data

Viewed from the chaos of existing production systems, the world of a simple, well-defined, well-disciplined architecture appears to be distant and unattainable. If the transformation to the atomic-centered environment had to be achieved all at once, such would be the case.

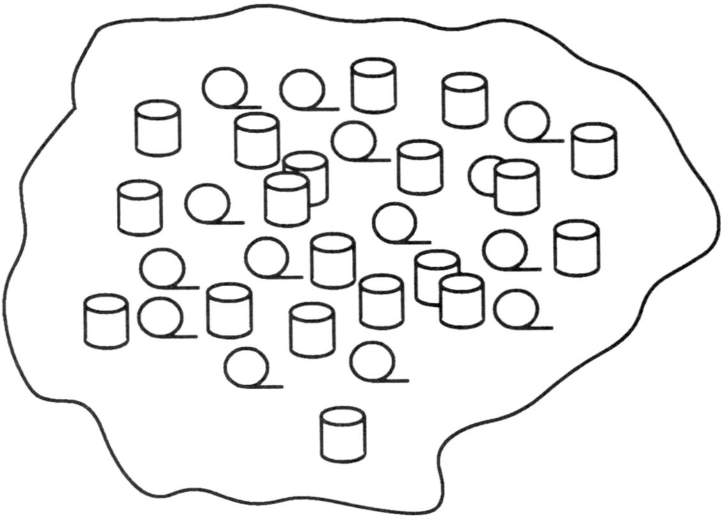

FIGURE 8.1 Production systems.
—current value data
—archival data
—summarized data
—projection data

But the reality is that the transformation to the atomic-centered environment can be achieved relatively easily because:

- the transformation to the atomic-centered environment does not require the rewrite of existing code;
- the environment can be created a single step at a time;
- the environment can be fit over the top of the existing production environment with absolute minimal disruption of the production environment.

The following model describes the steps a shop goes through to migrate from the existing production environment to the atomic centered environment.

THE DATA MODEL

The first step in going to the atomic-centered environment is the establishment of the data model. Refer to INFORMATION ENGINEERING FOR THE PRACTITIONER for an in-depth discussion of data modeling. The data model reflects the primitive data (and only the primitive data) of the corporation—the data that is at the center of the organization's universe. The data model must be built if the data model has not been created. If an adequate data model has already been built, there is no need to rebuild the data model from the ground up. Often, the architect can use existing data models as a *jump start* and quickly produce an adequate data model.

What characteristics of the data model are required to serve as a basis for the architecture? The data model should:

- reflect primitive data and only primitive data;
- be divided into levels—based on the amount of detail:
  - –the high-level portion of the data model that identifies the major entities—the major subject areas—of the corporation,
  - –the mid-level part of the data that describes what data elements there are, what keys there are, how they are grouped together, and how the groupings of data relate,
  - –there is a low level of data that describes keys, foreign keys, data characteristics, volumes of data and so forth,
- contain nonredundant, nonkey data elements;
- organize the primitive data according to its existence dependency criteria (that is, normalize data to the 4th level of normalization);
- represent the entire enterprise (or the subset of the enterprise that is to be integrated).

It matters little how the model is created and what conventions and constructs are used as long as the resulting model satisfies the above criteria. Once the data model is created, it can be used as a template to determine what the system of record looks like.

The system of record is the nonredundant detailed source of operational data. The system of record almost always is found in the existing production data. Whenever there is doubt as to the correct content or source of data, the system of record serves as a basis for reconciliation.

As an example of a high-level model, consider Figure 8.2.

Figure 8.2 is an entity-relationship diagram (ERD) for a financial

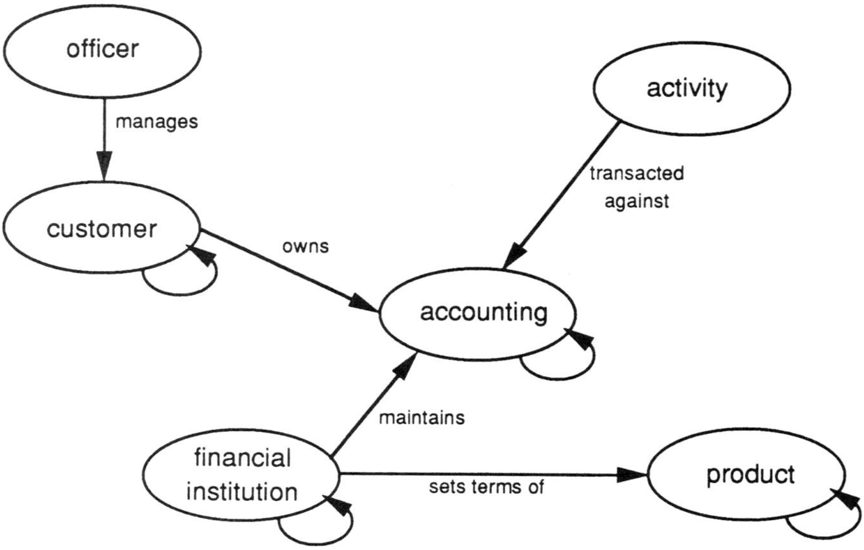

FIGURE 8.2 A high level data model for a financial institution.

institution. The entities (major subject areas) that have been identified are:

- officer;
- customer;
- financial institution;
- account;
- activity (transaction); and
- product.

The relationships that stem from the model are:

- officer to customer;
- customer to account;
- activity to account;
- financial institution to account; and
- financial institution to product.

The recursive relationships that are found in the ERD are from:

- product to product;
- financial institution to financial institution;
- customer to customer; and
- account to account.

ERD TO DIS

The ERD reflects only the primitive data of the organization and represents the data at a high level. The high-level data model is further broken down into detail by means of a data item set (dis). Each of the entities are broken into their own dis. The dis for a customer is shown by Figure 8.3.

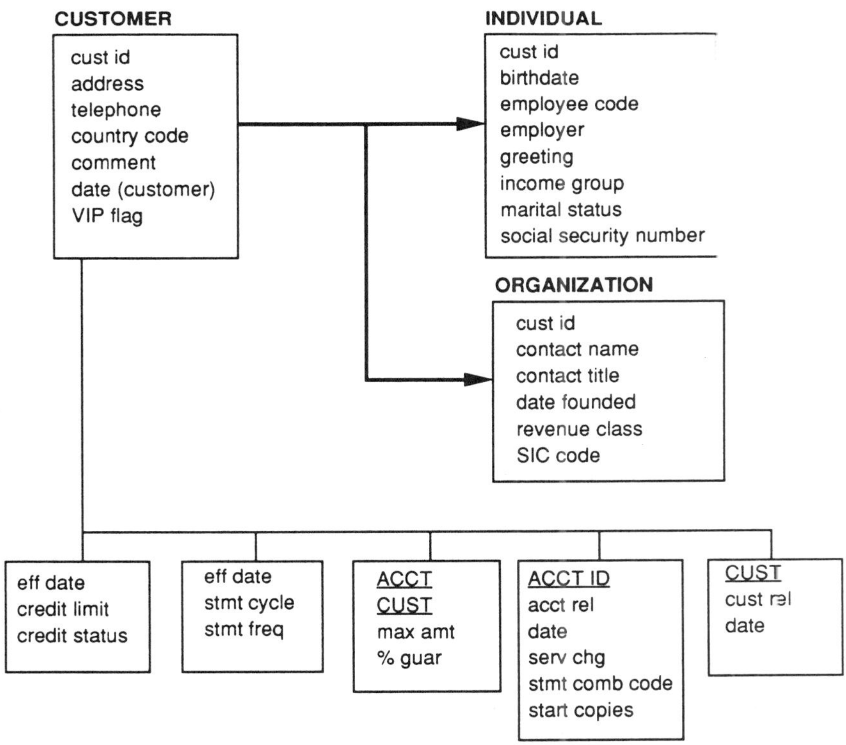

FIGURE 8.3 The DIS for a customer.

Figure 8.3 shows that each customer—one of the major subject areas—may have a customer identification, an address, telephone, country code, comment, date the customer established himself/herself as a customer and VIP flag. If the customer is an individual, there may be a birth date, employee code, employer, greeting, income group specifier, marital status, and social security number. If the customer is an organization, there may be a contact name, contact title, date of founding, revenue class, and SIC code. Each customer may have a credit limit and credit status with an effective date. Each time the credit limit or status changes, a new record of the effective date is kept.

The customer may have a statement cycle and frequency of statementing by date. The customer may have indirect liability that relates to another account and/or another customer. The indirect liability will have a maximum amount and a percent guaranteed. The customer may have a relationship to one or more accounts. When there is a relationship to an account, the information about the account relationship, date of the relationship, service charges associated with the relationship, statement combination indicator, and number of statement copies will be carried. In addition, the customer may have a relationship to other customers. Not shown in the diagram is the relationship a customer may have with an officer.

Low-level Model

Based upon the mid-level model that has been developed, a low-level model is built. Each of the groupings of data found at the dis level are transformed into a lower level by identifying:

- keys;
- physical characteristics;
- other relevant physical characteristics of the data;
- source in the existing environment.

Figure 8.4 shows how one of the groupings of data might be transformed to a lower level of design.

In Figure 8.4 the physical characteristics—CHAR (10), PIC '99', have been added. The key or keys have been identified, and other physical characteristics have been documented. Of course, each group of data at the dis level will have its own transformation. After the model has been created it is now *compared* to the existing production environment. The production environment is analyzed to determine how

Customer

Cust id	CHAR (16)
Address-	
Street	CHAR (25)
City	CHAR (30)
State	CHAR (02)
Zip	CHAR (09)
Telephone	CHAR (10)
Country Code	PIC '99'
Comment	CHAR (256)
Date (Cust)	CHAR (06)
VIP Flag	CHAR (01)

Key
- Anticipated 100,000 occurrences
- turnover rate - 5% per annum
- 75% individual, 25% organizational

FIGURE 8.4 The transformation of one of the customer groupings of data into a lower level model of data.

well the model matches the data that already exists, as shown by Figure 8.5.

As a detailed example of how the existing environment is analyzed, consider the existing car loans data, passbook savings data, home loan data, demand deposit data, and certificate of deposit, as depicted in Figure 8.6.

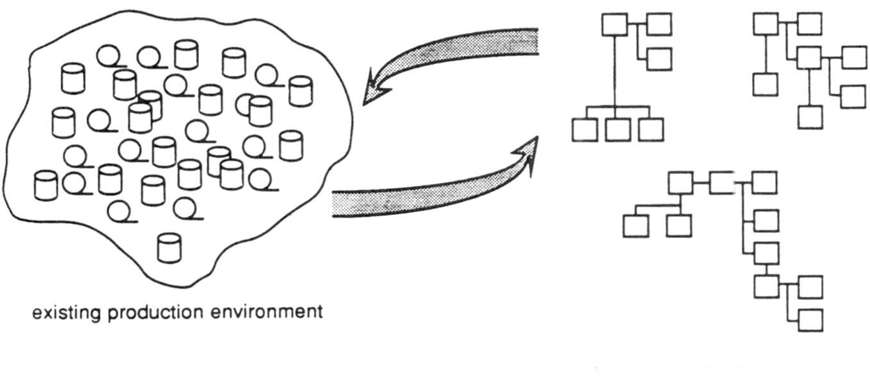

FIGURE 8.5 Comparing the model to the existing production environment.

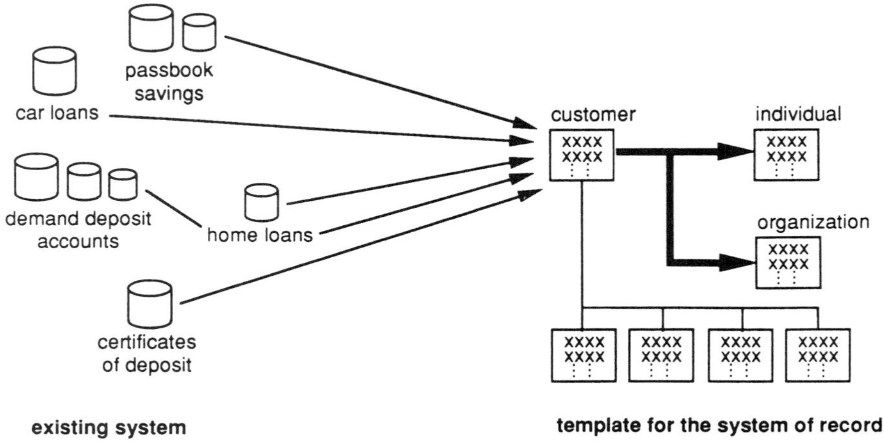

FIGURE 8.6 Comparing existing systems to the system of record (the DIS).

The data model for the customer is shown. Of course, in reality *all* the DIS would be compared to the existing environment. But for the purposes of this example, only customer data will be beat against existing data.

The first step in the analysis phase is to determine what data elements make up the data in the different environments. The data elements can be gathered from dictionaries, program listings, etc. Next, the data elements that have been gathered are compared to the model, as shown in Figure 8.7.

SYSTEM OF RECORD

The data elements in the existing environment which match the model form part of the *system of record.*

Using Figure 8.7 as a basis, the following system of record considerations can be made. When a record for car loans is compared to the model, cust id is formed from customer name. The model's address and name comes from the car loan's address and name. Country code is derived from address, although it does not directly appear as a data element in car loans data. The date of the customer record is the date the conversion from car loans to customer data is made. As the customer data changes (i.e., as a customer gets a new address) a new record

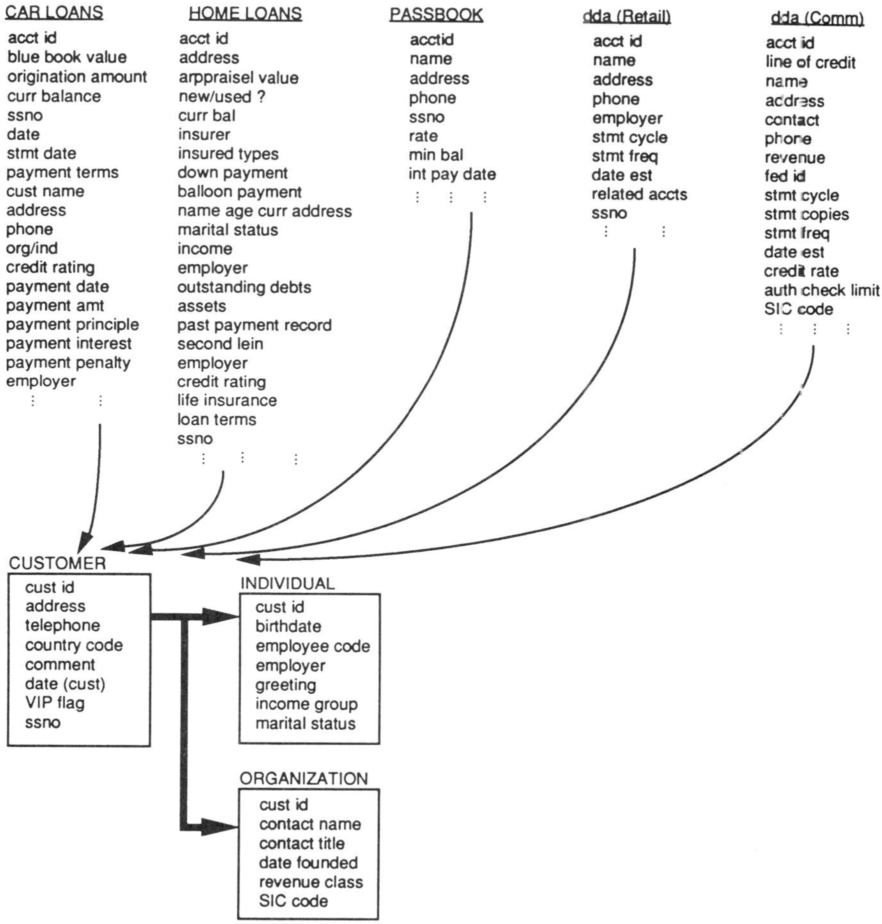

FIGURE 8.7 Comparing existing sytems to the system of record (the DIS).

reflecting the changed data and the date of the changed data is created. The VIP flag is set to a default value of N. SSNO from car loans is sent to SSNO in the customer data base.

If the car loan is made to an individual, the employer field is loaded from the car loans field of the same name. Other individual fields in the model are set to default values. If the car loan is to an organization, all organization fields in the model are set to default values.

In general, if a data element found at the car loan level is the same as that specified at the model level, the data element becomes part of the system of record. If no data element at the car loan level is found, then the value of the data element is inferred, if possible. An example of inference is the creation of country code from address, or the creation of date from the date of loan or update. If no existing data elements can be located, and the value of the data element in the model cannot be inferred, a non-null default value may be used. If no non-null default value is appropriate, a null value will be used.

The same sort of analysis and transformation occurs from each of the types of loans, passbook savings, dda processing, and so forth. Note that not all data elements are transported from the existing to the modeled environment. Only those data elements useful for dss processing are transported to the data model.

Another task facing the analyst is deciding which of two or more existing values of data is suitable for transformation to the data model. When there are more than one candidate data elements in the existing environment that may serve in the system of record (and only one data element ultimately may be selected), the analyst may select the appropriate data element using one or more of the following criteria:

- which data element occurs most often;
- which data element is most accurate;
- which data element is most compatible;
- which data element takes precedence over other data elements.

In the example shown in Figure 8.7, suppose a car loan was encountered for Kathy Allan. Using data from Kathy's car loan record shows that Kathy lives in Detroit, had her loan account record established in May, 1988, and is not rated as a VIP. The home loans are processed and it is found that Kathy Allan also has a home loan. The customer information that is available from Kathy's home loan application is included in her customer record. When there is a conflict in values—such as whether Kathy is a VIP or not, the analyst must determine criteria as to which value is correct.

Another consideration in the establishment of the system of record is the compatibility of keys. It is entirely possible that the data element found in one existing system forms a basis for being a key while the same data element in another system does not form a sound basis. For example, when Kathy Allan is found in the car loans system, her name is found as—"ALLAN KATHERINE". But in the home loan system her name simply appears as "ALLAN, K". Extra logic must be inserted to ensure that the match can be made. A typical match includes looking at address and/or employer to help determine when keys that appear to be the same, in fact, are different or the same.

Further complicating matters is the existence of incompatible codes among existing systems. As a simple example, in one system males are encoded as "1" and females are encoded as "0", while in another system, males are encoded as an "M" and females are encoded as an "F". If values that are encoded are to be part of the system of record, then there must be consistency in the content of the value of the encoded data element.

In short, defining the system of record from the existing environment requires:

- determining what data there is in the existing environment;
- determining the content and structures of the data model;
- resolving incompatible key values;
- resolving inconsistent encoded values;
- resolving the transformation of more than one existing data element into the system of record;
- determining what default values there should be;
- determining what null values there should be.

The transformation of data shown in Figure 8.7, while a good example in many ways, does not illustrate the time value of data that is found in the system of record. A better example is shown in Figure 8.8.

Figure 8.8 shows that savings deposits, CD withdrawals, and quarterly interest payments to account are existing systems and they are to be mapped to the model shown in Figure 8.8.

The same considerations of data mapping apply, as previously discussed. However, note that each activity has a data associated with it. The date on which the activity was found is attached to the data in the system of record. Another form of time dependency is illustrated by the simple table shown in Figure 8.9.

In Figure 8.9 there is a rate for an account type from one moment to another. Such an arrangement of data is called *continuous*, or *time span* data. The definition of data shown in Figure 8.9 is for the system of record.

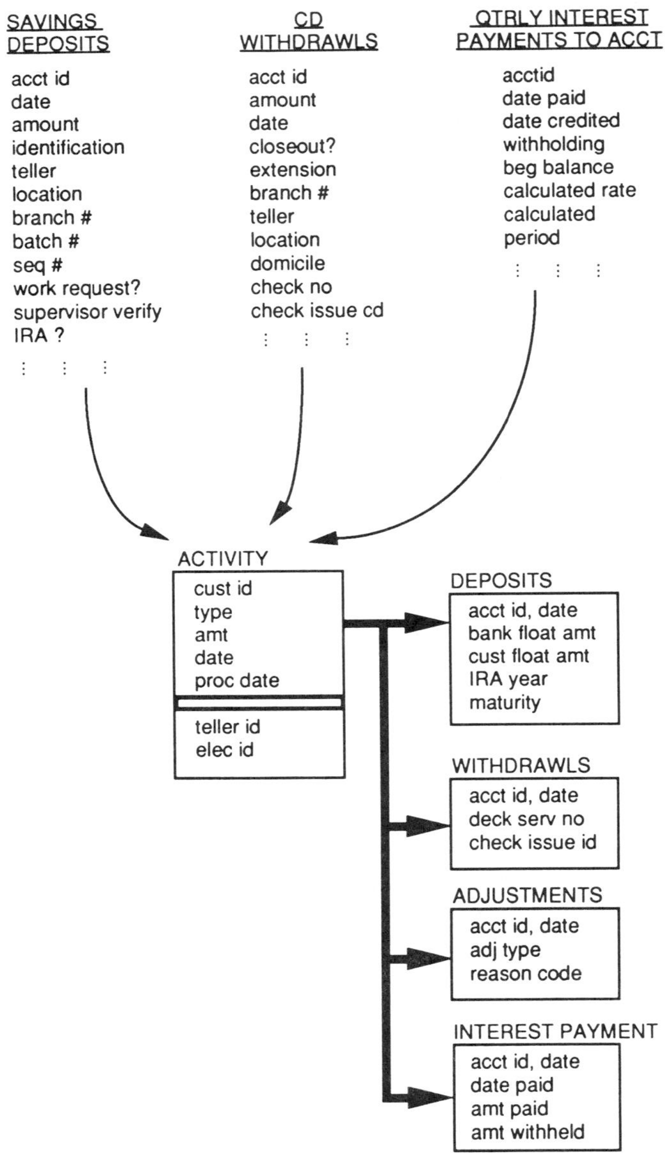

FIGURE 8.8 Transforming activity data into the system of record.

INTEREST RATE TABLE
acct type
beg date
end date
conditions
rate amt

FIGURE 8.9 A simple table showing the rate of an account over a period of time.

Populating Atomic Data

Consider how the data is populated. Figure 8.10 shows that car loan rates, home loan rates, bankcard rates, and signature loan rates are used as a basis for the system of record.

But effective beginning and ending dates are not to be found in the existing data. Instead, there is a current value to be found. Only as the current value of the rate is changed does the system of record have an occurrence of data written.

Another typical form of time variant data found in the system of record is periodic discrete data. Consider the two types of data—found in the system of record—as demonstrated by Figure 8.11.

The data in Figure 8.11 shows that at the end of the month, each account has its month ending balance recorded. A variation of the same monthly calculation shows not only month ending balance, but the monthly high balance, the monthly low balance, and the average balance for the month.

The first form of periodic discrete data—month ending balance—is easy enough to calculate. Figure 8.12 shows that all the contributing accounts are *frozen* at month end and their balances are shipped to the system of record. Calculating monthly high, low, and average balance is a different matter entirely. There are (at least) two ways to determine these values, as shown by Figure 8.13 and Figure 8.14.

Figure 8.13 shows that in the application, logic is inserted that keeps track, as each transaction is run, of the monthly high, low, and average. At the end of the month the data is transferred to the system of record. This method requires:

- manipulation of existing code to make the extra calculations;
- a few extra resources during production processing.

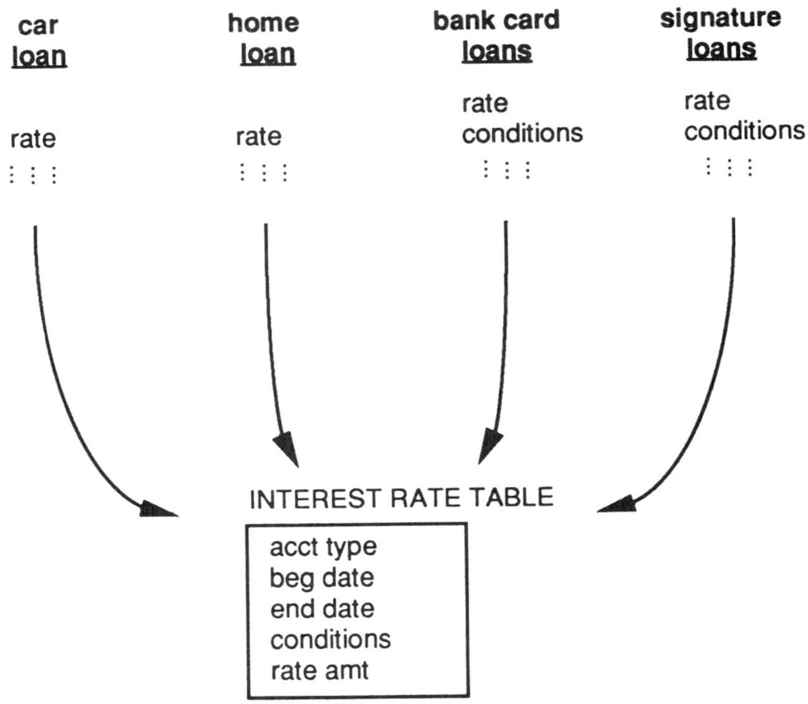

FIGURE 8.10 Populating the time span data.

FIGURE 8.11 Two forms of periodic discrete data.

Another approach is shown by Figure 8.14. In Figure 8.14 there is no need to manipulate existing code. Instead monthly activity is used to recreate the monthly movement of the balance. However convenient it is that this approach does not cause existing code to be disturbed, it is likely that *many* resources may be used in the storage and recalculation of monthly activity.

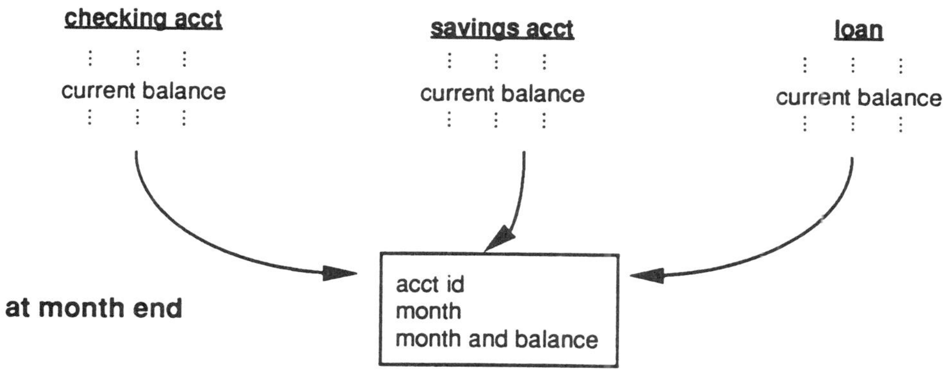

FIGURE 8.12 At month end.

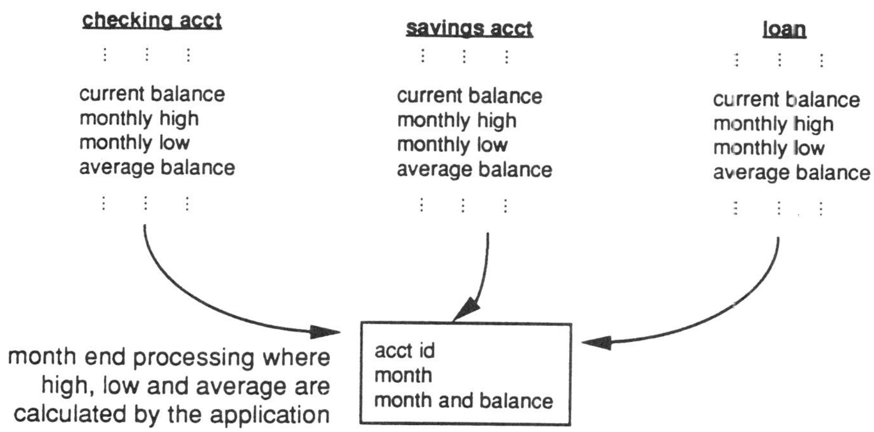

FIGURE 8.13 The application calculated high, low and average balance each month.

There are (at least!) two ways of viewing the system of record within the production environment. The simplest perspective of the system of record is simply as a subset of production data, as depicted by Figure 8.15.

Figure 8.15 shows that, using the data model, the data that forms the foundation for the system of record has been identified. But Figure 8.15 is inaccurate in that it shows that entire sets of data are either in or out of the system of record. Seldom is that the case. It is more normal for part of a data set to form part of the system of record, and

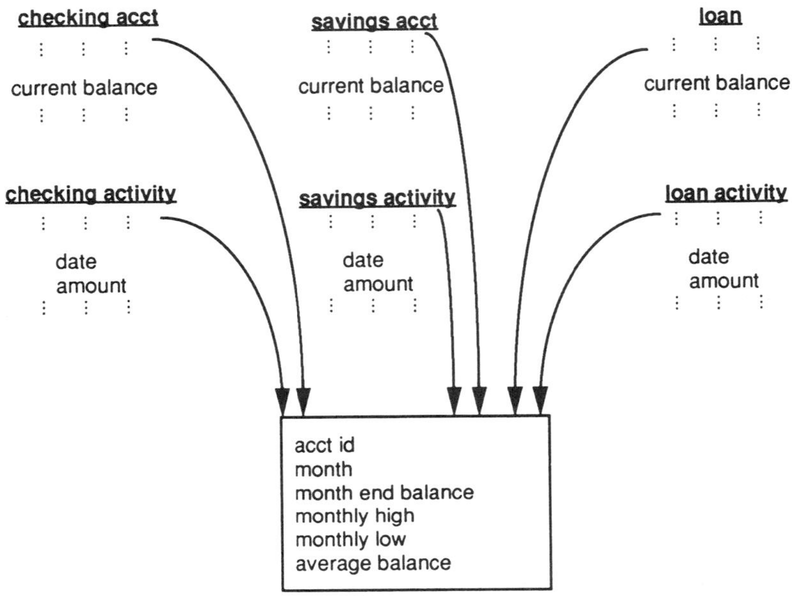

FIGURE 8.14 Month end input necessary where high, low and average are not calculated by the application.

part of the data to not belong in the system of record, as shown by Figure 8.16.

The content then, of the system of record, comes from the existing production database and the structure of the atomic database comes from the data model that has been built, as shown by Figure 8.17.

Extract Processing

The atomic environment is created from the production environment by means of extract processing. An extract program is a simple program that scans the production database looking for data. Based on the criteria given to the extract process, production data is selected and transported to the atomic level.

From a simplistic perspective, extract processing is done if:

- there is an extract process for each source of data, or
- there is a single extract program for all sources of data.

Figure 8.18 shows these two options.

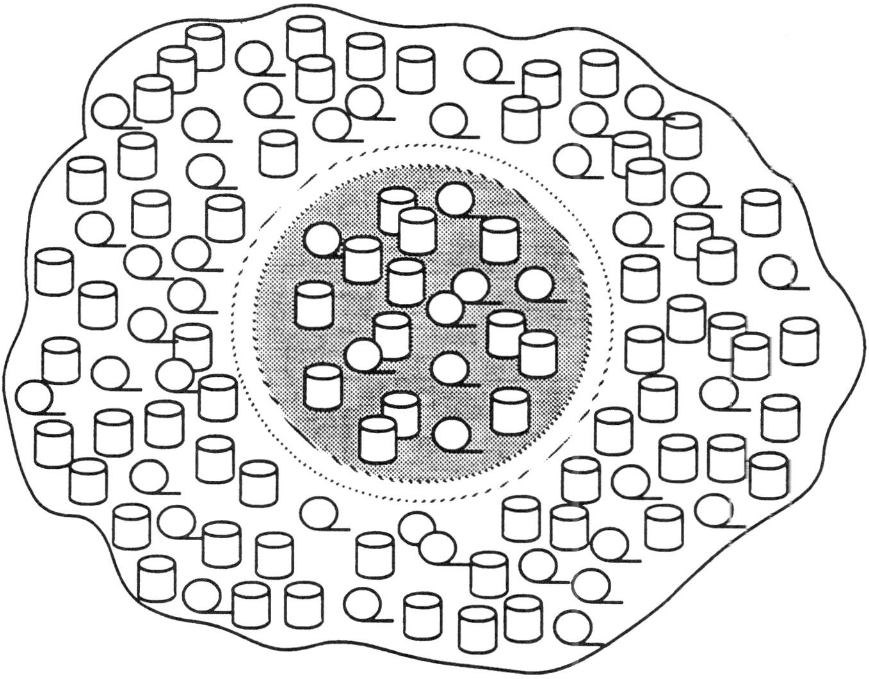

FIGURE 8.15 The system of record within the production environment.

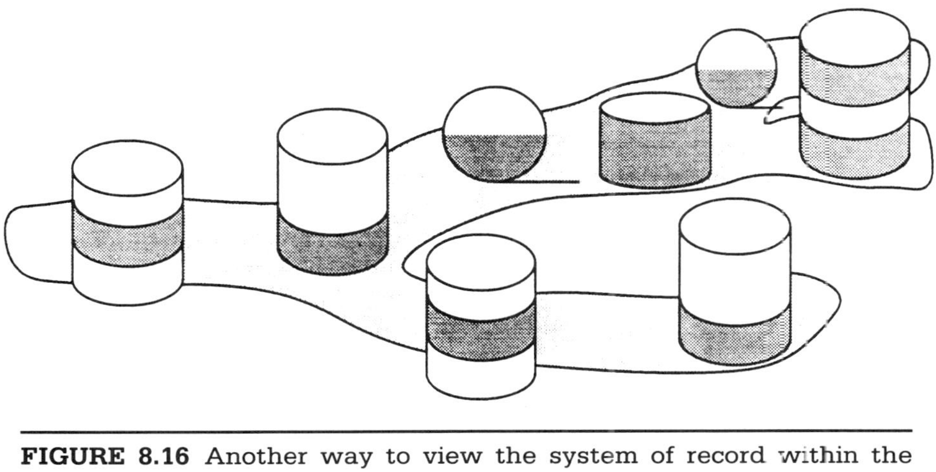

FIGURE 8.16 Another way to view the system of record within the production environment.

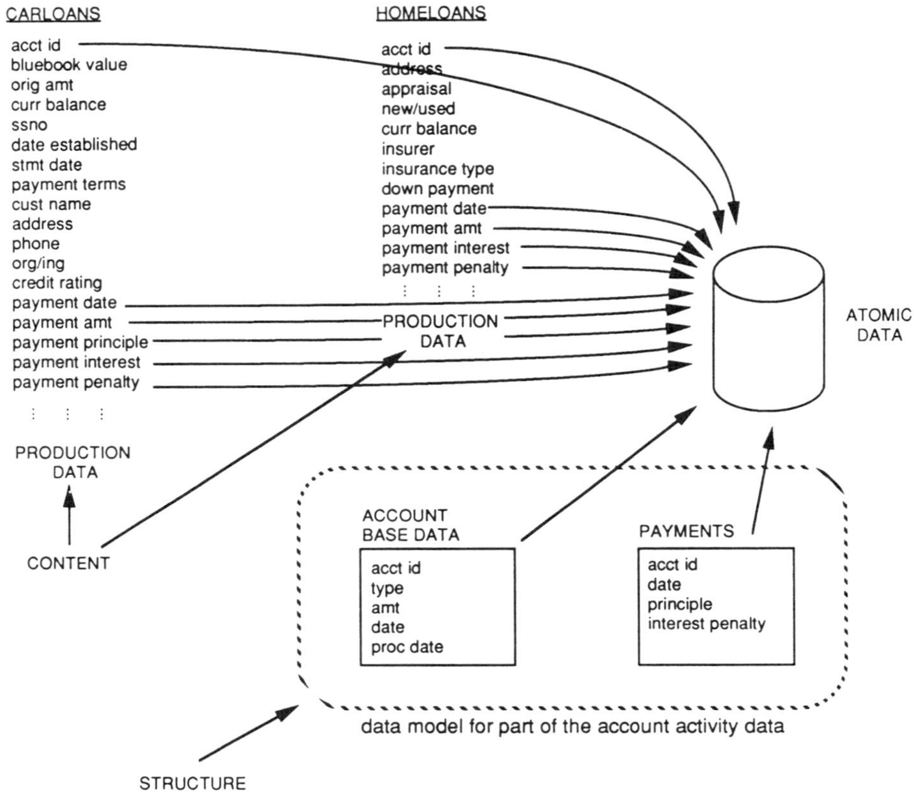

FIGURE 8.17 Not all data in the operational environment belongs in the atomic level of data.

One of the major issues of the population of atomic level data from the system of record that is found in existing systems is that of technology. Assuming that the atomic level data is to be built in ORACLE, it is a good bet that the existing systems are not built in ORACLE. Instead, existing systems are built in a wide array of technologies—CICS/VSAM, IMS, IDMS, Assembler, COBOL Masterfiles, FOCUS, etc. In fact, almost any technology may be expected at the existing system environment.

The first issue facing the designer is how to transport the data into ORACLE. The simplest approach is to use standard utilities. Vendor-supplied software is good for simple, straightforward movements of

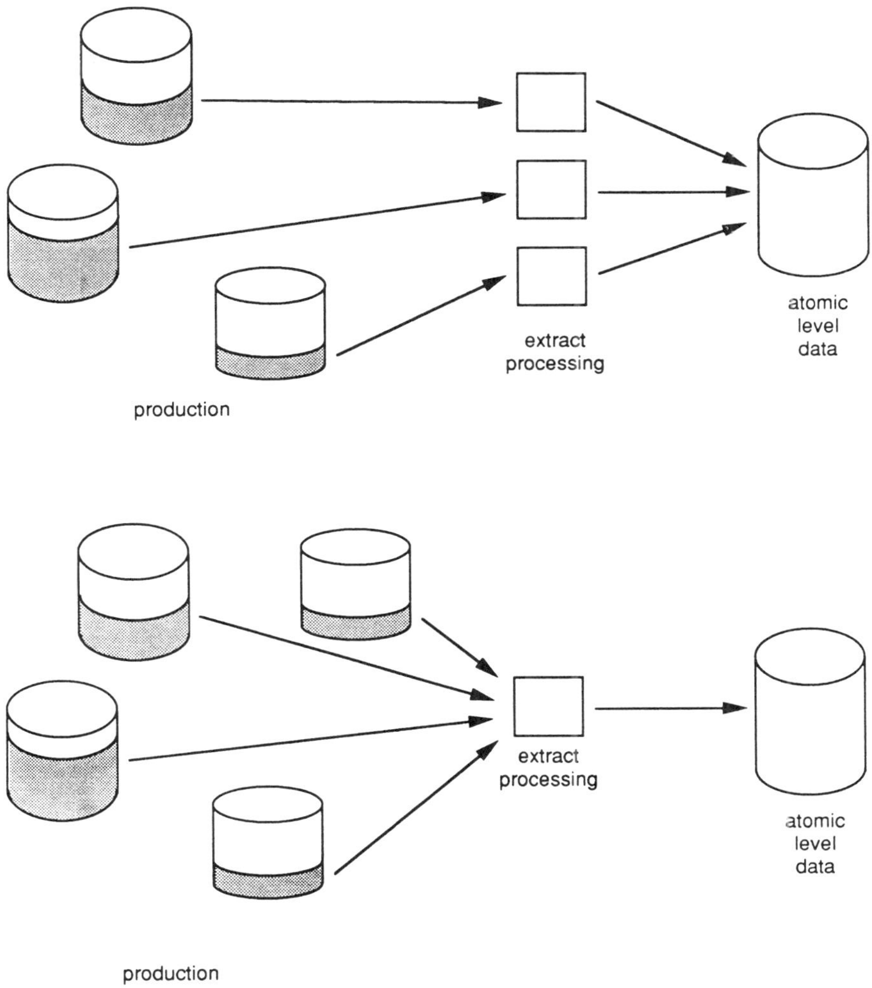

FIGURE 8.18 The two ways that extract processing can be done.

data. Occasionally the structure of the data becomes complex to the point that vendor-supplied software is not adequate. In this case, the designer must write customized programs in COBOL, PL/1, etc. Customized programs take more time to write and debug but are more versatile. With a customized program, most existing systems can be directly converted to ORACLE. Some existing systems are so complex that a direct conversion to ORACLE is not possible. (Fortunately, this is not a frequent.) When a direct conversion to ORACLE is not a possibility, it is always possible to write a conversion from the existing technology into a simple technology such as VSAM, then use vendor-supplied software to move the data into ORACLE. This circuitous route is advisable only when there is no other way to accomplish the conversion.

The techniques for conversion from existing technologies to ORACLE include:

- using vendor-supplied software;
- using customized code for a direct conversion;
- using customized code for an indirect conversion.

But the coding techniques that are appropriate are hardly the only considerations in converting data from existing technology to ORACLE. There are a variety of other considerations, such as:

- the resources used by the scan portion of the extract program and the effect of IMS, IDMS, CICS/VSAM, etc.;
- the total volume of data transported from existing systems into ORACLE, and the data communications capacity required;
- the frequency of extract processing runs;
- the ability to compress or otherwise scale down the volume of data extracted before the data enters the ORACLE environment;
- the creation of indexes upon entering the ORACLE environment;
- partitioning in the ORACLE environment.

In short, the technical considerations of extract processing must be considered in concert with such issues as the system of record, the design of the atomic database, and so forth.

A Staged Approach to Population

It is unusual to completely populate an atomic level database all at once. A more normal scenario is to populate first one part of the atomic level data, then another part. On day 1, an extract from one production database is written and part of the atomic level of data is populated. On day 2 another extract is written and another part of the atomic level of data is populated. The progression continues as shown by Figure 8.19.

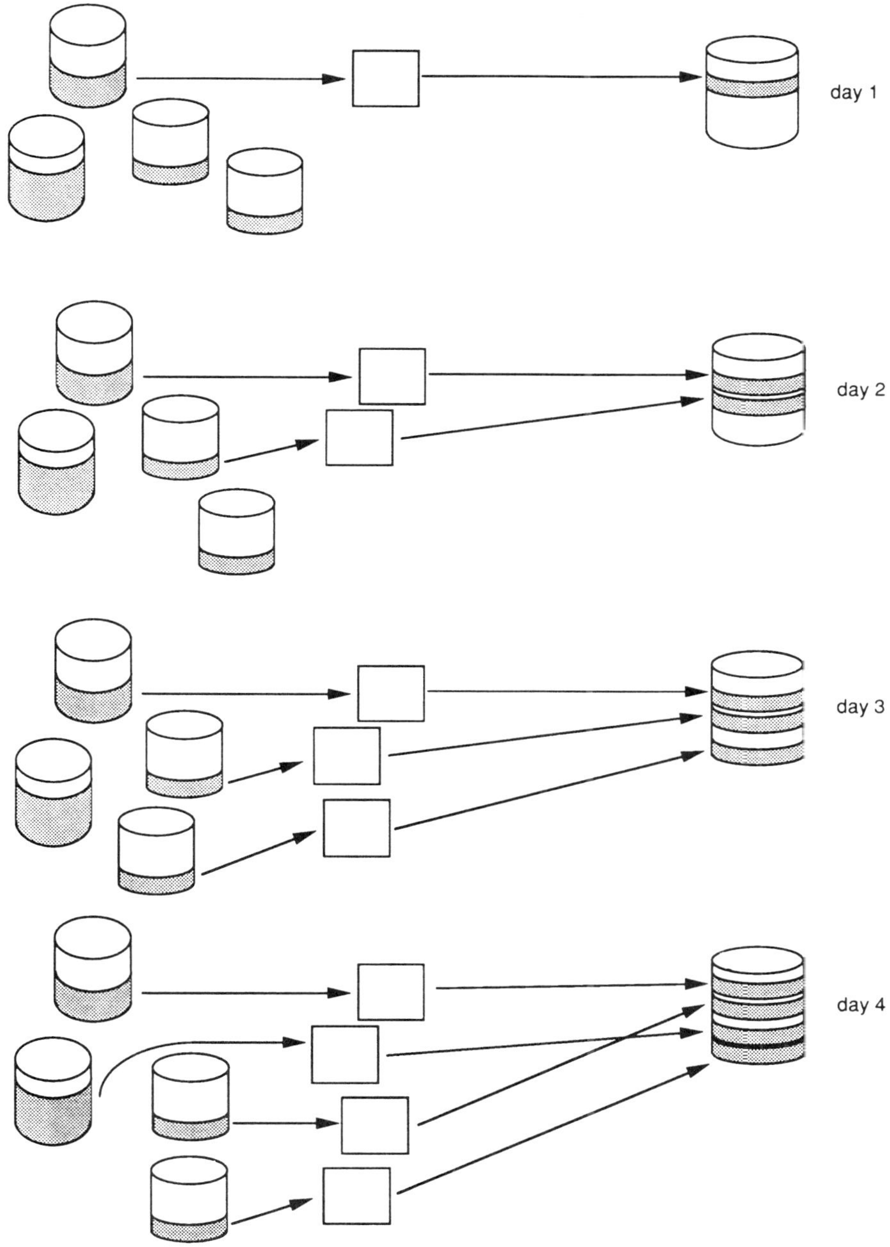

FIGURE 8.19 A typical progression of migrating to the atomic environment.

It may take *years* for the atomic level database to become fully populated. But that does not mean that the advantages of the atomic level cannot be enjoyed as soon as the first population of the atomic level data occurs.

The extraction process is one of the most critical aspects of the entire architecture. The architecture, to some degree, is limited by the extraction that occurs. The difficulty with the extraction process is in the volume of data that flows through the program. Under normal conditions there is—at least potentially—a very large amount of data that can flow from the operational (production) environment to the atomic environment. Some of the strategies for extract are:

- wholesale periodic extract;
- *delta* extracts, where only the changes are extracted;
- data base scans where selected records are extracted.

The advantage of being able to create the atomic environment a step at a time is twofold:

- the atomic environment can be created in an evolutionary, orderly fashion, and
- the benefits of the architecture, at the departmental and the individual levels can be enjoyed as soon as the *first* part of the atomic environment is populated.

As soon as the atomic environment is populated, both departmental and individual level processing can commence. Figure 8.20 shows the commencement of departmental and individual levels of processing.

Of course, over time as the atomic level data becomes more fully populated, then even more departmental and individual level processing occurs.

The interface between the atomic level and the departmental and the individual level is an important one. It is at this interface that the classical *derivation* of data is done. Figure 8.21 shows the interface.

What About Derived Data?

One of the foundations of the architecture is the difference between primitive and derived data. The data models that have been created reflect only the primitive data of the corporation. Derived data is often some of the most useful data there is, even though it is not directly

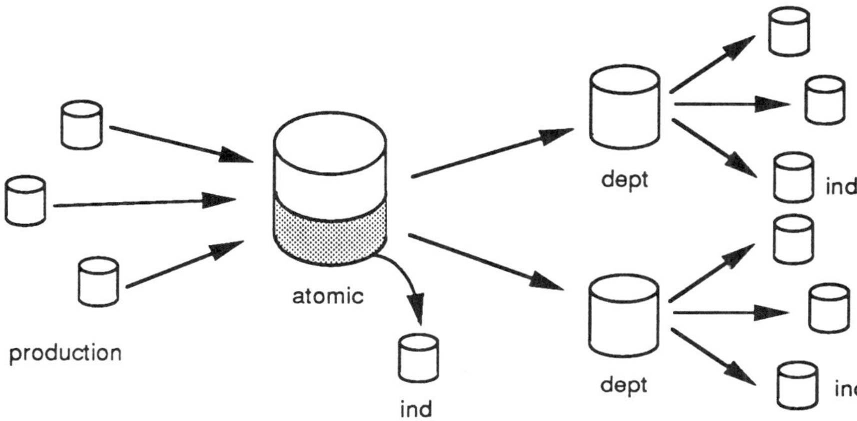

FIGURE 8.20 With the population of the first of the atomic level data, departmental and individual level processing commences.

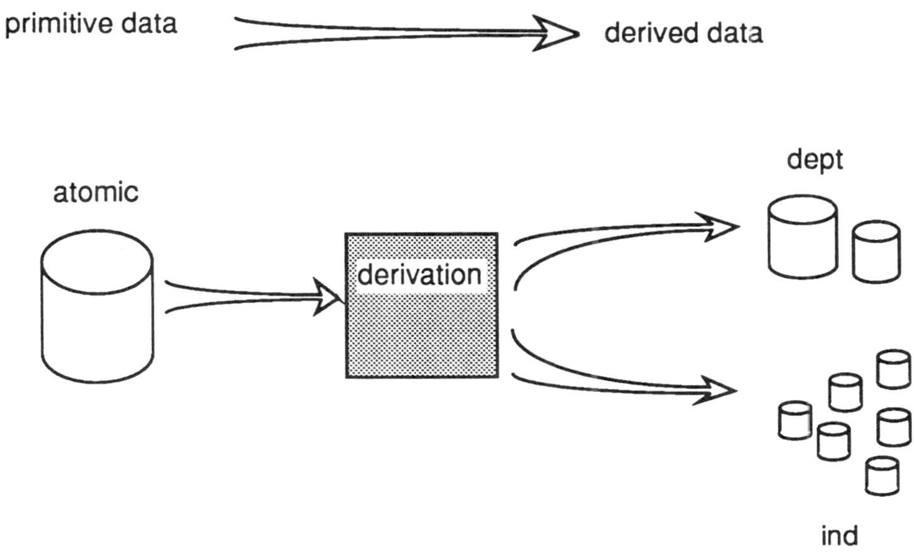

FIGURE 8.21 The interface between atomic and departmental/individual level data is where the transformation between primitive and derived data is made.

reflected in the data model. It is at the point where atomic level data flows into departmental/individual level data that the derivation of data is made.

Usually this derivation consists of:

- selection of subsets of data;
- summarization of data;
- calculations based on detailed data where detailed data is organized into subsets;
- creation of time dependent groupings of data, and so forth.

An example of each of these types of derivations will be given:

- summarizations—the total number of units shipped is calculated;
- subsets—units shipped are stored by type of end product, by dollar valuation per shipment, by plant, etc.;
- time dependent grouping—the monthly shipments by product line are calculated and stored. The monthly totals are kept for the past five years.

The steps in the migration to the environment are shown by Figure 8.22.

MIGRATION STEPS

The first step is the creation of the data model. The data model reflects only the primitive data of the enterprise. The next step is the identification of the system of record within the existing production environment. Next, the atomic environment is populated. Usually the population is done a step at a time in an incremental fashion. Following the population of the atomic environment is the usage of atomic level data at the departmental and individual levels. Departmental and individual processing grows over time. Next, the existing operational environment is re-engineered. The re-engineering occurs over a long period of time and occurs because of powerful motivations such as the need to use new technologies, the changing of requirements, and so forth.

One of the salient issues is just how long the architecture takes to put into place. The modeling (first) phase should take, even for a very large organization, no more than six months to complete. If studies have already been done on which the modeler can build, then the

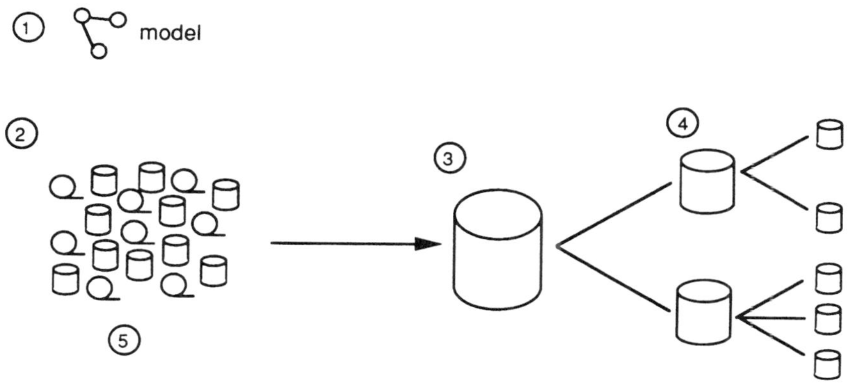

FIGURE 8.22 The steps in migration to the architecture.
1–creation of the model
2–identification of the system of record
3–design, population of the atomic level data
4–usage of atomic data at the departmental, individual levels.
5–gradual transformation of the operational environment

modeling effort should take even less time. The length of time required for modeling is greatly influenced by the fact that only primitive data is being modeled. Were both primitive and derived data to be modeled, the modeling effort would take much longer.

The second phase is the establishment of the system of record. To a large degree the length of time required for this part of the process depends on the state and size of the existing environment. As a rule, as long as the existing environment is not too large and too complex, no more than one month is required to identify the system of record. This estimate makes the assumption that adequate documentation and informed analysts are available for input.

The third step is the design and population of the atomic level database. The atomic database is directly patterned after the data model that was produced. It should take no more than one to two weeks to design the atomic level database.

Population of the atomic level database is another matter. The population of atomic level data requires the writing of extract programs and may occur in a staged fashion over many years. Of course, usually the most useful atomic data is populated first. But the *full* population of atomic level data does not occur for a lengthy period of time.

As soon as the atomic level data is created, departmental and individual usage of the data commences and continues as long as there is a need for dss processing.

Finally, the existing operational environment evolves over many years. Its evolution is slow and incremental and is a result of many factors.

Oftentimes, the atomic environment is created a single subject area at a time. A subject that is often the most popular is customer data. A lot of organizations have had an orientation toward accounts or policies and use the advent of atomic data as a vehicle to build customer databases. There is, however, no particular reason why customers must be the first subject to be tackled. Other subjects such as shipment, accounts, etc., are candidates as well.

THE AGENTS OF CHANGE

There are powerful motivations that push an organization toward the architecture that has been described. Some of those motivations are:

- the new audience using computers. Unlocking the doors to effective use of computers for end-users and dss analysts is not as simple as merely placing data, hardware, and software at the analyst's doorstep. Instead, an infrastructure must be created.
- the difference in patterns of hardware utilization. End-users and dss analysts use hardware in a fundamentally different way than traditional users. The ways in which hardware are used are incompatible in terms of technology and cost.
- the need for credibility. Once enough people start to do DSS analysis and end-user computing, it becomes apparent that there is a profound need for believability of data.
- the need for productivity. Just having data in an organization is not enough. The organization needs to have data organized so that it can be readily accessed. If the organization must go through the consolidation of data each time it desires to look at data in a different perspective, it might as well not have the data in the first place.

IN SUMMARY

The existing collection of data and processing—the *production* environment—in most shops can be described as *a mess*. It contains all sorts of data—current value data, archival data, summarized data, and so forth. Trying to do dss processing from the mess is not a good idea if the dss analyst cares about quality of data and believability of results.

The high-level data model that is needed to make sense of the mess usually has three levels—a high-level abstract model, a mid-level model whose attributes are grouped and identified, and a low-level where physical characteristics are identified.

The data model is used to identify the system of record within the existing environment. Once the system of record is identified, the extracts for the atomic environment can be written.

The atomic environment is populated over a long period of time. However, as soon as the atomic environment is populated with its first data, it can be used departmentally and individually.

QUESTIONS: CHAPTER 8

1. Name some types of data that are typically found at the nonatomic-centered production environment.
2. Any approach to rebuilding the production environment that requires a wholesale rewrite is likely to be a failure. T/F
3. The information map of the way information systems ought to be is called the ______________.
4. The data model reflects only primitive data. T/F
5. Usually there are ______________ levels of data models.
6. The high-level data model is called the ______________ or ____
7. The mid-level data model is called the ______________.
8. The low-level data model is called the ______________.
9. The basis for all atomic data is called the ______________.
10. Data attributes are identified in the ______________.
11. Physical attributes are identified in the ______________.
12. Major subjects are identified in the ______________.
13. Keys are identified in the ______________.
14. Groupings of data elements are identified in the ______________.

CHAPTER 9

Design Approaches/ Techniques for the DSS/ ORACLE Environment

The design considerations of the DSS/ORACLE environment are dominated by two factors:

- the bulk of data found at the DSS/ORACLE environment and
- the efficiency of access of data.

Not taking into consideration these factors can lead to very unsatisfactory DSS processing.

A third factor that becomes relevant at the moment of design is that DSS requirements, for the most part, are unknown. The very essence of much DSS processing is heuristic, analytical processing where, of necessity, requirements are not known until the current process is complete.

The classical approach of starting with user requirements and working backward into a database design simply is not applicable to DSS processing, in general. That is why there is a big emphasis on data modeling and not on process modeling when constructing the DSS environment.

In some cases in the DSS environment there is the opportunity to anticipate *some* analytical requirements. For example, regardless of the analytical processing to be done, the developer in a retailing environment knows that the orders to be analyzed ultimately will be traced back to the consumer, or that in a financial environment the banking activities that are analyzed must be related to the customer. The *very general* set of DSS requirements may be able to be anticipated, but detailed specific requirements will seldom be forseen. The DSS developer then must build the DSS environment based on a data model and only very generic processing requirements.

DESIGN TECHNIQUES

The following are some general design techniques/approaches that may be useful in building DSS/ORACLE environments.

Time Stamping

Every unit of DSS/ORACLE data must be time stamped in some form. The usual is to add the time element to the key of the data being stamped. The practice is to concatenate the time stamp to the lower part of the key. There are three forms of time stamping:

–continuous;

–event discrete; and

–periodic discrete.

In addition, individual columns may be time stamped or, more commonly, rows of data may be time stamped. Some examples of time stamping are:

```
ACCOUNT NUMBER        - Key
ACTIVITY ID NUMBER    - Key
ACTIVITY DATE         - Key
ACTIVITY TYPE
AMOUNT                          a financial
LOCATION                        event discrete
TELLER                          record
ID
ELECTRONIC ID
CASH BOX BALANCE
CASH BOX SEQ NUMBER
PAYEE

CUSTOMER ID           - Key
FROM DATE             - Key
TO DATE               - Key
```

```
NAME
ADDRESS                                a customer
CREDIT RATING                          continuous
ANNUAL INCOME              record
EMPLOYER

ACCOUNT                    - key
MONTH ENDING               - key
AUG BALANCE
LOW BALANCE                            an account
HIGH BALANCE                           periodic
PENALTY                                discrete
STOP PAYMENTS                          record
INTEREST
```

Partitioning Data

Because of the very large amounts of data collected in the atomic DSS/ORACLE level of data, the partitioning option should be carefully considered. Partitioning of data allows large collections of data to be managed gracefully. Access of data, recovery of data, indexing, and so forth can all be enhanced by partitioning of data.

Partitioning of data in ORACLE can be done at at least two levels—the ORACLE level and the application level. As a rule, there is much more flexibility in doing partitioning of data at the application level.

Partitioning of data can be done many ways (or in a combination of many ways). Some criteria by which atomic data can be partitioned are:

- geographic area;
- marketing division;
- product line;
- organizational unit; and
- random separation of data

Some of the criteria for proper partitioning of atomic data are:

- partitioning subdivides data exclusively (i.e., each partition contains an exclusive subset of data);

- partitioning subdivides all data (i.e., no data in the database is excluded from being in at least one partition);
- partitioning divides data so that there is roughly the same amount of data in any partition;
- partitioning can be extended so that future growth of the data evenly populates the partitions;
- partitioning can be extended to more partitions if necessary;
- partitioning divides data into units which are accessed as a unit (i.e., most processing can be satisfied within one partition);
- the data within each partition has a homogenous definition;
- partitioning of data divides data into partitions that do *not* necessarily have an equal probability of access.

As an example of partitioning of data for an atomic database, a designer has used two criteria—geography and time division by year—to partition monthly sales information

```
REGION                  - Key    partition
YEAR                    - Key    partition
MONTH                   - Key

PRODUCT A SALES
PRODUCT B SALES
PRODUCT C SALES
OTHER SALES
TOTAL SALES
```

There are four regions—Northeast, Southwest, South and West. There are three years' worth of data. The records in the database look like:

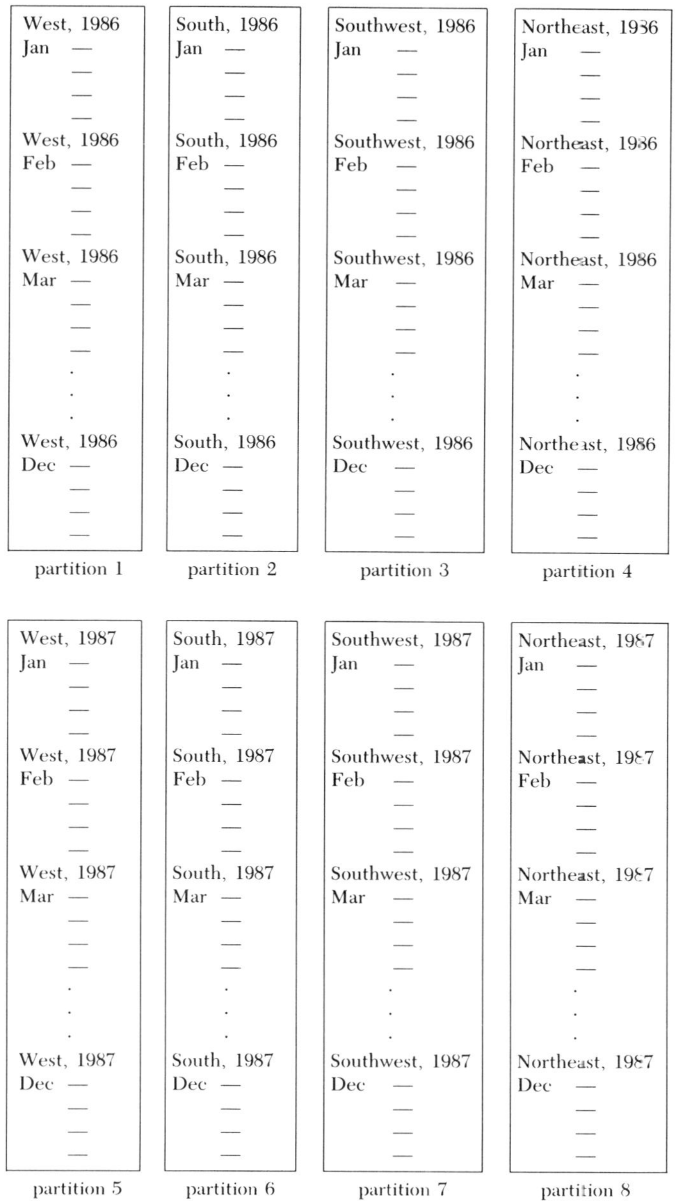
West, 1986
Jan —
West, 1986
Feb —
West, 1986
Mar —
West, 1986
Dec —
partition 1
South, 1986
Jan —
South, 1986
Feb —
South, 1986
Mar —
South, 1986
Dec —
partition 2
Southwest, 1986
Jan —
Southwest, 1986
Feb —
Southwest, 1986
Mar —
Southwest, 1986
Dec —
partition 3
Northeast, 1986
Jan —
Northeast, 1986
Feb —
Northeast, 1986
Mar —
Northeast, 1986
Dec —
partition 4
West, 1987
Jan —
West, 1987
Feb —
West, 1987
Mar —
West, 1987
Dec —
partition 5
South, 1987
Jan —
South, 1987
Feb —
South, 1987
Mar —
South, 1987
Dec —
partition 6
Southwest, 1987
Jan —
Southwest, 1987
Feb —
Southwest, 1987
Mar —
Southwest, 1987
Dec —
partition 7
Northeast, 1987
Jan —
Northeast, 1987
Feb —
Northeast, 1987
Mar —
Northeast, 1987
Dec —
partition 8

Sparse Index

Given the volume of data that is anticipated at the atomic ORACLE level, sparse indexes are almost a necessity. A sparse index is built at the application level in ORACLE. A sparse index is a table that has been effectively subsetted from a large table. It is much more efficient to process against the sparse index than it is against the full database.

As an example of a sparse index, consider a claims table for an insurance company. The data in the claims table is defined:

```
CLAIM NUMBER            @Key
POLICY NUMBER
BY
DATE
AMOUNT
LOCATION
CLAIM TYPE
SETTLED
SETTLEMENT COSTS
```

There are 2,000,000 claim entries a year added to the table. A sparse index is built on the column *settled*. If the value of settled is N, then an index entry is created. In other words, the sparse index is built for all claims that have not been settled. The sparse index entry is for about 1,500 claims per year. It is much more efficient to first access the sparse index to answer queries against unsettled claims.

Of course, another sparse index can be created if it is found that data were regularly being accessed along some criteria. For example, a sparse index on claim type could be created. Where claim type denotes *collision*, a sparse index could be created. To analyze all collision claims, it is efficient to first access the secondary index.

The designer must keep in mind the work required to keep the sparse indexes up to date. If a column is updated, of course, there is the chance that its sparse index must likewise be updated. However, most atomic ORACLE databases are loaded once and are seldom, if ever, updated. In this case, usage of a sparse index is ideal.

Indexing

Given the amount of data that is anticipated at the atomic level, it is mandatory that the data be indexed. It would be unthinkable to build an atomic database that was not indexed. In addition, once data is loaded into the atomic level, it tends to be stable, so update of the index usually becomes a minor problem.

However, the loading of the index each time the results of an extract is made and the volume of data are not trivial considerations. The following are some guidelines/techniques for managing indexes in a ORACLE atomic environment:

- specify no more than 3 indexes per table;
- load the indexes when the workload permits;
- partition data (this reduces the size of any index);
- use clustering, where applicable (this can greatly reduce the number of index entries;
- build sparse indexes whenever there is a predictable pattern of access of a minority subset of data.

Low-level Summarization

On occasion the granularity of atomic data is too low. By raising the granularity of the data, the number of rows at the atomic level can be greatly reduced. Consider a simple example from a telephone company.

A telephone company wishes to store monthly phone activity by customer at the atomic level. On the average, there are 100 phone calls per month per customer. Storing the details of each phone call at the atomic level adds up to many, many rows of data at the atomic level. The designer decides to condense each month's customer records accordingly:

```
ACCT NUMBER
NUMBER OF CALLS
NUMBER OF LONG DISTANCE CALLS
TOTAL PHONE MINUTES
TOTAL BILL
NUMBER CALLS@8:00-5:00, M-F
```

The amount of space required to store the above information is significantly less than the amount of space required to store each phone call. In addition, the calculation of number of calls, total bill, etc., is done once as the data is stored. There is a huge savings in elevating the granularity of the data.

Note, however, that some utility of the atomic level of data is lost. The query—how many phone calls were made to Peoria, Illinois—cannot be answered by the data that has been stored. The designer must carefully consider what queries are preempted by elevating the granularity of the data.

Of course, a multi-leveled atomic database can be built. At the *regular* atomic level data is elevated and is managed by ORACLE. At the detailed level, where the actual detail of all phone calls is kept, data is stored on VSAM or on magnetic tape files and is only infrequently accessed.

Data Filtering

Given the amount of data that is anticipated at the atomic ORACLE level, data filtering is in order. Data filtering refers to the selective storage of only data elements that have a high probability of access at the atomic level. In other words, as data is extracted from the system of record in the operational environment, only selected data elements are transported to the atomic environment.

As a simple example, consider the data that is found in the operational environment of a financial system for transactions and activities:

OPERATIONAL DATA	*ATOMIC DATA*
ACCT NUMBER	ACCT NUMBER
ACTIVITY DATE	ACTIVITY DATE
AMOUNT	AMOUNT
PAYEE	PAYEE
ID	LOCATION
ELECTRONIC ID	
CASHBOX BALANCE	
CASHBOX SEQ NUMBER	
TELLER ID	
LOCATION	
. . .	
. . .	
. . .	

In the transition between operation to atomic data, certain data elements are *lost*. Teller Id, Id, Cashbox Balance, etc., simply will not be useful for DSS processing supported by the atomic level of data.

Therefore, those data elements are not transported to the atomic level of data. This has the effect of reducing the total amount of data at the atomic level. Of course it precludes certain kinds of DSS processing. But if the probability of access/usage is extremely low, the tradeoff is justified.

Rolling Summarization of Data

Based on the notion that the older data becomes, the less useful its detail is, the process of rolling and summarizing data at the atomic level is a viable design alternative.

The process of rolling and summarizing is best illustrated in terms of an example. Suppose a telephone company keeps track of phone traffic on a daily basis, by hour. A record of data for a day's worth of phone activity looks like:

1:00 – 2:00 a.m.	253 calls	
2:00 – 3:00 a.m.	178 calls	a daily record
3:00 – 4:00 a.m.	310 calls	of phone calls
. .	. .	
. .	. .	
. .	. .	
11:00 – 12:00 p.m.	450 calls	

The phone company wishes to store the history of phone calls in its atomic database. Attempting to store each day's record adds up to a lot of atomic data. Instead, the phone company stores data thusly:

MON	TUES	WED	THURS	FRI	SAT	SUN	WEEK 2	WEEK 3	WEEK 4	MONTH 2	MONTH 3	....
–	–	–	–	–	–	–	–	–	–	–	–	....
–	–	–	–	–	–	–	–	–	–	–	–	....
–	–	–	–	–	–	–	–	–	–	–	–	....
–	–	–	–	–	–	–	–	–	–	–	–	....

At the end of the month, the three weekly and seven daily totals are added together to create a new month's total. At the end of the week, the seven days' totals are added together to create a new week's total, and so forth.

In this fashion, the most detail is stored about the most recent data, and the least detail is stored for the oldest data. The technique of rolling summarization is useful for minimizing the space and processing required against atomic level data. Of course, the designer must be aware that some amount of detail will be lost as time goes on.

Dynamic, Temporary Subsets of Data

One of the most useful techniques for managing large amounts of data in the face of heuristic processing is the selection and transport of likely subsets of data at the outset. In selecting and separating likely data, much unnecessary processing can be avoided.

For example, suppose an analyst is charged with analyzing defective parts manufacturing. Instead of starting to do analysis on the manufacturer's atomic data (most of which is not about defective parts), the analyst first collects information about which parts are defective. Then the analyst collects atomic data—inventory, assembly, raw goods, etc.—information about only the defective goods. After having created a *mini atomic* environment that relates *only* to defective goods, then the analysis starts. The difference is that analysis is done *only* on goods that are known to have had defects and *much* less data and processing is involved than if analysis had started with the full atomic database.

Of course, at the end of the analysis, the selected data is discarded. And, if the analysis is very lengthy, it may be desirable to occasionally refresh the subset of data on which analysis is being done.

Another useful application of the approach of saving temporary files is that of saving the results of joins, especially large joins. Even in a nontransaction-oriented environment such as the DSS environment, the amount of resources required to do a join is considerable. The frequency with which joins are done is limited when there is a large amount of data. Therefore, when a large join must be done, it makes sense to store the results of the join, even after the processing against it is completed in the eventuality that further, unanticipated processing will be done.

Purge Criteria

Unless the atomic environment is expected to be large and to contain data with a modest to low probability of access, it should not contain data with *no* probability of access.

Purge criteria should be specified for every atomic database, ensuring that unneeded data is removed. This simple technique (which has been around for as long as there has been data) should not be overlooked by the designer who seeks to keep atomic databases of a manageable size.

Selective Inversion

A combination of previously mentioned techniques is that of selective inversion of data. Selective inversion occurs where tables are accessed regularly on other than the primary key. (In truth, selective inversion is a specialized form of secondary indexing.) Selective inversion is best illustrated by an example.

Suppose a database is built for an insurance company's policies. There are many policies and policies are keyed (indexed) by policy number. An analyst wishes to study all policies whose coverage is over $50,000. The analyst creates a small table, as shown:

```
COVERAGE AMOUNT     - Key
COVERAGE TYPE                        an inverted table
POLICY
```

The table is small, and the key is coverage amount. It is very efficient to operate against the inverted table, albeit for a limited amount of queries. Of course, to link a policy or class of policies back to the original policy table, the linkage is easily performed by means of a join.

Piggybacking Extracts

Since operational data must periodically be scanned and it is likely that there will be a large amount of operational data, the minimum number of operational scans there are, the better. A design technique is to *piggyback* as many scan criteria into a single scan as possible.

As a simple example, suppose one extract is looking for all insurance policies, whose premium date is September. Another scan is looking for all policies that have coverage more than $100,000. The two scans could be combined into the same scan with multiple criteria:

```
SCAN1

LOCATE POLICY
WHERE
PREM DATE = 9                COMBINED SCAN

SCAN2                        LOCATE POLICY
                             WHERE
LOCATE POLICY                PREMDATE = 9 OR
WHERE                        COVERAGE > 100,000
COVERAGE > 100,000
```

Storage of Report Files

On occasion a large report must be created. To build the report much supporting information, oftentimes called report files, must be gathered. A simple practice that is usually inexpensive and may save considerable effort is the temporary saving of the report files *after* the report is issued, for up to 30 days.

In the event that there are minor problems with the report, saving the report files may preclude having to gather the basic reporting information again.

Preallocation, Preformatting of Space

On occasion, the behavior of data is known in advance. When this is the case, the designer may use this knowledge to physically influence the location of data to best advantage.

For example, suppose a designer knows that monthly production by product line is to be put into a design support atomic ORACLE database. The designer knows that the months will always be stored, in order. There will never be 13 months. Even if monthly production for a part is zero, there will be a monthly production total. In every case, month 6 will be inserted after month 5. In short, the data is *well behaved* in terms of its occurrence.

In addition, assume that data is generally accessed for the entire year, product line by product line. In other words, normal access is from product line month n to product line month n + 1. In this case, it makes sense to physically position month n's data adjacent to month n + 1's data. A simple way to do this is, at the first of the year insert a row for each month of the year, in order. A value of zero is used for monthly production because monthly production is not known at the time data is inserted. Then, on a month-by-month basis, the monthly production values are updated.

The same effect can be achieved in several other ways—through clustering of data or through the creation of arrays of data in a row. The designer must determine whether a simple loading/update technique, clustering technique, or array in a row technique is most appropriate.

Referential Disintegrity

In an operational environment, referential integrity is a most important feature. The up-to-the-second validity of information in the operational environment is of the essence. But in the DSS/ORACLE environment, the importance of referential integrity is less important due to the volume and usage of the data, and due to the aging process of the data. Over time, the up-to-the-second accuracy of a relationship becomes less important. And doing massive summarizations of data seldom involves looking at the referential integrity relationships of each of the units of data. Thus it is that with DSS/ORACLE data, referential integrity of data takes on a very different dimension.

As a rule, the tight referential integrity constraints of the operational environment are relaxed in the DSS/ORACLE environment. However, on occasion *some* referential integrity information will need to be carried forward. For example, consider a manufacturer's order information. In the operational environment, the order information appears as:

```
ORDER NUMBER
SUPPLIER NUMBER
LINEITEM (1)        AMT     COST     DELIVERY DATE
LINEITEM (2)        AMT     COST     DELIVERY DATE
LINEITEM (3)        AMT     COST     DELIVERY DATE
    .                .        .             .
    .                .        .             .
    .                .        .             .
LINEITEM (n)        AMT     COST     DELIVERY DATE
SHIP TO LOCATION
TOTAL COST
DISCOUNT
```

In the operational environment, if more information about the order is desired, such as information about the supplier or the parts ordered, the supplier or the parts table is accessed. However, in a DSS environment there may be no parts of supplier table to go to. Even if there is a parts or supplier table to go to, it may be very complex and/or very difficult to locate the right data. In this case, it may be useful, at the moment of extract, to include information other than order information that has a good chance of being used with order information, such as:

```
ORDER NUMBER
SUPPLIER NUMBER
SUPPLIER NAME
SUPPLIER ADDRESS
SUPPLIER CONTACT
```

```
SUPPLIER PREFERENCE CODE
LINE ITEM (1) AMT DESCRIPTION V/M STANDARD LOT COST DE-
LIVERY DATE
LINE ITEM (2) AMT DESCRIPTION V/M STANDARD LOT COST DE-
LIVERY DATE
LINE ITEM (3) AMT DESCRIPTION V/M STANDARD LOT COST DE-
LIVERY DATE
        .   .           .   .           .   .   .
        .   .           .   .           .   .   .
        .   .           .   .           .   .   .
LINE ITEM (N) AMT DESCRIPTION V/M STANDARD LOT COST DE-
LIVERY DATE
SHIPTO LOCATION
SHIPMENT RECEIVED VERIFICATION
DATE RECEIVED
TOTAL COST
DISCOUNT
DATE PAID
```

The data in the order number DSS/ORACLE table is distinctly denormalized and very likely will contain redundant information. It will also be very easy and efficient to process. As long as constant update is not occurring on the data (which in a DSS environment is seldom the case), the problems of redundancy are minimal, and in fact lead to efficiency at the time of execution.

No Update of DSS Data

As a rule, there should be an absolute minimum of update processing in the DSS/ORACLE environment. (The few deliberate cases discussed previously are, in any case, the exception, not the norm.) The mode of processing in the DSS/ORACLE environment is one of insertion and loading of indexes. Only under very exceptional circumstances should update of data be allowed.

As a rule, it is better to insert adjustment records than it is to change an existing value. Where there are many adjustment records that gravitate to the atomic environment, periodically, in a batch mode all adjustments are applied. But there should be a need for batch adjustments very, very infrequently.

Public Summary Data

The identification and storage of public summary data can save huge amounts of processing. For example, accounting calculates a monthly

TOTAL REVENUE value and stores it in the atomic level. When departments need that value, there is no need to go through all the monthly data for the recalculation. The careful storage of public summary data can greatly enhance the processing required at the DSS/ORACLE level.

Preconditioning of Users

Even though this is not strictly speaking a design technique, the preconditioning of users is an important aspect of the DSS/ORACLE environment. Users must be told that when they access a large amount of data they will not get response time in the order of seconds.

	frequent access	infrequent access
experienced users	native SQL	prepackaged SQL or native SQL
casual user	prepackaged SQL	ORACLE forms

Queries that access large amounts of data take a fair amount of time to complete.

Longer queries, such as ones that require large joins, should not be done during the processing day. Massive requests must be done out of harm's way, either overnight or on the week end. Preconditioning the user can be one of the most effective things the designer can do.

In addition, for regularly run queries, a certain amount of prepackaging can be done. This saves the user from having to create the query and also prevents the user from creating a *run away* transaction.

As a rule, the interface to the DSS/ORACLE environment can be streamlined by encouraging different levels of users to use different interfaces. The following matrix describes the interface:

IN SUMMARY

In summary, this chapter has discussed design techniques applicable to the DSS/ORACLE environment. These techniques include:

- time stamping of data;
- partitioning of data;
- sparse indexing of data;
- indexing of atomic data;
- data filtering;
- rolling summarization of data;
- creating dynamic, temporary subsets of data;
- elevating the granularity of data;
- purging atomic data;
- inverting selective columns;
- piggybacking of extracts;
- storing report files;
- preallocating, preformatting of space;
- creating arrays within rows;
- referential disintegrity of data;
- no updating of DSS data;
- creating public summary data; and
- preconditioning users.

QUESTIONS: CHAPTER 9

1. The design considerations of the DSS/ORACLE environment are dominated by the need to manage ______________ amounts of data and the need for ______________ of access of data.
2. Requirements for DSS processing are PREDICTABLE/UNPREDICTABLE.
3. Every unit of data in the DSS/ORACLE environment is ______.
4. The three forms of measuring time variancy are ____________, , and ______________.
5. Because of the large amount of data that needs to be managed at the DSS/ORACLE level, ______________ of data should always be considered.
6. Partitioning of data in ORACLE can be done at two levels—the ______________ level and the ______________ level.
7. When data is partitioned, the size of the unit of recoverability and reorganization is INCREASED/REDUCED/STAYS THE SAME.

8. Partitioning data /reduces/increases/does not affect/ the total amount of data in the database.
9. Name some ways (5) that data can be partitioned on.
10. A sparse index in ORACLE is always built at the ____________ level.
11. A sparse index always creates redundancy. T/F
12. It is much more efficient to access a sparse index than a full table IN EVERY CASE/SOMETIMES/NEVER/WHEN/APPLICABLE.
13. Because of the size of data, DSS/ORACLE data MUST ALWAYS/ MAY BE/MAY NOT BE indexed.
14. The maximum number of indexes for DSS/ORACLE data should be ______________.
15. Indexes always have to be loaded as the data is loaded for ORACLE DSS data. T/F
16. The most fundamental design issue of atomic DSS data is that of the level of ______________ of the data.
17. The more fine the data the MORE/LESS data there is.
18. With very granular data, many requests may be satisfied. T/F
19. Data that is not used for DSS processing can be ____________ as data flows from the operational to the DSS world.
20. A technique of keeping new detailed data and aging the data is called ______________.
21. One technique for minimizing the loading of an index is to create data and index it on an as-needed basis. This technique is called ______________.
22. Whenever possible, new extract requirements should be ______ with existing extract processing.
23. Upon producing a report, the report file should be SAVED/DISCARDED.
24. Preallocation and preformatting of space can be used to _______ data.
25. Users should be ______________ as to what the appropriate expectations for DSS processing are.

APPENDIX A

Answers

CHAPTER 1: THE EFFECTIVE DSS/ ORACLE Environment

1. operational
2. development life cycle; requirements gathering; use of DSS, operational systems; audience served; usage of hardware; type of data operated on
3. no
4. heuristic; non repetitive
5. IS
6. trend analysis; actuarial analysis; demographic analysis; ad hoc reporting
7. TRUE
8. IS
9. STABLE
10. UNSTABLE
11. set at a time
12. FALSE
13. primitive
14. derived

15. SOME
16. clerical
17. management
18. CAN
19. processing

CHAPTER 2: EFFECTIVE DSS/ ORACLE SYSTEMS—THE ISSUES

1. 4GL technology; personal computer
2. MAY
3. IS NOT
4. accuracy/credibility; timeliness/accessibility; cost of processing
5. TRUE
6. SHOULD
7. MIGHT BE
8. information cycle
9 END USER

CHAPTER 3: AN ARCHITECTURE FOR EFFECTIVE DSS/ORACLE SYSTEMS

1. magnetic tapes
2. sequentially
3. TRUE
4. redundancy
5. directly
6. no
7. an index; a randomizer
8. 2–3
9. ACCESS and UPDATE
10. MIS
11. much hardware; relaxed response time criteria
12. unfriendly
13. extract
14. taken offline; run overnight; run on another processor

15. explosive
16. FALSE
17. foundation data; DSS basis data; an information warehouse
18. operational data; external data
19. TRUE
20. departmental data; individual data
21. CAN BE
22. public summary
23. can
24. CAN BE
25. administrative; directional
26. continuous, event discrete; periodic discrete
27. MAKES MANAGEABLE
28. system of record
29. TRUE
30. granularity
31. MORE
32. MORE
33. the cost of handling data
34. TRUE
35. MAY or MAY NOT
36. EFFICIENT

CHAPTER 4: OPERATIONAL DATA/ EXTERNAL DATA IN SUPPORT OF THE DSS/ORACLE ENVIRONMENT

1. MOST OF
2. IS NOT
3. IMS, IDMS, CICS/VSAM, TPF, FOCUS, ADABAS, Datacom DB, Model 204
4. SOME
5. key structure; data elements; grouping of data elements; structure of data; encoding/decoding structure
6. FALSE

7. TRUE
8. system of record
9. TRUE
10. TRUE
11. TRUE
12. IS NOT

CHAPTER 5: ATOMIC LEVEL DSS/ ORACLE DATA

1. non redundant
2. redundant
3. MUST BE
4. continuous; event discrete; periodic discrete
5. continuous data
6. event discrete
7. periodic discrete
8. A LITTLE OR SOME
9. 24 hours
10. TRUE
11. extract
12. RARE
13. sequential; batch
14. 1
15. 3 or 4
16. SELDOM
17. partitions
18. adds nor subtracts
19. MUST BE
20. subject
21. the ability to manage large amounts of sequentially-oriented data; the ability to interface with a wide variety of technologies
22. SOME
23. living sample; "true archival"
24. MAYBE

CHAPTER 6: DEPARTMENTAL/ INDIVIDUAL LEVEL DATA IN THE DSS/ORACLE ENVIRONMENT

1. the atomic level
2. the atomic level; the departmental level
3. operational; directional
4. frequently
5. infrequently
6. keeping or increasing
7. markets
8. internal
9. external
10. pulled
11. likely

CHAPTER 7: PROJECTION DATA/ PROJECTION PROCESSING IN THE DSS/ORACLE ENVIRONMENT

1. historical; projection
2. TRUE
3. future
4. IS NOT
5. MAY/MAY NOT
6. MAY
7. working budget; baseline budget; most current budget

CHAPTER 8: MIGRATION TO THE DSS/ORACLE ARCHITECTURE

1. current value data; archival data; summary data; projection data; external data; end user data
2. TRUE
3. data model
4. TRUE
5. 3

6. ERD, major subject area
7. dis; data item set
8. physical model
9. system of record
10. dis, mid-level model
11. physical model; low-level model
12. high level; ERD
13. dis; mid-level model
14. dis; mid-level model

CHAPTER 9: DESIGN APPROACHES/ TECHNIQUES FOR THE DSS/ORACLE ENVIRONMENT

1. large efficiency
2. UNPREDICTABLE
3. time stamped
4. continuous, event discrete, periodic discrete
5. partitioning
6. system; application
7. reduced
8. DOES NOT AFFECT
9. geography; line of business; business organization; time; random; product line, etc.
10. application
11. TRUE
12. WHEN APPLICABLE
13. MAYBE
14. 3 or 4
15. FALSE
16. granularity
17. MORE
18. TRUE
19. filtered, discarded
20. rolling summarization

21. dynamic/temporary subsets of data
22. merged; piggybacked
23. SAVED
24. physically calculate
25. preconditioned

APPENDIX B

Database Glossary

access—The operation of seeking, reading, or writing data on a storage unit.

access method—A technique used to transfer a physical record from or to a mass storage device.

access pattern—The general sequence in which the data structure is accessed, that is, from tuple to tuple, from segment to segment, etc.

access time—The time interval between the instant when an instruction control unit initiates a call for data and the instant when delivery of the data is completed from the device control unit.

address—An identification (number, name, label) for a location in which data is stored.

addressing—The means of assigning data to storage locations, and subsequent retrieval on the basis of the key of the data.

algorithm—A set of statements to solve a problem in a finite number of steps.

alias—An alternate label used to refer to a data element.

application blocking of data—The grouping of different occurrences of the same type of data by the application programmer. The application programmer takes care of data placement, location, deletion, overflow, etc.

archival database—A database copy saved for historical, recovery, or restoration purposes.

atomic—The smallest addressable unit within a system.

atomic level data—Archival (time variant) data at a low level of detail with a moderate probability of access positioned to serve as a foundation for DSS processing.

attribute—A property that can assume values for entities or relationships. Entities can be assigned several attributes; for example, a tuple in a relation consists of values. Some systems also allow relationships to have attributes.

audit trail—Data that is available to trace activity; typically used for database transactions or for terminal activity.

availability—A measure of the reliability of a system, indicating the fraction of time when the system is available divided by the amount of time the system should be available.

backup—To restore the database to its state at a previous point in time. Backup is often achieved from an archival database, that is, a snapshot of the database at a specified time.

batch—Computer environment in which programs (usually long-running, sequentially-oriented) exclusively access data and user activity is not interactive.

batch environment—A sequentially dominated mode of processing; in batch, input is collected and batched for future processing throughout the day. Once collected, the batch input is transacted sequentially against one or more databases.

batch window—The time when the on-line system is available for batch or sequential processing. The batch window occurs during non-peak processing hours.

block—A basic unit of data structuring; the physical unit of transport and storage. A block contains one or more records. This is sometimes called a page.

blocking—The combining of two or more physical records so that they are jointly read or written by one machine instruction.

block splitting—A data management activity that allows a fully packed block to be split into two or more blocks, where each new block contains some free space.

buffer—An area of storage that holds data temporarily while data is being received, transmitted, read, or written. Is often used to compensate for differences in the speed or timing of devices.

Buffers are used in terminals, peripheral devices, storage units, and in the CPU.

checkpoint—An identified snapshot of the database or a point at which the transitions have been frozen or are quiescent.

checkpoint/restart—A means of restarting a program at some point other than the beginning, used after a failure or interruption has occurred. Multiple checkpoints may be used at intervals throughout an application program. At these points records are written giving enough information about the status of the program to permit its being restarted at that point.

cluster—A means of storing data together based on a common key value.

cluster key—The key around which the cluster is built.

code—(1) To represent data or a computer program in a form that can be accepted by a data processor. (2) To transform data so that it cannot be understood by anyone who does not have the algorithm to decode the data before its presentation.

column—A vertical table cut in which values are selected from the same domain. The column is named in the heads.

commit—A condition issued by a group of operators or transactions when the changes to a database are concluded satisfactorily and can no longer be canceled or rolled back, except as a whole by a later special command to undo the entire group.

compaction—A technique for reducing the number of bits required for storage without destroying any information content.

concatenated index—An index over multiple columns.

control database—A database containing data other than that directly related to the function of the application. Typical control databases are terminal data bases, security data bases, audit data bases, tables data bases, etc. Although control databases are necessary, it is mandatory that they be implemented properly.

DASD—Direct-access storage device.

data—A recording of facts, concepts, or instructions on a storage medium for communication, retrieval, and processing by automatic means and presentation as information that is understandable to humans.

data element—An attribute of an entity; a uniquely named and well-defined category of data that consists of data items and that is included in a record of an activity.

data model—(1) The logical data structures, including operations and constraints, provided by a DBMS for effective database processing. (2) The system used for data representation (e.g., the ERA or relational model).

decompaction—The opposite of compaction. Data is stored in a compacted form but must be decompacted upon use to make sense to the user.

derived data—Data about multiple customers or multiple events.

derived data element—A data element that is not necessarily stored but that can be generated when needed (for example, the age given the date of birth and current date).

direct access—Retrieval or storage of data by a reference to its location on a volume, rather than relative to previously retrieved or stored data. The access mechanism goes directly to the data in question, as is normally required with on-line use of data.

direct-access storage device (DASD)—A data storage unit on which data can be accessed directly at random without having to progress through a serial file such as tape. A disk unit is a direct-access storage device.

dss data (decision support systems)—Data used in a free form fashion to support managerial decisions.

encoding—A shortening or abbreviation of the physical representation of a data value, for example, male = M, Female = F.

encryption—The transformation of data by means of an algorithm from one form to another so that the data is unrecognizable in its transformed representation. Encryption is done for security reasons. Should an unauthorized person stumble on the transformed data, the data would be useless without the transformation algorithm.

entity—A person, place, event, or thing of interest to users at the highest level of abstraction.

entity-relationship-diagram (ERD)—A high level schematic of data at its highest level of abstraction

foreign key—An attribute that is not a primary key to a relation in a relational system, but whose values are values of the primary key of another relation's tuples.

format—The arrangement or layout of data in or on a data medium (for example, a buffer) or in a program definition.

heuristics—A method of obtaining a solution through inference or trial-

and-error that uses approximate methods while evaluating the progress toward an acceptable goal.

index—The portion of the storage structure maintained to provide efficient access to a record when its index key item value is known.

interactive—A mode of processing combining some aspects of on-line processing and some aspects of batch processing; in interactive processing. The user can directly interact with data over which he or she has exclusive control. In addition, the user can cause sequential activity to occur on the data.

I/O (input/output)—The means by which data is stored on DASD. I/O is measured in milliseconds while computer processing is measured in nanoseconds.

join—An operation that takes two relations as operands and produces a new relation by concatenating the tuples and matching the corresponding columns when a stated condition holds between the two.

key—A data item or combination of data items used to identify or locate a record instance (or other data grouping).

key, primary—A key that is used to uniquely identify a record instance (or other data grouping).

key, secondary—A key that does not uniquely identify a record instance; that is, more than one record instance can have the same key value.

line—The hardware by which data flows to or from the processor. Typically lines go to terminals, printers, other processors, etc.

line time—The amount of time required for a transaction to go either from the terminal to the processor or from the processor to the terminal. Typically line time is the single largest component of on-line response time.

living sample—A representative database, typically used for analytical work in the fact of a very large data base. Periodically, the very large database is stripped of data so that the living sample represents a cross section of the large database. Then statistical activity can be done against the living sample database without disturbing the large database.

load—To insert data values into a database that was previously empty.

loading—The automatic recording of data concerning attempts to query, load, augment, or update the database.

lockup—The event that occurs when a database is being used exclusively and other programs desire to access the data base but cannot.

magnetic tape—The medium most closely associated with sequential processing; a large ribbon on which magnetic images are stored and retrieved.

master file—A concept from sequential processing where a given file holds the definitive data for a given system.

message—The data input by the user in the online environment that is used to drive a transaction or the data that is output to the user as a result of the execution of a transaction.

navigate—To steer a course through a database by using such devices as indexes and pointers to arrive at and examine a record and data item values.

normalize—To decompose complex data structures into normal form structures.

null—An item or record for which no value currently exists or may ever exist.

numeric—A representation using only numbers and the decimal point.

on-line storage—Storage devices, especially the storage media they contain, under the direct control of a computing system, not off-line or in a volume library.

operating system—Software that enables a computer to supervise its own operations, automatically calling in programs, routines, language, and data, as needed for continuous throughput of different types of jobs.

operational data—Data used to support the day-to-day operations of an organization, usually at a detailed level.

operations—The organizational unit responsible for making the computer environment operable.

overflow—The condition in which a record (or segment) cannot be stored in its home address; that is, the storage location logically assigned to it on loading. It may be stored in a special overflow location or in the home address of other records. The area of DASD where data is sent when collisions occur or where records go when they must be written and there is no space in primary DASD.

peak period—Time (day, month, etc.) when the system experiences the greatest volume of transactions or activity.

populate—To place occurrences of data values into a previously empty database. See also *load*.

precision—The degree of discrimination with which a quantity is stated. For example, a three-digit numeral discriminates among 1,000 possibilities from 000 to 999.

primary key—An item whose value uniquely identifies a record or tuple.

processor—The hardware at the center of processing; processors are divided into three categories, mainframes, minicomputers, and microcomputers.

processor cycles—The hardware internal cycles that do many functions that drive the computer, such as initiate I/O, perform logic, move data, and perform arithmetic functions.

projection—An operation that takes one relation as an operand and returns a second relation that consists of only the selected attributes columns, with duplicate rows eliminated.

purge date—The date on or after which a storage area is available to be overwritten. Used in conjunction with a file label, it is a means of protecting file data until an agreed release date is reached.

queue time—The amount of time a transaction spends after being transmitted to the processor before going into execution Queue time is dependent on many factors: the system load, the level of integrity, the priority of the transaction, etc. Queue time can become the largest factor in poor online response time.

query language—A language that enables a user to interact directly with a DBMS to retrieve and possibly modify its data.

random access—To obtain data directly from any storage location regardless of its position with respect to the previously referenced information. Also called *direct access*.

random access storage—A storage technique in which the time required to obtain information is independent of the location of the information most recently obtained. This strict definition must be qualified by the observation that we usually mean relatively random. Thus magnetic drums are relatively nonrandom access when compared to magnetic cores for main memory, but relatively random access when compared to magnetic tapes for file storage.

record—An aggregation of values of data items or elements.

record-at-a-time processing—Access of data a unit at a time (that is, a record at-a-time, a tuple at-a-time, etc.)

record type—The category to which a record instance belongs, as defined by the record format in the database schema.

recovery—The restoration of the database to an original position or prior condition, often after major damage to the physical medium. See also *rollback* and *commit*.

reorganization—Process of unloading data (in a poorly organized state) and reloading (to a well-organized state). Reorganization in some DBMS is also done to restructure the database.

repeating group—A collection of data that can occur several times within a given record occurrence.

response time (user)—The amount of time the user has to wait between entering a transaction and receiving a response. Response time is a function of communication line time, processing time, and amount of processing activity.

row—A nonempty sequence of values in a table and the smallest unit of data that can be stored into and erased from a table.

scope of integration—The formal English language definition of what the boundaries of the system are and are not.

secondary index—An index composed of secondary keys rather than primary keys.

secondary key—An attribute that is not the primary or ordering key but for which an index is maintained.

secondary storage—Storage facilities forming not an integral part of the computer but directly linked to and controlled by the computer (for example, disks, magnetic tapes, etc.).

security—The protection provided to prevent unauthorized or accidental access to a database or its elements; the updating, copying, removal, or destruction of the data base; or the changing or running of a proscribed application.

select—To identify a subset of stored data that meets specified criteria.

set—A number of distinct objects with a membership criteria. In a network or CODASYL-type of database, a set is a named logical relationship between record types consisting of one owner record type, one or more member record types, and a prescribed order among the instances of member records.

set-at-a-time processing—Access of data by groups of data, each member of which satisfies some selection criteria.

SQL—A language used in relational processing

subject data base—A database and related system designed to support business functions and their applications by managing the data for a particular subject area.

system of record—The final authority as to the accuracy of data. By definition, the system of record is correct. There can be only one system of record.

table—A relation that consists of a set of columns with a heading and a set of rows (that is, tuples). See also *relation*.

transaction—A command, message, or input record that explicitly or implicitly calls for a processing action (for example, updating a file). A transaction is atomic with respect to recovery and concurrency.

transition data—Data sharing both primitive and derived characteristics

tuple—A group of related fields in a row of a relation; a row of the relation or table.

update—To change values in all or selected entries, groups, or data items stored in a data base; to add or delete data occurrences of their relationships.

user—A person or process issuing commands and messages to the information system.

variable fields—Fields that may or may not occur in a given record.

variable-length fields—Fields that may vary in length when they occur.

view—An external relation that consists of attributes retrieved or derived from one or more base relations joined and projected as given in the view definition.

BIBLIOGRAPHY

ORACLE manuals:

"ORACLE RDBMS with the Transaction Processing Subsystem," March 1988, Version 6.0.

"ORACLE for DEC VAX/VMS Installation and User's Guide," ORACLE Part No 1001.

"ORACLE for IBM VM/SP Installation and User's Guide," ORACLE Part No 1003.

"ORACLE for Sequent/Unix Installation and User's Guide," ORACLE Part No 1008.

"ORACLE ERROR MESSAGES and Codes," ORACLE Part No 3605.

"ORACLE Utilities User's Guide," ORACLE Part No 3602.

Date, C.J. *AN INTRODUCTION TO DATA BASE SYSTEMS*, Reading, MA, 1974—a leading early book on SQL and normalization.

Inmon, W.H. *DATA ARCHITECTURE: The Information Paradigm*, QED Information Sciences, Inc., Wellesley, MA 02181—the best description of the system of record, atomic level data, DSS data structures, etc.

Inmon, W.H. and Friedman, L.J. *DESIGN REVIEW METHODOLOGY FOR A DATABASE ENVIRONMENT*, Prentice Hall, Englewood Cliffs, NJ 07632—a treatise on design review, written originally for IMS but useful for anyone doing design review. In addition, there is a section on the standard work unit.

Inmon, W.H. *ORACLE: BUILDING HIGH PERFORMANCE ON-LINE SYSTEMS*, QED Information Sciences, Inc. Wellesley, MA 02181—a text describing design techniques for high performance in ORACLE. Part of a video course on the same subject.

Inmon, W.H. *INFORMATION ENGINEERING FOR THE PRACTITIONER*, Yourdon Press/Prentice Hall, Englewood Cliffs, NJ, 07632—a good description of data modeling, process modeling, and the system of record. Also mentioned are the atomic level data structures and the target architecture.

Inmon, W.H. *INFORMATION SYSTEMS ARCHITECTURE*, Prentice Hall, Englewood Cliffs, NJ 07632—a primer on data modeling and the architected approach to building systems.

Index

A

Q

R

S